THREE BABIES

Biographies of Cognitive Development

CONSULTING EDITOR: *L. Joseph Stone*
Vassar College

THREE BABIES

Biographies of Cognitive Development

JOSEPH CHURCH, *editor*
Brooklyn College of The City University of New York

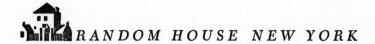

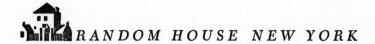 *RANDOM HOUSE NEW YORK*

PREFACE

THIS volume consists primarily of the life histories of three babies from birth to age two (in the case of one baby, Benjamin, almost to age three), as recorded by their mothers. By design, these accounts stress the babies' cognitive development, their coming to know and to adapt to their surroundings and to know and manage themselves. Incidentally, there are numerous observations of the babies' affective and motivational development, of their personality development, of their coming to be individuals with idiosyncratic life styles. The records, inevitably, have their shortcomings, some of which I point out along the way. This is not simply because the mothers, like everybody else, are fallible, but because the task of being simultaneously a mother and a dispassionate, analytic observer of one's own baby's behavior is a painfully demanding one, and we should be humbly grateful that these records even came into existence.

Despite omissions, ambiguities, and possible inaccuracies of interpretation, and even though the babies are a highly selected, unrepresentative sample who begin very early to reflect the intellectual, symbol-minded, person-centered orientation of their parents, these biographies contain data of a kind very hard to come by. They describe flesh-and-blood babies living and developing in the material, emotional, and symbolic context of family, neighborhood, and society, and of physical space and objects and relationships.

Even after all the debatable observations have been discounted, enough remains to show that these babies are very different from the mythical creatures postulated by learning theorists, psychoanalysts, and educators of various persuasions. They are not empty organisms. They are not id-driven, self-seeking sensualists masquerading as innocent, cuddlesome babes. They are neither creatures of vacuous innocence, in mortal danger of being corrupted by knowledge and discipline, nor demons steeped in original sin who must be beaten into submission and broken to the demands of civilization. They are alert, affectionate, responsive, variegated in their emotions, and hungry for experience. They are also, in various proportions, perverse, negativistic, volatile, sly, shy, timid, fearful, irritable, greedy, and full of guile and altruism. They are atypical in their families and in their own bright precocity, but they are typical in that they embody all the normal characteristics, endearing and exasperating, of ordinary babyhood. They slobber, drool, vomit, urinate, and defecate like any other babies. Like any other babies, they can melt a parent's viscera with a smile of uncontaminated loving radiance. They are young human beings.

These accounts are offered, first, to the student to help him know more concretely the raw material of human psychological development. They are offered to the general reader in hopes that he will find pleasure and excitement either in learning about an unknown realm of human experience or in being reminded of something he once knew. Even the experienced parent may find in these accounts things he never knew, since the moment-to-moment demands of coping with babies and all the rest of life can easily blind parents to the marvels of infantile behavior and development. The reader should be warned, however, against using the behavior reported in these documents as a standard against which to measure the development of some other baby. These accounts do not provide age norms—even among these three babies of similar background there are wide disparities in the ages at which particular forms of behavior appear, no matter how constant the sequence of emergences. These accounts are also offered to the advanced scholar in the hope that they will contribute to his understanding of developmental phenomena and suggest new lines of empirical research. It is my conviction that the serious developmental psychologist can find in these pages leads to formal experimental procedures that will provide the foundation for a sophisticated cognitive psychology which in its pursuit of rigorous abstractions does not lose sight of the realities of its subject matter.

These records are the product of a now-abandoned project to collect a great many such biographies, with the idea that some secure generalizations could be inferred from a large number of roughly comparable observations. The assignment proved impossible for most of the original participants, although several mothers contributed valuable fragmentary accounts. The present biographies are the only ones that spanned the entire first two years, and it is to the everlasting credit of the three mothers that these documents exist. For it must be remembered that these mothers are the authors of this volume, and it is only to protect the pseudonymity of the babies (and their friends and relations) that my name appears by itself on the title page. The highest tribute I can pay the authors of this book is that I twice tried to do what they have done, and failed.

The mothers' observations were guided by a schedule, devised by the editor, that sought to sensitize them to often-neglected forms of behavior without unduly narrowing their field of attention. Besides some specific items of behavior that they were asked to be on the alert for—most of these will be evident in the actual records—the mothers were asked to record whatever they found amusing, surprising, or puzzling. The observation schedules have since gone through several revisions, incorporating some of these mothers' observations, some observations sent in by other parents, observations drawn from the literature, and some that I have made, and have been partially codified as a series of formal experimental tasks. The six areas of functioning covered by the latest version of the schedule are: perception of objects and object attributes via all the exteroceptive modalities; orientation to space and the perception of spatial relations, including causation; personal and social awareness; affective reactions to medical personnel and procedures; imitation; and self-awareness. In addition, I am continuing work on tasks dealing with the perception of two-dimensional objects and space, including pictorial space, and the characteristics of early language. The test items include interview questions, observations, and formal experimental procedures. I have tried out a number of these items with babies of diverse ethnic origins in Honolulu and am satisfied that the tasks are a suitable device for studying early cognitive functioning and development. It is my intention to embody these tasks in a systematic study of individual and group differences in cognitive development, to try to relate particular patterns of cognitive development to varieties of parent-child relationships, and to test the predictive power of the tasks for later intellectual achievement. But let it be noted that findings obtained by the formal methods now under development can never have the richness and depth of the present records.

As an editor, I have tried hard not to spoil the flavor of the original texts, although occasional polishing of style and deletion of repetitive passages seemed called for. I have tried not to resolve true ambiguities, although I am sure that occasionally, in trying to make something clear, I must have falsified it. In some cases, I have signalled obscurities with a question mark in brackets; in other instances, I have suggested possible interpretations in a note.

As editor, I have both edited and editorialized. In notes inserted in the text between brackets I have tried to indicate what I think are important specimens of behavior and to relate specific bits of behavior to more general principles and issues. I have tried to follow a middle course between commenting on everything that struck me as noteworthy and letting the narrative flow on without interruption. Needless to say, I have singled out for comment and emphasis those items of behavior which best fit my theoretical biases. Other people, reading the texts through a different set of theoretical lenses, may find quite different patternings of meaning. I have done a certain amount of cross-referring among the records and have added observations of related behavior from other sources.

In lieu of a tabular chronology of behavior, I have tried to provide a highly detailed index, with items classified in as many different ways as I can think of. This index should make it easy to retrieve specific bits of behavior and also to make comparisons among the three babies.

Note that the order of presentation of these biographies is arbitrary. The reader is free to approach them in whatever sequence he prefers. All three accounts differ from each other both in the mothers' style of reporting and, of course, in the temperament of their subjects. I have tried to say something about these special characteristics in the introductions to the individual biographies. All three accounts, each in its own way, are rich in information, and I cannot sufficiently express my appreciation to the mothers who have allowed me to make public these fragments of their personal lives.

JOSEPH CHURCH
Brooklyn College of
The City University of New York
September, 1965

CONTENTS

THREE BABIES

Biographies of Cognitive Development

PART I

DEBORAH

❊❊❊❊❊❊

DEBORAH, *born the day before Benjamin (whose biography begins on page 107), was, like Benjamin, an unplanned but eagerly welcomed baby born to middle-aged parents. Debbie, however, is a first-born, whereas Benjamin is a third child, fourteen years junior to his sister. Since Debbie's and Benjy's parents know each other well, their life histories have been more closely intertwined than is apparent in the records.*

Debbie's father is a psychiatrist, of a strong philosophical-literary bent, and her mother is a physician who did not practice after Debbie's birth. As will be seen from the record, the parents' general orientation to child-rearing is founded on a strong faith in the natural powers of growth and maturation nourished by abundant love.

The family lives in a modern suburban house which had to be enlarged to provide a bedroom for the new baby. Debbie's maternal grandmother lived nearby, and an overgrown miniature poodle was also an important figure in her life.

The record kept by Debbie's mother is a rich one, but it is more summary and interpretive than Benjamin's and Ruth's

(whose biography begins on page 163). Although the latter two
records describe a greater number of specific incidents, tied more
to specific times and dates, they less often convey the whole
personality of the baby.

Debbie's physical and motor development were remarkably
precocious (as was corroborated contemporaneously by several
observers) and therefore should not be taken as norms against
which to compare babies in general. Debbie is a very bright
child, but so are Benjamin and Ruth, and her rapid physical
maturation seems unrelated to her intelligence.

Debbie's nursery-school teacher, describing her just before
and after her fourth birthday, stresses Debbie's variegated functioning, her ability to shift from constructive, highly controlled
activities to gay abandon, the diverse things in which she
engages, and the way she adapts to the pattern and pace of her
playmates. She is easily dominated by one little girl, and can
cope with her buffetings only by sucking her thumb in doleful
isolation. She nevertheless continues to seek this little girl's
companionship, and even manages by diplomatic maneuvers
sometimes to make her own ideas prevail. Although she continues to be very adult in her manner and conversational skills,
she shows considerable disobedience, defiance of authority, and
behavior calculated to outrage the grownups.

BIOGRAPHY

DEBBIE was born on December 8 at 1:13 P.M. She measured 18 inches long and weighed 5 lb. 14 oz. Her color was good and she cried spontaneously.

During this period of five days in the hospital Debbie and I have had some scant opportunity to get acquainted with each other at feeding time (she is breast fed) and, more remotely, through nurses' comments and odd-hour observations through the nursery window.

She seems muscularly strong—is able to hold her head up unwaveringly in vertical or supine position for two or three minutes at a time, has a good grasping reflex, coughs and sneezes with adequate force. She comes for nursing crying rhythmically and with "real tears" in her eyes, and the breast brings quiet immediately. She nurses steadily for ten minutes, pulls forcefully away from the nipple for one burp without re-gurgitating, and cries for more. After nursing she does not sleep in my arms, but seems content to be cuddled and rocked while she peers up at my face.

She eats well except for the 2 A.M. feeding, when she most obviously prefers to sleep.

Nurse's report: "You're going to have some time with that one. She stops crying when she hears one of us walk through the door. She doesn't wait until she can see us at all."

Debbie was discharged from the hospital on December 13, weighing 5 lb. 11 oz.

Second week.

DEBBIE seems to follow a fairly regular schedule of her own
devising. She consistently refuses the 2 A.M. feeding and she remains awake and active and often vociferous between her 2 P.M.
and 6 P.M. feedings. This four-hour period seems to be some sort
of disorganized, rather chaotic exercise period. She is not in
pain or fretful, but most alert to any stimulus—household sounds,
subtle alterations in light direction or intensity, texture of
blanket or jersey nightgown, etc.

Hunger cries remain specific, not so much by tone as by
rhythm of cry. [*Note 1: When the editor first saw these notes
some months later, Debbie's mother could no longer recall the
particular character of the hunger cry.*]

She follows people accurately as they walk about the large
rooms, and our poodle, too. We have never observed the typical
eye-crossing and ocular muscle imbalance in her that is often
present in the newborn. [*Note 2: The editor has seen few cases
of such imbalance, either, and doubts that it is nearly as common
as the literature would lead one to believe. Cf. Woodworth,
1938, pages 576–577.**]

We have installed a plastic butterfly mobile above her criblet
—more or less in desperation to help her through her wakeful
(and bored?) afternoons. She watches it with obvious concentration for fifteen or twenty minutes at a time, and definitely prefers the blue-toned butterfly to the others (green, pink, yellow,
blue and green). [*Note 3: Such early preferences can be determined for certain only if the baby's head is braced in the midline
and actual measurements are made of the time spent looking at
each color. Color preferences at slightly older ages have, however, been demonstrated by: Staples, 1932; Valentine, 1913–14;
and, more recently, by Spears, 1964.*] Music turned on (radio)
during these periods seems to please her, too. She notes its

* References to the literature are grouped at the end of each chapter and
are arranged alphabetically.

appearance by moving her eyes toward the source and if it disappears seems restless for several minutes.

Follows familiar figures through doorways with her eyes and stares constantly at the door for their reappearance for up to ten minutes—is not distracted from this "waiting" by closer stimuli for long, and turns eyes and/or head back toward the doorway.

Third week.   December 22

DEBBIE now measures 19½ inches and weighs 6 lb. 4 oz. Pediatrician suggested cereal once daily. She continues her previous schedule as before, except that she cries for her 6 P.M. feeding by 4:30 or 5 P.M. and then sleeps soundly from 6 to 10 P.M. when I waken her for nursing. [*Note 4: It is conceivable that Debbie could have skipped both her 10 P.M. and 2 A.M. feedings and slept through. There is no way of knowing whether Debbie's mother's waking her was in the interests of the mother's milk supply or was a remnant of her earlier pediatric training.*]

I continue to bathe her by sponge bath method on the kitchen drainboard. She seems to be rather ticklish generally, so we handle her firmly but as briefly as possible at bath times to reduce stimulation as best we can.

Debbie very definitely smiles at familiar faces—and more fully so if these faces smile at her. Strange smiling faces elicit only a serious stare. [*Note 5: Both Debbie's smiling and her strange-familiar discrimination are remarkable at this age. (Bayley, 1932)*]

Return to criblet after nursing is accompanied by a sigh of seeming relief, and sight of the mobile brings forth a smile of greeting from her. She reaches up toward it frequently now. [*Note 6: Likewise remarkable. (White, 1963)*] She still prefers the blue butterfly and follows it through all its gyrations.

She cries with impatience if not out-and-out anger at being properly sat at a 30–45° angle and strains forward fitfully. Seems happy again at being held or propped in upright position.

She flails angrily at being swaddled or being dressed or held in any way that restrains the movement of her limbs, but despite this is not a hyperactive infant. Think it's merely that she already uses arms and legs for investigation of her surroundings. [*Note 7: Peter Wolff's (1959) observations show a differential reaction to tight versus loose swaddling, the former producing calm and the latter agitation.*]

1 month, 8 days.   January 16

DEBBIE now measures 20 inches long and weighs 8 lb. 9 oz. She nurses and eats cereals and fruits. Debbie takes both her cereals and her fruit with adequate interest and thus far without much evidence of likes or dislikes.

She does not usually hold onto breast while nursing, but uses her free hand to feel the fabric of my blouse, or a button which she sees and grasps. She studies patterns and tries to follow them with an outstretched finger briefly. She looks up at my face and grins (interrupting sucking for a few seconds) when our eyes meet. She still paces her nursing with one interruption for burp (has never regurgitated a drop), which she indicates by spitting out the nipple, but never by crying with "gas."

She reaches for toys which she sees nearby, but not for those definitely far away (these she stares at). [*Note 8: In answer to the editor's query, Debbie's mother reported that Debbie had opened her fingers and grasped one of a set of keys on a chain.*] And she bats at toys dangled above or in front of her, occasionally grabbing one after considerable effort to do so. This brings forth a chuckle of satisfaction.

She also chuckles and laughs outright at "funny faces" made by her Daddy. She invariably responds to being called by name by turning to the source of the call (visible or not) and by a look of suspenseful but pleasurable waiting attentiveness. This response is specific to the words "Debbie" and "Loo Lee." She pays no particular attention to other words called out in the same voice unless they resemble phonetically the two noted above (such as "every" or "Noo Nee"). [*See Ruth, Note 3, page 168.*]

2–3 *months.   February*

BY NOW Debbie's afternoons are less eventful and she occasionally naps for thirty minutes or so.

She has discovered her hands, stares at them many times a day for three or four minutes at a time, watches them as she wiggles fingers, extends and flexes them, rotates wrists. She also clasps her hands together and stares at them out in front of her at arm's length. [*Note 9: Such behavior is more usual at 4–6 months, although Benjamin showed it at three months, eighteen days, and Ruth at eight weeks.*]

While nursing she has several times engaged in repetitive exercises in close-range and distant differentiation—grasping successively farther away fingers on my hand, letting go of each as she spies the next one and grabs it instead. Good control in this with very little weaving and random misses. The thumb is now in opposition at all times and she uses it, together with forefinger, for picking up some small objects.

Bath time is now in the kitchen sink. Tolerates some splashing well and grins and coos at having face or scalp washed. Less ticklish generally—seems to recognize different sensation when genital area is soaped or sponged.

Increasingly vocal: engages in answering-type conversations with both parents lasting four or five minutes, total body straining prominent as she tries to vary her tonal range, or make various lingual and labial sounds. [*See Benjamin, 2 months, 1 week, page 112, and 2 months, 25 days, page 113, and Ruth, Note 5, page 168.*]

Laughs at being jiggled, and also at the poodle's wagging tail or its sneezes, and in response to our laughter.

In the past week she has omitted her 6 A.M. feeding, too, and takes her 10 P.M. only because she is awakened and coaxed a bit. She is still being breast fed.

2 months, 3 weeks.   March 2

DEBBIE measures 20 inches long, weighs 10 lb. 3 oz. She eats cereal and fruit, and has added vegetables. She has had the triple vaccine and first polio shot. Screamed at the injection but was soothed by mother's low "tru-tra-trooing" to her.

Her first injection was followed by low fever and a cold. Debbie was not fretful during these three to four days of upper respiratory infection, but slept a bit more than usual and had some loss of appetite for solids.

Debbie's interest in her mobile persists and she continues to greet it with smiles and outstretched arms on her return to the crib. She now screams at it in perfect good humor when it is not in motion, as though to make it move. And she lies on her back and kicks the crib mattress, shaking the crib and jiggling the mobile a bit. Then she laughs.

She has begun to practice hearty crows of glee when approached or offered food, or at the dog. She also makes guttural sounds of all volumes when playing by herself, along with sounds of impatience when she can't reach or do a thing as she wants to. If her frustration isn't remedied, she very rarely progresses to rage—more usually diverts her own attention to something else.

Reaches for and gets two different toys, using both hands simultaneously. Strains toward the dog whenever he is visible. Recognizes the sound of dog's collar bells at all times, and smiles in the direction of sound even if dog is in another room. [*Note 10: Note the spatial orientation required to be able to localize sounds from an invisible source, as contrasted with orientation reported earlier to sounds produced in the same room.*]

Has begun to play with larger fuzzy stuffed toys, especially a big red fox. This poor toy gets cuddled, batted, licked, bitten, and is now missing its red felt tongue and its button nose which she picked at specifically.

She now turns onto her back at will and we find her most

mornings in her crib not only on her back but crossways, head and shoulders behind the crib bumper, holding it out at arm's length while she studies the pictured animals on it. Greets us gaily in passing and returns to her "reading." [*Note 11: It is doubtful that Debbie sees the designs on the bumper as representations of anything.*]

She observes her full arm in action at length. Raises and lowers it from the shoulder, bends elbow and wrist, and watches with interest.

She now stands against me for burping and has done so for two to three weeks. She struggles mightily to climb up me, using arms and feet to reach two favorite books on the shelf behind my head. Both of these are selected from among many books no matter how changed the relationships. One has on its spine an orange portrait of Shakespeare which she likes and recognizes, and the other a black Borzoi imprint. With effort she has lately been able to reach them and scrapes at these two small pictures with a fingernail.

3 months.

WHILE NURSING, she has practiced (three different occasions) for ten to fifteen minutes each time a sort of peek-a-boo by hiding her face behind a fold of my blouse, pulling it away and grinning when she sees me again.

Also repetitive practice of picking up and dropping toys (rattles) or her shirt fabric without watching the process, but, rather, staring off into space idly or actively. Peers at the object only if it hasn't fallen just exactly where she expected to find it, then locates it, and picks it up. [*Note 12: Again note Debbie's orientation to unseen space on the basis of auditory cues.*]

Now raises head to watch and listen to her wind-up "Lullaby Bear," drops it when the tune is finished, and goes immediately off to sleep.

On first exposure to mirror last week, recognized mother, looked from mirror to person several times to check up. Then looked at herself and ducked her head "shyly" as she stared from under eyebrows at her image. By now she is quite at ease with it all, and sometimes smiles at herself. Reaches toward self image and stares into own eyes with forehead against mirror seriously. (Had never seen another baby "in the flesh" before this.) [*Note 13: It is doubtful that Debbie recognizes her reflection as her own, but her behavior is strikingly advanced.*]

Debbie is an alert child—her sensory perceptions are multiple and constant. This month she has begun to "look" a question at me whenever a new sound or smell (flowers) or person impinges on her. And the "word" for it removes the questioning glance. By now, door-slams, hammering, dog-barks, telephone, door-bell, etc., are all familiar to her and accepted without question, though she still hears them and listens to them.

An electric door-planer induced an imitative high-pitched scream from her on one occasion. When the planer stopped and she continued, she apparently heard herself, stopped abruptly, with a wide-eyed expression. When I said, "That was Debbie," she laughed and in a few seconds repeated it and laughed again. [*Note 14: Imitation of inanimate sounds does not usually occur until 9–12 months of age. Note the self-discovery in Debbie's hearing her own voice, and the beginning comprehension of language here, above, and below.*]

She recognizes and responds to a number of phrases, among them: "Take a nap," "Bye-bye butterfly," "Where is your foot?" "Sippy-sip" (of milk), "Take a bath," "Hold on" (grabs both hands of parent and strains upward to be lifted from crib or playpen), "Burp?" [*Note 15: Here we must be mindful that these phrases are ordinarily used in a context of things and behavior that carries some part of the meaning.*]

Usually a cheerful, responsive child, Debbie threw two brief (two to four minutes) global physiological storms early this month, both characterized by diffuse motility and screams of rage, and both brought on when her supper time had been inadvertently and unavoidably postponed by thirty minutes or more. Both appeared without any warning, and only when the food was placed before her. Suddenly too aware of hunger, perhaps, to be able to eat. [*Note 16: Note the goal-gradient effect, the increased intensity of response as gratification approaches, which can be observed in both children and adults in many everyday situations. See Benjamin, Note 14, page 124.*] These brought from the harassed mother a firm nah-nah-nah-nah (her first scoldings), and immediately, both times, Debbie stopped crying, "asked" for a moment's cuddling and soothing talk, and then ate happily as usual, though perhaps with more gusto.

One other item: Having caught her thumb in a plastic safety-pin-shaped rattle a week ago, she has since refused to play with it (previously her favorite teether) despite being reintroduced to it at intervals. [*Note 17: Observe the one-trial learning.*]

Something happened during the first week or so of this third month which "almost overnight" made Debbie seem less an infant and more a baby. [*Note 18: Debbie's mother is probably referring to the widely observed phenomenon of the baby's "becoming human."*] Hard to define explicitly, it somehow involves a further steadying of her afternoon schedule, a wider range of vocal and facial expression, increased motor control, greater capacity and assurance in areas of enjoyment, waiting, and involvement with her entire world.

4 *months.* *April 6*

DEBBIE measures 23 inches and weighs 11 lb. 6 oz. Puddings have been added to her diet. She has had another triple vaccine and her second polio shot.

This time Debbie began to scream and shake with racking cries and sobs as soon as she approached the doctor's examining room. Increased volume of sound when he appeared, but responded quickly to soothing after her second injection, and was willing to be calm in his office thereafter. [*Note 19: Note both the learning involved here and the retention of learning over a one-month span. See 2 months, 3 weeks, page 10.*]

Debbie has by now insisted that her 10 P.M. feeding (still breast fed) be omitted, so essentially is now on three meals a day. Eats everything offered with fair interest, though she seems to dislike sweet foods (squash, sweet potato, pineapple, pudding), and to prefer beans and spinach and other less sweet tastes.

She continues to drop and retrieve objects at will, to manage two or three at once, selectively, and to try to exercise vocal magic on her mobile. [*Note 20: Lest the baby's attempts to influence physical events vocally appear hopelessly stupid, we should remember that he learns early that vocal magic does in fact work on one class of things—people—and he then has the task of learning to discriminate between influenceable and non-influenceable objects. As an aside, we might wonder whether the use of voice-actuated feedback apparatus for experiments in "verbal learning" reinforces the magicalism of young subjects. We might further bear in mind that babies learn quite early about blowing on things with their breath, which has an effect on how their skin feels and on match flames and bits of paper.*] She has increased her peek-a-boo experiments with simple head-turning, blankets, etc. She has shown considerable eagerness to drink from a cup but has very little facility with it thus far.

She shows marked interest in standing with minimal adult support. And when told to "Sit down," she thinks very hard, then her knees bend, and down she sits. This is a game with her of her own devising which brings forth much giggling and laughter. [*Note 21: Since this standing-sitting game requires parental cooperation, it seems not quite accurate to describe it as of Debbie's own devising.*]

Humor and appreciation of her own games occur with two other activities: (1) she delights in finding herself somehow above either of us, reacting with boundless glee and much looking down at us; (2) she thinks that chewing alternately on right and left index fingers of a parent while standing supported by their thumbs is completely wonderful. She looks at us with knowing eyebrow-cocking glances, grins, and much laughter.

She has also devised a "kissy-kiss" game on her own which delights her and soaks the cheek or nose of parent with gooey saliva. She seems to enjoy this both as infant and as parent-imitation and takes on a most gentle-eyed intent expression as she comes in to bestow the kiss.

She now greets self in mirror with wide-arm welcome gestures and huge grin. Pays no attention to parental image, and reaches out to touch own image very rarely now.

She greets Daddy at homecoming with outstretched arms and much laughter, and also her grandmother (providing the catch-phrase "Are you Nana's little girl?" is uttered first).

She reacted with screams and much crying to her first meeting with a year-old boy who approached in an aggressive manner, and has refused to "go to" one woman who appeared rapidly and noisily at Debbie's crib. After their departure, she, both times, put her hand up to mother's mouth to be kissed and then all seemed well again. [*Note 22: Note that such discriminations among people need not be only on the basis of facial features but may involve styles of movement, tones of voice, and odors as well. See Note 23.*]

Vocalization now includes *g, gl,* and rolled tongue sounds, also occasional *h* and *n* sounds.

Debbie has during the latter half of this fifth month discovered her feet—reaches for them, handles and chews on them. Also insists on using them as prehensile hands—grasps arm of parent, toys, etc. with them and with toes of one foot with considerable motor skill. She also has begun to rub her eyes when sleepy and to scratch stomach and buttocks whenever they itch.

There were two major occurrences this month. First, the addition to the house was completed and Debbie moved into her own room from the living room. Took this easily and well—showed marked interest in new spatial relationships and indicated that she needed to have new routes from her wing of the house repeated several times (watched fore and aft as we progressed slowly) and then accepted it all in apparent comfort. Second, on April 25 (age 4 months, 17 days) Debbie demanded supplementary feeding and the pediatrician suggested sudden and total weaning from the breast. Despite all my good intentions to do this gradually, she made the transition to the bottle with no murmur of protest or confusion, although it took her bowels a week to accommodate to cow's milk.

Concomitant with the discovery of her feet, Debbie finally succeeded in her attempts to turn from back to stomach. Turning over extends her reach and she seems to take her enlarged scope as a matter of course.

She also sits alone now, pushing away from the support, though when fatigued, or with extended interest in her feet, she tends to end up nose on toes.

Two "errors" in perception this month: (1) she mistook a curly-fabric black jacket on a chair for her black dog and reached and strained toward it from across the room, uttering something suspiciously like "dg, dg, dg" over and over again and with increasing confusion in her facial expression when it didn't come to her as her dog does [*Note 23: Even though personal recognition may involve perception of a complex of convergent attributes, one striking (although perhaps irrelevant) feature can be enough for recognition (correct or incorrect), that is, it can "stand for" the totality. Inversely, changing one feature (as by putting on a hat) can alter the Gestalt beyond recognition.*]; (2) awaking from a nap in her crib to find a stoutish grey-haired woman looking down at her, she responded as she does to her grandmother and it was only after a moment had gone by, when she was picked up, that she realized that it was not grandmother, reared back at arm's length, studied the face a moment, smiled tentatively, and then settled down to accept the new person.

5 months.   May

DEBBIE's height is 24 inches, weight 12 lb. 8 oz. Meats have been added to her diet. Triple vaccine and third polio shot. Took this visit to pediatrician with some visible tension and readiness to cry, but did not. Watched all other children with interest though with a "poker face."

Debbie has by now become so active and so curious and observant of everything that impinges on her that she has begun to take, without any action on our part, fairly long afternoon naps. This is not to say that she is a hypermotile baby, but is so busy "working" on some project or watching everything visible or following adult conversations with her head swiveling to watch each one speak in turn, or engaging in answering conversations with a parent (even in another part of the house), that she at last feels the need of rest in the afternoon.

She is now capable of projecting expected passage of parents from area to area while out of sight and of her dog, too, often apparently listening for audible clues to their progress.

She manages two and three toys of medium size well, picking and choosing easily and with good motor control. She finds tiny flecks, specks, and flakes on rug or couch and picks them up accurately.

She watches leaves, shadows, and smoke with interest but has never yet sought to grab them. She seems to have fair depth perception and does not attempt to grab things out of range, though she may strain and kick to indicate that she wants to get near enough to make grabbing practical. [*Note 24: This observation raises, without answering, the question of how close a stimulus has to be before the baby attends to it. There is some reason to believe that there are distinct limits to the baby's visual and auditory range, and that it is not until toddlerhood that the child can detect things at great distances from himself, or at least perceive them as constant.*]

She continues to be most responsive to those she knows and to her dog, and seems to think "going to" each parent alternately is a great game. Accepting of strangers, though not an automatic grinner at them. She is not frightened, but stares seriously, smiles quietly if she likes what or whom she sees and then "moves in" quietly and even sweetly.

Facial mobility and expressiveness increased with ability to smile, during solo play, at parent who may not be smiling at her; or not to smile when smiled at, as she chooses. Eyebrow cocking, ducked head, coyness, lusty shouting, grins, etc. [*Note 25: The reader should bear in mind that these emotional expressions reflect the development of variegated self-world relationships and in this sense can be considered cognitive phenomena.*]

She has begun to try to take toys with her from crib to bathroom and to other parts of the house. She likes jangling toys and noisy toys now, whereas before she seemed uncertain how to react.

She sits up in her bath and it's a problem to keep her from grabbing everything within reach and sucking on it. Occasionally puts a sponge or a brush back upon its shelf and chooses another object to immerse. [*Note 26: Debbie's ability to place an object on a shelf implies an orientation to space quite different from that involved in simply letting go of unwanted playthings.*]

She has begun to alternate kicks and makes some effort to take alternate steps when standing with support. She has a fair sense of rhythm and will adjust large arm or leg wavings to fit whatever is on the radio, often with due regard to lesser or off-beats in addition to the major beat. While standing, she often bounces, wig-wags her hips, or stamps in time to music with her left foot. [*Note 27: It is probably more accurate to say that Debbie's reaction to music includes a variety of body movements.*] She obviously enjoys this and coos happily or looks "smug."

She more and more studies eyes and mouth in a face intently and tries to imitate oral movements and vocal sounds, although we have made no effort to have her learn sounds or words.

Has learned the "Bronx cheer" and delights in it. Also many polysyllabic sounds which she uses for solo play accompaniment. Squeals and shrieks are prominent. She likes to be whistled or sung to as before.

Fairly mobile now, she gets about from room to room by rolling over and over, with odd wriggles and stretches, rocking and teetering on hands and knees with frog-leaps forward. She is able now to pick up dropped toys on the counter behind her head, easily and without any need to use her eyes. [*Note 28: Debbie's mother seems to be saying that when Debbie is being bathed in the sink she can then simply reach out to where the toy has fallen and retrieve it. This implies that this region of*

*space is so stably defined that the sound of the plaything's im-
pact immediately gives its location relative to Debbie.*]

On one occasion, she experimented hesitantly, but on her
own initiative, with a game of give-and-take with a favorite toy.
The concentration was intense for fifteen to seventeen minutes
and left her quite tired.

A visit from a seven-month-old crawler engaged Debbie's
most intent watching during one afternoon, and the next day she
definitely tried to mimic, with some success, the other child's
actions (crawling mainly). [*Note 29: Students of imitation would
do well to remember that there may be a considerable delay between the stimulus-action and the act of imitation.*]

Having seen and watched TV on one brief occasion, she has
since intermittently stared at the picture tube when the radio
(but not the TV) is first turned on, as though expecting it to
light up.

Mirror now usually evokes boredom. Reflection seen in a window wall apparently alerted her to the fact that a barrier was
there and she immediately put both palms on the glass, leaned
forward and proceeded to look right through at her dog outside,
as she had been doing from across the room anyway. (Our
house is modern and largely glass.) [*Note 30: In such cases one
must observe carefully that the child is indeed looking* through
the glass and not at *it.*]

This month Debbie has learned to clamp her jaws and lips
firmly together in rejection of food. Cannot say that she dislikes
any specific food, but rather that on occasion she just does not
want her meal. That this is sometimes arbitrary may be indicated by the fact that if she happens to taste a bit of the rejected food on her lip, she may then eat with gusto—but not
always. [*Note 31: Negativism is by no means rare at this age.*]

6 months. June

DEBBIE measures 25 inches and weighs 14 lb. Egg yolks have
been added to her diet. When Debbie was vaccinated, she cried
only at the doctor's approach and examination. She liked being

dressed and taken out of the cubicle, and all was sunny again. On the day following her six-month day, Debbie cut her first two teeth (lower incisors). No preliminary fretfulness, but as the teeth actually erupted, during a thirty-minute period, she cried with real pain. She then "asked" to finish supper, and, suddenly very tired, went to bed early for the night, omitting her customary play period. The next morning all was as usual with her except for occasional tongue exploration of the two new teeth as she ate.

Her lusty enjoyment of life has taken a bound forward in the past week. Her crib is a complete shambles these mornings, her crows and squawks and shrieks are heard easily all over the house and yard. She moves flexibly and quickly, and she is quite capable of flinging herself unpredictably toward a goal, even from a height. Takes watching now at bath and dressing times. [*Note 32: The baby's fearful withdrawal from the edge of a precipice is taken as evidence that he sees the spatial relation of self to drop-off. Debbie's quite different behavior does not mean that she does not see the "visual cliff" (Gibson and Walk, 1960) but only that she sees it as attractive rather than repellent. I have called this reaction, observed in some other babies (see Ruth, age 7 months, 27 days, page 199) and in some puppies, the "Geronimo effect."*]

We have begun to bathe her in the tub where she can splash and kick and play with toys or washcloth with more space and freedom. She relishes the entire procedure. Lies down on her back contentedly for a shampoo, sits up with glee, apparently thinks having face and feet washed is some kind of a joke. Dressing afterward is eased if she has a toy to play with.

Introduced to her first cracker on her six-month day. She managed it quite well—gummed and nibbled her way through it, held fragments in each hand and dropped only small crumbs. The gooey smear on fingers she licked off and sucked off, leaving Mother with only a few soggy crumbs on the face to wipe up.

Since then she has shown great interest in cookies, and if she spots one placed beforehand among the toys in her bounce-chair tray, she immediately begins to toss out and to drop whatever objects block her view of and access to the cracker. [*Note 33: The provision of a bouncing chair, previously unmentioned, implies encouragement of whole-body activity and muscular control. It is important to note Debbie's visual discrimination of edible from inedible, and of the figural cookie from the potentially distracting jumble of background.*]

She prefers to play with two or more objects at once, rather than one, and either picks up each one in sequence or shifts toys from hand to hand in order to pick up others.

6 months, 6 days.   June 14

DEBBIE has finally succeeded in creeping, much to her obvious delight. She has spent the entire day practicing this new skill and takes off most earnestly in straight-line, fifteen- to twenty-foot excursions, hands patting the floor rhythmically and loud enough at times to be heard all over the house. She accompanies herself with gleeful crows and ahh-ahh sounds. [*Note 34: Once again, the precocity of Debbie's motor development should be signaled. Characteristically, a child practices new skills for their own sake; later, they may be functionally subordinated to other activities. In the case of creeping, getting to a destination is at first a minor consideration, whereas it later becomes dominant, with creeping merely the means to an end.*]

This sixth month seems to have been a month of powerful self-assertion, and she has learned to be quite no-ish on occasion. For instance, she can now take or leave her dog's advances and will sometimes flail annoyedly to push Ollie away; she can delay her usual gay greetings to familiar persons for a moment or two, first giving an ornery, knowing expression as she watches the newcomer's reaction; she shakes her head no-no to reject food or cup; she indicates the end of a meal firmly by clamped lips and sudden interest in anything away from her feeding table, lunging toward it; she pushes proffered toys away and picks up one of her own choosing.

Humor appears when she delays greetings as mentioned above. Also she apparently relishes a little joke when she "goes" to one person and then turns away to "go to" another. Also when she wags an arm in poorly coordinated waving actions as Daddy comes into or goes from the room.

On several occasions also she has enjoyed plugging up a whistling parent by poking an index finger into the lips and laughs at this. [*Note 35: These observations are important, because they remind us that babies do not lead lives of hard-headed pragmatism but begin at an early age to explore situations in terms of their emotional possibilities, and to manipulate situations to bring out new meanings.*]

She has once or twice made high-pitched soft humming sounds utilizing a range of two to four notes when she has been about to drop off to sleep. These somewhat resemble singing, as though she is lullabying herself to sleep. (She has no such sleep ritual, though she invariably enjoys Mother's singing at odd intervals during the day.)

Now that she creeps so well, she has the full run of the house, and her pitty-pats give adequate clues to her whereabouts, as do her vocalizations. She clambers into closets, low cupboards, and every nook and cranny, leaving a wake of scattered objects behind her as further testimony of her progress.

Interest in bottle has definitely diminished, and she much prefers the cup at all times. She eats neatly, drooling or slobbering only very rarely and slightly. She opens mouth only when previous spoonful has been swallowed and manages with ease seven to nine consecutive swallows of fluid from her cup.

6 months, 18 days.   June 26

FOUND Debbie inexplicably sitting up in the middle of the floor on two occasions last week. Today she devoted the entire day to mastering this change of position. [*Note 36: Debbie apparently began to creep before she was able to get into a sitting position without help.*] Sprouting like a mushroom here and there about the house in the midst of her more routine creeping, she repeated the action of sitting up more than sixty times today. Early in the day, thumps were frequently heard as she dumped herself backward or sideways to continue creeping, but by afternoon she was adept at pivoting back onto hands and knees. She remained cheerfully matter-of-fact during these long workouts and never became fretful, which she almost never is anyway.

7 months. July

HAVING become able to sit up by herself last week, Debbie by now is busy pulling herself up to standing position alongside chairs, sofas, cabinets. She does this by pulling with the arms and pushing with the legs, although she sometimes uses arm or leg power predominantly.

By virtue of this new skill, she now can get up into cabinets or planter-boxes or fireplace—all of which are six to twelve inches off the floor—and these activities keep Mama busier than before.

She enjoys her new game of creeping back and forth up-into-and-down-out-of her reclining chair in its flat position, and does this three or four times in a row every other day or so. We now also use her chair as a convenient toy box, and she frequently creeps from distant corners of the house to it and kneels beside it as she selects the toy she wants next.

All these actions have served to teach parents that an occasional prohibition is now in order (fireplace and electric outlets and wires are the three No's for now). Our first "No" was ignored repeatedly (we admonished and removed her with hopeful but unsuccessful attempts at diversion). Now, however, a few days later, she either pauses halfway in her approach to a taboo object and looks around waiting for the word, or dashes headlong for it at double pace, apparently hoping to reach the object before the word comes. [*Note 37: According to the usual criteria, a child cannot be said to have learned a taboo until he obeys it. However, the behavior of children (and dogs) shows clearly that they can learn taboos and still try to evade them. See Benjamin, 11 months, 3 weeks, page 138, and Ruth, 8 months, page 201.*] If she succeeds in getting the forbidden fruit, then she either works on it at double pace or appears momentarily confused or hesitant, as though again waiting for the word "No."

With all this increased mobility, she has begun on occasion to resent being laid down for diaper change and cries with muttered syllables to tell me that it's no fun to be treated in this manner.

Her pattern of growth remains essentially as before—daily schedules fairly stable, with an occasional day-long interruption for "growing," a day on which she sleeps very little and works steadily at some project. On these days she never has been fretful or cranky despite frustration and lack of sleep, and to date has never waked up during the night.

She remains mainly a morning napper, with variable afternoon siestas. She revels in a family get-together from mid-afternoon until bedtime, and her main group play with parents and dog and toys follows a 5 P.M. supper and continues until bedtime at 6:30 or 7, depending on signs of fatigue.

This being July, she has long since been introduced to the swimming pool, and this she enjoys fully. Creeping about on the flagstone walk, locating fragments of dried leaves to crunch and crumble, climbing into and out of a small wading basin, mingling with neighbors and other children (she pats, slaps, pokes, and stares at them, as well as creeps after them as she chooses), and being taken into the water for sozzling and splashing and kicking are great fun for her.

As for "poking," she pokes a forefinger into eyes, mouths, ears, cups, toward light sockets. [*Note 38: This probing exploration of the environment illustrates the baby's response to "demand qualities," the way that characteristics of the environment tell us how to behave—a chair is to sit on, a baby's cheek is to pinch—as does the exploration of textures described below.*]

She continues to investigate textures of objects (dog fur, brick fireplace, mirror, leaves, sidewalk) as she has for several weeks now with extended forefinger or a rhythmically rubbing palmar surface.

Rhythm continues to interest her—she now bangs toys or slaps

with her fist, or bobs up and down alongside a chair while standing, in time to singing commercials and some music on the radio,
or to songs sung by a parent. She will stand up next to the radio
speaker and feel its vibrations and pat it in time to music also.

Her "speech" now consists of monologues conducted in a
range of tones and volumes, and encompasses polysyllabic
speeches involving *bl, br, mr, nah, gl, gr,* interspersed with *oo,
ee, ow,* and *o, eh, ah* vowel sounds. She emits forceful "Ha's"
when she accomplishes something worthwhile and looks toward
parent.

7 months, 16 days.   July 24

DEBBIE has rejected bottle totally and completely for several
days now, despite its being offered, and will use cup only. She
has begun to "chew" solemnly, even her liquids, so some junior
foods are being introduced. She seems to enjoy this and smiles
appreciatively up at the adult. Her appetite is still at the four-
month level, and fairly steady except for fluids which she seems
to alternate on a two-day-off, one-day-on basis.

She has a new game of peek-a-boo of her own invention and
which evokes broad smiles and laughter from her. This involves
her ducking down out of sight behind the sofa arm and then
popping up again repetitively.

She also has begun to take toys with her as she creeps about
the house, either carrying a soft squeaky-toy in her mouth as she
goes, or clompety-clomping around with a block or rattle in one
hand making an odd sound pattern as she travels.

She has long since (two or three weeks) been able to detour
around obstacles, and goes in back of doors or around boxes to
locate long-lost toys. [*Note 39: Notice that such behavior con-
tradicts the findings of delayed-response experiments. The difference may be in who it is that "hides" the toy, the experimenter
or the baby. Such retrieval of hidden objects is not ordinarily
observed, however, much before age one. See Benjamin, 11
months, 3 weeks, Note 25, page 138.*] Anything else, of course,
she mauls her way over.

She plays well for ten or fifteen minutes in another room without any direct supervision, returning to home base to crawl up Mama's leg and be greeted for a moment or be offered a sip of liquid. Then off again about her business. [*Note 40: Again, experimental findings about the baby's brief attention span must be questioned. How long the baby pays attention to something seems to be a matter of what it is the baby is expected to pay attention to.*]

7 months, 22 days. July 30

SHE has begun to walk along the full length of couches or around coffee tables. She usually brings a small toy up with her, places it on the table, grabs it again later, drops it on the floor, goes down on one knee to retrieve it (holding onto sofa or table with the other hand) and back up again. She goes from table to chair, too, with pleasure in the reaching.

She is quite expert now at kneeling, pivoting on one foot, standing on tiptoe to reach a higher object, rotating her trunk from the waist to pick up a fallen toy behind her as she stands.

8 months. August 8

ON THIS, her eight-month day, she notified us as usual at 6:30 A.M. that she was awake and wet, and, as usual, we found the crib a shambles (toys scattered, blanket crumpled into a ball at the foot end, etc.), and Debbie standing at the crib side ready to welcome us with a broad grin and outstretched arms, also as usual. The only thing different was that she had completely removed her rubber pants and soaked diapers, and was dressed only in her little jacket.

These mornings, after changing, she resumes solitary play with chattering—occasionally she naps again for thirty minutes —until she hears us stirring and the radio on about 7:30, when she shouts to us to come get her. She then joins us; creeps into bathroom to sit on floor and watch Daddy shave, into bedroom to climb into the dog's basket, into kitchen while coffee and toast are prepared. She eats at 8 A.M. or so—with variable gusto and no impatience beforehand.

Thereafter, she plays for a while, climbs into her toy box and sits amidst the toys, flinging some out, fingering, studying, or chewing others. Then a period of following Mama all about the house as the chores are done, making no particular demands on parent, but investigating whatever catches her interest.

Bath time follows at 9:15 or 9:30, depending on whether she seems receptive to the idea on being asked "Bath?" [*Note 41: Note how word and routine converge to enable Debbie to understand what is said to her.*] She plays with plastic toys in the tub, sucks on the washcloth with noisy swallowing and some choking on bath water. Sleepiness supervenes during the dressing, with eye-rubbing, slight irritability, and yawning. To bed with relief and rubbing of nose against the sheet and asleep immediately.

8 months, 8 days.   August 16

AN active period of change since the last entry. Debbie's been a busy little person and parents have been busy trying to note the events.

In creeping about the house, she frequently stops, elevates her bottom, and peers out between her legs at the upside-down world, rights herself and looks again to check impressions and repeats the process several times. [*Note 42: Note both the playfulness and seriousness of Debbie's exploration of spatial relations. Note, too, that she is exploring not only space but also her own body's orientation therein.*]

Standing up by the refrigerator she seems fascinated by a raised metal applique brand name, and with tip of index finger investigates the similar shapes of *e* and *o* over and over again, ignoring the other letters.

She creeps pell-mell from remote corners of the house whenever the telephone rings, and soon appears at my knee, oo-ing and ah-ing, to talk on the phone. [*Note 43: Debbie's mother probably means that Debbie wants a turn at being talked to on the phone. Even children who use language cannot at first talk back to a telephone, although they obviously recognize the voice at the other end and understand what is being said.*]

The same pertains to the doorbell and she sits seriously watching the entry of whatever visitor has appeared.

She has begun to clap hands together on her own (no adult demonstrations of this in advance), but welcomes our mimicry of her action with a wise, eyebrow-cocking smile.

She also now begins to clap and then seemingly listens for the "patty cake" words to begin before she goes on.

She has begun to clap two toys together and always seems exceptionally pleased with this action and its resulting sounds.

She follows Daddy to the door and stands at the window waving an arm wildly as he disappears from view. On his return she scrambles to the nearest point of view of the foyer and on recognizing him she laughs, waves, jabbers, and rushes headlong toward him again. [*Note 44: Presumably Debbie, like other babies, is alerted to her father's homecoming by the idiosyncratic sound of his car. Again, though, her daily physiological cycle probably readies her to expect her father at a particular hour.*]

She spies sunny spots on the rug, sits beside them and makes shadows in the spot with extended hand or arm. She does not try to grab the shadow.

She recognizes that sound will soon come from the speaker in the living room after the switch in an adjoining room is clicked on, and she interrupts her play and sits with turned head to await the sound. If music appears she bounces and bangs happily at once. [*Note 45: Note this additional instance of classical conditioning, but note, too, the lag between the conditioned stimulus (the click of the switch) and the unconditioned stimulus (meaningful sounds). It would be tedious but worthwhile to catalogue all the possible pairings of stimuli to which the baby is exposed, and to determine which connections get established and which do not.*]

She stands eagerly beside the tub while the bath is being drawn, reaches in to put a hand under the stream, and dumps toys in. She indicates impatience at panties and diaper by push-

ing and tweaking them. If rubber pants are lowered as she
stands there, she steps out of them neatly without help and
then yaps at me to remove those diapers please.

8 *months, 12 days.*   *August 20*

VISITED yesterday by a strange baby, one month younger than
Debbie, who cried and pouted when in need of solace. Debbie
watched this, walked around the coffee table closer to the baby,
and then began to cry, too. When the other baby was picked up
by its mother and lowered the intensity and urgency of its cry,
Debbie stopped crying and went back about her business.
[*Note 46: Note the contagion of affect unrelated to either
Debbie's state or any particular sympathy for the baby. But
note, too, the learning reflected in what follows.*]

And today, in the midst of busy play with familiar toys, she
suddenly looked up at me with a definite pouting lower lip
(new for her), screwed up her face and began a rather "theatrical" forced crying. This stopped when she was picked up—
no soothing required. Later on in the day after two naps she
tried this maneuver again and this time Mother merely looked at
her and extended lower lip gradually. At this, Debbie laughed
at the silly change in Mother's face and the episode was over.

8 *months, 18 days.*   *August 26*

CUT one upper incisor on August 22 and the second one erupted
today. Discomfort attending these a bit more pronounced than
with lower incisors. Crying and compulsive biting relieved by
aspirin and ice chips in a handkerchief. The days were otherwise unremarkable and she was not prolongedly fretful.

Given a new set of colorful nesting plastic cups, she investigated them earnestly. When a parent later piled them up like
blocks she watched each one put in place and then knocked the
whole pile down with a wide-flung arm. She appeared disappointed or taken aback by this, so the parent then repiled them.

This time, she most definitely sought to remove only the top one (and failed). Lower piles using three or four instead of the total twelve gave her success on her next attempt and she managed to grasp and remove the top one or two quite neatly. Play on her own with these same cups on successive days demonstrates her interest in trying to put one atop another. Movements too gross, however, and she fails. [*Note 47: It seems likely, too, that Debbie could not perceive the size relations involved in stacking the cups.*] After a few attempts she leaves this game to play with something else.

Debbie's relationship with her dog (and of Ollie with Debbie, too) is developing nicely and gives us some silent amusement. She grabs the wagging tail, pokes fingers into the dog's eyes and mouth. Slaps at the dog (in imitation of adult petting, perhaps) but not too uncontrolledly, fingers the shiny foot pads, singles out one by one the various dangling tags on Ollie's collar for study and turns them over in her fingers or between the fingers of one hand. They also share shredding paper games, and on state occasions Debbie will deliberately give her dog a piece of her cookie, much to the delight of each of them. She's usually able to hand the cookie fragment to the dog between fingers or thumb and finger—though on occasion it sticks to her sticky palm and Ollie can't get it easily. At this she flings the hand to loosen it, or rubs her extended palm on a surface to scrape it loose, then tries again to pick it up properly.

8 months, 25 days.   September 2

WRITING a letter in the dining room this morning, heard a strange call of alarm from Debbie. I looked up to find her up on a chair and peering down anxiously. She'd gotten up without aid, but needless to say she was given aid in getting down again and pronto! [*Note 48: Here Debbie exhibits a more conventional "visual cliff" response. See Note 32, page 20.*]

Since last entry, Debbie has begun to show some boredom with the feeding process. She plays with anything available, traces out with a finger tip the patterns on her feeding-table top, makes a great thing of touching the "baby" on the jar label or her plate. [*Note 49: This may be the first indication that Debbie recognizes a pictured object.*] She also swivels her head to follow any distracting sound or movement. She engaged a few times in a foot peek-a-boo, nudging my knee with her foot, then withdrawing the whole leg again up into the seat when I reached or looked for the foot; and this with a little smile of secret enjoyment that she has so often when she invests an act of hers with humor. [*Note 50: This game implies some comprehension on Debbie's part that what may be visible to her may be invisible to her mother.*] She still shows no interest in holding the cup (nor did she the breast or bottle either), but does grab for the spoon frequently to "help" guide it to her mouth or dish. She also has developed a major interest in finger painting with her food and returns gooey fingers repeatedly to the paint pot for more. Profligate with her material, but when finished she is eager to have hands wiped off a bit, after she has first done her best to suck and lick them clean. [*Note 51: Such a desire for cleanliness of the fingers seems to be universal in infancy and is probably motivated by the fact that sticky or dirty fingers interfere with smooth tactual communication with things.*] She now prefers to get down and play right after her solids and comes back at intervals for sips of her milk which she prefers to drink while standing up at my knee or alongside a low table.

9 *months.* September 10

HEIGHT is now 26½ inches, weight 15 lb. 13 oz. No untoward response to the doctor's office or to the doctor. Seemed curious but a little reserved during the examination.

Today Debbie selected a tomato from a full basket of tomatoes awaiting canning this afternoon, bit into it and in a few moments had eaten essentially all of it! This occurred on a linoleum floor—a few seeds, scattered shreds of tomato skin on baby and floor and a puddle of juice were all that remained. This accomplished, she was intent on choosing another when parents decided one was probably enough. [*Note 52: It may be that Debbie is here asserting her readiness for a more mature diet.*]

Debbie has experienced her third trip to the supermarket and seemed to enjoy all the crowds, noise and colorful displays. She has been such an alert, watchful, participating infant that we have sometimes protected her from too great a barrage of strange stimuli such as a large grocery store provides. Previous trial trips were overstimulating to her, with early fatigue and request for cuddling afterward. Not so this time.

Rides in the car have always been accepted by her, but now that she sits up she not only studies the dashboard items but reaches for them; and she evinces interest in other cars, trees, and other large bits of scenery. Stopped for red light or parked for a moment, she watches and follows, with head and trunk motions if necessary, pedestrians, passing cars, children skipping along, bicycles—all that heaves into view.

Cooler weather has necessitated dressing Debbie in more than her panties with or without a jacket. She puts up with all this new manipulation quite well—fingers the corduroy, pats her trousered knee, and watches the buttoning of bib-front with deeply flexed neck. She seems pleased with a new garment and preens a bit in feminine fashion.

The appearance of a rocking-horse in our household demanded that she creep right over, stand up to this unstable creature, and look the gift in the mouth. She walked around it, stepping nimbly over protruding rockers and, not at all upset by its unpredictable motion, proceeded to tangle its tail, jangle the stirrups, pull on the bridle, poke at its eyes and ears. Riding was good and she cried when we attempted to stop it too soon.

Now that the ground is too cold and damp for her to be allowed to creep about the yard, we procured a small stroller. This is the greatest thing that ever happened, to judge by her response, and she revels in daily rides around the neighborhood. She studies all passing flowers and shrubs, stares up at tree leaves, sits for fifteen to twenty minutes to watch chipmunks and squirrels busy at work under the oak tree. She strains to reach playing neighbor children or their dogs whom she knows and accepts. We find this very nice. She has never been one much for swaddling as a wee infant or for restraint (as in a bouncing chair or play pen, which soon bore her), so this ability to stay put and let the world come to her is a change.

Her first exposure to steps: climbed directly and forthrightly up the whole flight of six (no risers to these steps) and then proceeded to back down them again, ever so nicely. But still does not back down off chairs, though she is up on one chair or another a dozen times a day, and asks for help in getting down again. We help her back down and she takes an increasingly active part in this maneuver.

9 *months, 10 days.   September 18*

VARIOUS things necessitated the day-long absence of both parents for four consecutive days. Debbie remained at home in the care of a grandmother whom she knows and likes. The grandmother is familiar with the baby and the baby's usual reactions and the "schedule," so this was an easy separation.

Debbie responded to this quite well—ate and slept as usual during most of the day but, according to report, became a little more restless and dissatisfied than usual toward late afternoon, requiring a bit more entertainment and supervision than is ordinary, and went to bed one-half to one hour earlier than usual.

During these four nights she awoke at the 10 to 12 P.M. diaper-change time (most unusual for her), cried and was not soothed until she had had a thirty- to forty-five-minute play period with both parents. The play she instigated was very like the alternate "going to" each parent with patting the adults and quiet humming sounds that she usually engages in at the termination of her post-supper play time.

She repeated this night-waking, but diminishingly, until last night, when she slept right through as usual.

On my first day home with her again, she was more clinging and more demanding of attention than ever before, but on the second day was back to normal.

9 months, 13 days.   September 21

DEBBIE succeeded in getting herself down off a chair without help (except for Mother's asking "Get down?") this morning and once down she stood beside the chair and banged the seat jubilantly with an arm and had a look of elated triumph on her smiling face. She then repeated this new accomplishment many times, sitting and standing on the seat between ups and downs, taking toys up with her and crowing and ha-ing often.

Her "speech" these days varies from crooning to crowing and lusty shout in tone, with occasional highpitched "singing" during solitary play. She uses repetitive compound words—"dip-dap," "na-na," "ma-ma," "da-de," "ee-vow," "ha-vlah"—along with other combinations of "tsah-ti-doo," "bah-bi-moo-na," resembling real words in a sentence as far as phrasing and inflection are concerned. [*Note 53: This account suggests that Debbie, at an unusually early age, was using "expressive jargon." It is impor-tant to note that the child may learn the cadences and melodic characteristics of speech, as well as the phonetic intonations of his native tongue, before he uses any words.*] Her only query-inflections use single sounds like "eh?" "ah?" "oooh?" "fa?" etc. She continues occasionally to talk quietly in her crib before dropping off to sleep (never cries) and is chatty after an oc-casional nap, before she stands up and imperiously summons company. She has never been tearful or groggy or cranky on awaking, except for those four night-waking episodes.

She recognizes the same phrases mentioned previously and now, in addition, reacts appropriately to such phrases as: "Want a cookie?" "Get down," "Here comes Daddy" (she looks toward the door expectantly until she can hear him and begins to creep to the door before he is visible), "Give it to Mommy," "Pick it up," "Go get it," "Are you wet?" "Easy, easy," "Are you hungry?" "Drink?" etc.

"Give it to Mommy" is an outgrowth of her give-and-take games, of course, with the words added as we realized that her increased mobility was making all sorts of unsavory objects available for sampling and tasting, etc. She will remove a dried leaf or small stone or whatever from her mouth and hand it to either parent on request. She also plays give-and-take to this request with cookies and toys and just very recently has been able to wait to take it back until we say "Debbie take it," and also to turn my pronated fist over and try to open the hand to find a vanished object. [*Note 54: Debbie's searching for a hidden object is evidence of "conservation," an awareness that things continue to exist even when they leave one's perceptual field. At an earlier age, the child acts as though things that go out of his ken go completely out of existence. It seems likely, though, that at least a few privileged objects, such as the father who disappears in the morning and reappears in the evening, are "conserved" at a very early age (see above). Note, too, that not all attributes of objects remain invariant (e.g., size, color, or shape), nor do all objects: smoke and clouds dissipate, ice melts, soap bubbles and balloons burst, food disappears from the plate, hot foods grow cold, fat congeals, wounds heal—in short, change and inconstancy are as much a part of experience as stability. This behavior also indicates that Debbie is probably capable now of discrimination learning, with position as the discriminative clue. Compare Ruth, Note 31, page 190.*]

Her orientation to space is changing—she pokes finger or fist or spoon into cups; she picks dry cereal or cookie fragments out of bowls and cups and eats them with gusto and excitement, she puts smaller odd-shaped toys into a pan or a dish, she pokes fingers through the holes in doughnut-shaped stacking toys (and tries but fails to impale them on their spindle). [*Note 55: All these examples show a new awareness of enclosed space, of a distinction between inside and outside.*] She peers around labeled jars and cans to see the design on sides and back and tries to turn them herself, with uncertain control. She brings toy to coffee table, gets down and then brings another up onto it— then picks up and chooses and pushes away and pulls toward her. She is likely to put toys back where she found them and then go back to where she had been playing and do the next thing on her whimsical agenda. [*Note 56: These examples show not only Debbie's growing command of spatial relations among objects but also, as implied in the word "agenda," some ability to organize behavior in time.*]

She also flings one to three toys ahead of her and creeps to them, flinging them again and so on for the length of the house. She has two or three times done a bit of flinging or rolling of toys back and forth with a parent for six or seven exchanges before she calls a halt to this fatiguing nonsense by grabbing the toy and creeping away with it or just leaving the scene to go do something else.

APPETITE AND FEEDING: Having contentedly maintained the four-month level of intake for the past four to five months, Debbie is at last gradually beginning to increase her food consumption. And now too, for the first time since then, she begins to show signs of impatience and eagerness as the meal is prepared, whimpering as she follows me about the kitchen and banging and oh-ohing at her table before that first mouthful.

She does much less "finger painting" but peers into dish or cup to see the food level go down. She is much interested in finger-foods and manages all sorts of dry cereals, tomato, and other bits of adult food.

She only "mmms" now on feeding herself and not to fed spoonfuls as before.

She gulps her milk in long drafts of eleven to fifteen swallows, and comes up for air with deep inhalations afterward. She "begs like a puppy" at the family table sometimes, in hope of a bit of Mama's food after her own meal has been eaten.

She sometimes goes through a routine of one bit of dry cereal for Debbie, one for Ollie, now one for Debbie, and one for Ollie during her after-supper play-and-nibble session.

MUSIC: Much body participation to any selection with a clearly audible (it may be syncopated rather than regular) beat. Sometimes hums in continuation of a piece just ended and to some pieces which are mainly rhythm-percussion arrangements (as in some jazz and in one particular record for children), supplying her own "tune" as it were. She evinces a bit of perplexity and/or sadness to some Impressionistic music (Delius) and to some markedly atonal modern music. She still loves to be sung to and still plugs up a whistling parent as before.

HOUSEHOLD "CHORES": She appears at bedside to "help" make the bed most mornings—pulls and pats blankets, swats the pillow. [*Note 57: Even at nine months of age, Debbie has opportunity for identification with the mother.*] She follows the vacuum cleaner with interest and begins to think dustmops might just possibly be for riding on. She is so nosy about contents of refrigerator and high shelves where baby foods and cookies are kept that she presents a real traffic hazard. She sometimes sobs at the door as her Daddy leaves for work (*long* absences a new experience after the reduced schedule of summer) but accepts soothing readily.

ATTENTION SPAN: Quite capable of concerted doing or watching for fifteen to thirty minutes. Not always easily distractible from whatever she is doing. She has several times, after an interval of a whole night's sleep, gone directly back to the last (and obviously unfinished) bit of exploration or manipulation of the previous day as soon as she's up again the next morning, creeping to it despite all sorts of competing stimuli. [*Note 58: Debbie's ability to recall what she was doing before she went to sleep accords well with the principle of retroactive inhibition, but one does not expect a Zeigarnik effect, a tendency to resume interrupted tasks, as though the individual finds it hard to tolerate the lack of completeness, at so early an age.*]

NURSERY RHYME: "This Little Piggy" is familiar to her. She smiles up at Mother, wiggles and separates toes, laughs in anticipation of the "wee-wee-wee-wee" little pig makes. On the floor, she also touches Mother's toes (I wear toeless sandals) and looks up expectantly.

CURIOSA: Last week she discovered the bookshelf over the couch in the den—sidled along the couch seat peering at the thirty to forty volumes on the shelf with interest, but when she came to the Shakespeare volume that had so interested her months ago (and which she had not seen in the interim) she said "Ha" and immediately reached up to touch it—and only this one book. This is one of the larger and lighter-colored volumes on the shelf, though there are others rather similar, and there are brighter, more richly decorated books present which one would think would be more striking. Can't explain her behavior except on the basis of memory. [*See 2 months, 3 weeks, page 11.*]

MOTOR ACTIVITY: Impatient with creeping, she frequently skitters to and fro up on hands and feet, often using toes rather than whole sole of foot. She scoots along the linoleum floor sliding a tiny piece of paper under the tip of one index finger, daintily and with good balance despite the precarious position.

9 *months, 3 weeks.* *September 29*

I FEEL a need for some sort of summing up to help reach a description of the changes in Debbie's tenth month. As her seventh month was rather a "no" month with beginning self-assertion, her eighth and ninth months were devoted to intense development of various motor skills. The first half of her tenth month seemed to be rather in straight line progression with an easily discernible continuity. But now some sort of rather indefinable major transformation seems to be occurring, similar in scope to that change at age three months from newborn to infant that was so subtle and yet so pervasive.

Comfortable and adept with all her previously acquired motor-manipulative skills, she now combines several activities simultaneously rather than in tandem, e.g., she can eat, play with a toy, smile at Mother and bounce to the music all at once and without interruption of any one by the other, etc. [*Note 59: Here we see an example of functional subordination, the ability to coordinate part-activities into a higher-order whole.*]

Along with this she has begun to show a new assertiveness and self-expression: (a) now does not necessarily respond to name; (b) occasionally has rejected proffered milk with such vehemence that the cup has gone flying with fine resulting mess; (c) first momentary frown when a strange but already favored visitor paid marked attention to the dog; (d) unable to reach a toy while being dressed, she unhesitatingly leaned forward and bit the obstructing parental arm [*Note 60: Although babies do indeed bite people, the editor has never heard of a baby's aggressively biting an inanimate object, though he may scream at, strike, or kick such. It is a moot point whether the baby has some dim appreciation that biting is painful to people (and so is a way of getting them to do things) but not to things, or whether non-human objects simply do not appear as bitable to him as people.*]; (e) fairly frequent tears and expression of self-pity at being changed (we keep expecting her to indicate discomfort with wetness, but no difference; it's mainly the imposed supineness, I think), although at other times she's all giggles and helps by elevating one leg at a time to get rubber panties back on; (f) on two occasions she has ducked her head and scooted in the other direction on being asked "Nap?"

Her facial expressions now begin to foreshadow the toddler's rather than the baby's—momentary wistfulness, flashes of "poor me" looks, appraising stares of intense seriousness and suspended belief or judgment, daydreaming for a second or two. [*Note 61: Here we can see the beginnings of an "interior life" reflected in Debbie's variegated facial expressions and, we presume, their corresponding feeling states.*]

And we now begin to hear little sighs of boredom, and occasional aimless efforts to think of something new and different to do sometimes punctuate Debbie's play. Also, although she has always maintained good contact with me during her play periods, she now seeks out increased cuddling, snuggles for a while during long periods of concentrated play (has cut her nap time down to an hour or so in the morning and often only fifteen to thirty minutes in the afternoon, so these little lap-sits afford a much-needed rest period). She also now, although rarely, refuses liquids from the cup, so when this happens we offer essential fluids by bottle later, during one of her passive moments. She usually takes some fluid this way but with obvious amusement at such an inefficient and old-fashioned method. This has not occurred more than four or five times, when she has been just "too busy" to bother with drinking more than six to eight ounces from the cup in a day. Bottle offered otherwise is uniformly rejected. She has begun to suck her thumb now and again when tired but fighting off sleep.

So, we think we see a baby comfortably consolidating old advances, a bit bored while waiting for the next developmental step, eating more, as though a growth spurt were on the way, regressing just a bit to more baby-like ways (but new for her) as a way of working off irritations.

There might be several environmental factors contributing to this also—summer vacation over, Daddy is now away most of the day, and with summer's end outdoor living has been markedly diminished and rain has even curtailed her stroller rides. (The four-day absence of Mother preceded this and she had apparently recouped fully for a week before these new changes.)

10 months.   October

DEBBIE's period of boredom has passed and she has found new activities to occupy her time and keep her busy and content once more. Her impatience with creeping has been mitigated somewhat by two things: (1) She finds she can creep into and through various narrow or low apertures, which entails much twisting of torso or up-and-down undulation, as in creeping beneath chairs or couches or between wall and chair leg. Much of this cat-like action pleases her and she laughs or screeches with pleasure as she completes a difficult passage.

(2) In addition she has been practicing new positions, such as playing on her knees, pulling herself up into a squatting position, and raising herself up from squatting to standing with varying amounts of holding on. She stands leaning against chairs clapping hands in time to music and sometimes taps one foot too and grins broadly at such enjoyable activity. She has also developed changes in her sitting position—tailor fashion and with legs straight and widespread as she manipulates a toy.

As for finer movements, she pulls Daddy's shoelaces and curtain cords, and works the dog's leash off its hook. She increasingly helps guide the spoon to her mouth, finger feeds with considerable skill, retrieves food particles from her chair or lap, chews well with mouth closed and lateral motion of jaws, licks her lips and uses her hand to get wayward crumbs off chin or cheek into her mouth. [*Note 62: Such acts require fairly advanced body localization. Debbie is neater than most babies, but all show something of the same behavior around this age. Older children are less fastidious, perhaps because they are better able to disregard such distracting stimulation.*] She can let go skillfully enough to make piles of two and sometimes (rarely) three small blocks or stacking cups, has been able on many different occasions to put doughnut blocks onto the spindle (though this ability deteriorates rapidly with fatigue), she can lift covers off pans to find "hidden" toys. She strokes her dog and her own and her parents' faces with real gentleness and tenderness of facial expression.

Much interest in textures still, with palmar stroking of various objects (bricks, hair, velours, sand, etc.) and with pleasurable repetitive tactual comparisons of, for instance, contiguous areas of linoleum, varnished wood, and rug.

She has added "Bye" and "Hi" to her limited vocabulary, accompanied by raised arm gestures and occasional finger waving.

We have observed her in several episodes of "silly" giggling and rapid head- or torso-wagging when some accomplishment in solo play especially pleases her, or when she recognizes a familiar bit of music.

Taking pictures of her unawares becomes ever more difficult. She now recognizes the quiet click of opening the camera from another room and interrupts her play to wait expectantly for Daddy to reappear holding the little black box to his eye.

10 months, 1 week.   October 15

As OF today Debbie has six teeth, having cut her second two upper incisors without particular incident.

Having not seen her grandmother for three weeks, the sudden and silent appearance of this familiar face around a corner caused Debbie to shriek "Nana" and creep rapidly to the doorway to be greeted, grinning all the while.

By now she is quite adept at standing alone and pushing herself up from a squat. She cruises, with great interest in reaching things that used to be just out of reach on tables, etc.

Pivoting on her padded little rump puts many more toys easily within her reach than before she could sit up. Finished with one, she is likely to put it behind her, seemingly absentmindedly, as she focuses her attention on another. But then, after several minutes she reaches behind her, knowingly and without looking, to find it and put it to use again.

Pivoting is useful to her in the tub now, too—she reaches the soap dish, the fixtures, toys along edges of tub. Has begun to use a small blue stacking cup to drink from in the tub. Manages well with finger tips and adequate head tilting. (Still never attempts to help hold her cup or glass at feedings.)

Finer actions—grasps two or three smallish objects in one hand as she wanders about the house; also rotates a toy neatly, using finger tips only, as she scrutinizes it.

As for "toys," she vastly prefers those objects she finds for herself (empty boxes, jar lids, soap wrappers, etc.) to any toy designed for children, with the exception of several stuffed animals for which she shows affection and interest. [*See Ruth, 8 months, page 200.*]

Debbie surprised us today by bringing "Red Fox" on request from her room to the dining room (a distance of forty feet through several rooms—and a major feat for her to creep the distance both ways, dragging this twelve-inch-high animal with her on the return trip). We had not realized she knew its "name" or that she could distinguish between it and "Bear" and "Heffalump," but she demonstrated to us then that she knew each of these equally well by bringing them, too. [*Note 63: Debbie clearly demonstrates here the phenomenon of "passive language," the ability to understand things said to her before she herself has begun to talk. The fact of passive language indicates that* language is first learned more nearly according to a Pavlovian model than an operant one. See Benjamin, 10 months, 9 days, page 136, and Ruth, 10 months, 1 day, page 209.]

10 months, 20 days. October 28

A TEN-DAY visit by paternal grandparents from the Rockies. Debbie accepted their arrival at 2 A.M. (was awakened for this event) smoothly, took their presence in the household as entirely normal, reveled in the special attention, but when fatigued would seek out Mother for a few moments' respite and private-or-personal attention. Showed her grandfather a bit of feminine coyness and seemed to realize this was "funny," for she would laugh as she robbed his breast pocket or flirted with him. (These were games specific to him, just as her play with jewelry was specific to her grandmother.) [*Note 64: If we recall Debbie's opportunities for feminine identification, we will hesitate to ascribe her flirtatiousness to innate constitution.*]

A child's rocking chair was given to Debbie. She immediately got up onto it and stood in it as though it were a chariot, undismayed and even jubilant at its rocking motions. She manages to make it rock by shifting her weight from one foot to the other and beams broadly at this. She also goes to her chair occasionally and rocks it (standing up in it) in time to music and humming quietly to herself.

10 months, 25 days. November 2

INTERMITTENT ventures in walking unaided during the past week or so (one to three steps at a time) have now given way to determined if unsteady excursions of six to ten steps. As she becomes more confident she now quite frequently goes about with a spool or a cookie in her hands, stopping every once in a while to nibble as she stands, before going on to take four or five more steps. Then down she goes—bump! Rises again, most often by pushing up from a squat but sometimes by raising rump up on all fours with slow elevation of head last.

With this increased mobility, she now will "go get" Red Fox, Teddy Bear, Heffalump, Baby (doll), Bear, Daddy's shoes, Mommy's shoes, ball, cookie, on specific request (verbal only, no gestures) and goes rambling through the house to find and bring them. [*See Note 63.*]

Also she turns and walks toward her bathroom or her bedroom on being asked "Are you wet?" "Bath?" or "Nap?"; to her feeding table ("Eat?" "Are you hungry?") and to the telephone or door whenever bells ring.

Dancing to music now is more variable, with hip-wiggling, bouncing, head-shaking, arm-waving, toy-banging, all while standing. She occasionally dances for several moments through an entire piece, and often, too, will interrupt her play for a brief bit of dancing as some phrase or rhythm catches her fancy.

11 months, 10 days.   November 18

HAS found her stomach—enjoys a singsong game of "Patty-pat the tummy." Has also found her ears, both of them—this follows much interest in parents' and dog's ears by a month or so. Will engage in "Where's Daddy's ear? Daddy's other ear? Debbie's ear? Debbie's other ear? Ollie's ear? Red Fox's ear?" etc., at considerable length and with much laughter. [*Note 65: It is not clear whether Debbie has just discovered these bits of anatomy or has begun responding appropriately to their names.*]

She has developed forceful head nods and shakes, accompanied by explosive "Ess" or "Nah" on being asked questions regarding either food or the state of her diapers. These actions are so vehement at times that they knock her down, laughing. [*Note 66: It has been asserted, as by me, that "yes" comes as a much later development than "no." Debbie's behavior calls this thesis into question.*]

Other verbalizations are: Ollie, babbee (baby), bass (bath), ditty (Teddy Bear), Guk Guk (Thank you), plus DaDa, Mama, Nana, dg (dog). Accompanies her play with shouts, shrieks, screeches, laughter, repetitive syllables, jargon "sentences." She asks for explanations or names of things by "Sss-ah." [*Presumably "What's that?"*] Satisfaction with an act accomplished is frequently heralded by a loud "Ah." Pleasure at seeing something which pleases her brings forth a musical "Oooh." Clucking and kissing sounds occasionally. [*Note 67: Notice that this report of active vocabulary follows by only thirty-three days the account of passive understanding (Note 63). Note, too, that the words reported here overlap only partly with those to which we know she reacted.*]

Yesterday felt confident enough about walking so that she demonstrated it before a visitor and at a neighbor's house (previously only walked in parents' presence, at home). However, the next day was marked by "regression": decided fatigue, need for cuddling, insistence that we feed her, and refusing to drink from cup. We offered her a bottle, and she lay down on the floor to drink it, the first time she has accepted a bottle in two or three months, her eyes partly closed. After an ounce and a half, she "came to," smiled around the nipple, and after a few more sucks she got up and began striking the bottle. Then she flung it away, a distance of six or eight feet. Thereafter she behaved normally and refused another bottle offered later in the day.

Has been developing intermittent interest in spoon-feeding herself, sometimes allowing Mother to fill the spoon for her, at other times refusing any help at all! Fortunately she tends to grasp the spoon pronately and is fairly successful at getting it to her mouth. Also demonstrates consistent right-handedness in this as well as in grasping for toys, although the left hand comes up to help steer missed particles of food into the mouth. Food preferences still exclude the sweeter tastes generally, with peas being consistently unacceptable for six months now. Jello, ice chips, and ice cream make her laugh as they melt in her mouth. Pieces of apple, pear, banana seem preferable to cookies. Crisp crackers please her. While she is not a ravenous eater, food interests her and she is quite neat about it even though she insists on finger- or spoon-feeding herself much of the time.

Spends thirty to forty-five minutes at a time with large magazines, with minimal help asked for in turning the pages. Dislikes tearing them and demands help when this occurs. [*Note 68: The child's distress at something's being torn or broken implies that he has some sense of its integral state. We do not know when such reactions first occur, or what things they may be particular to. We would expect great variability, however, so that the baby may object vociferously to being given a broken cookie, even though he himself will destroy it in eating it.*] Alternates use of hands properly when turning pages forward or backward. She stops now and again to examine a picture or advertisement, with happy "ooohs" and some pointing at dogs, people's faces, or certain red or blue colors. (Never yellows, greens, or purples.)

MOTOR ACTIVITIES: Piles and repiles paperback books and works hard to stand them on edge. When successful is very pleased and wants parents to "look" (indicates this by catching our eye and ah-ing). Piles two floating toys in her bath, puts doughnut rings onto any spindle-like object (sticks, fingers). Much repetitive putting and taking of small objects like pieces of dry cereal into cups or jars or from coffee table to floor and back up again, entailing much squatting and standing and great concentration. Still offers occasional ones to her dog or a parent.

Responses to language: "Pat . . . (the doggy, Red Fox)" results in patting. "Soft" brings forth stroking motions. "Love . . . (Red Fox, baby, Daddy or doggy)" causes her to cuddle close, "Easy!" and she calms down her actions.

11 months, 16 days.   November 24

DEBBIE still invests the incongruous or the unexpected with humor, as, for instance: (1) finding a parent lying on the floor (laughs and sits on the poor parent, preferably the head), (2) coming across any toy in a strange place, or (3) as she enters a room seeing any "ridiculous pile" of objects (parent built) such as a milk carton, a block, a plastic doughnut ring and a rattle one atop the other. [*Note 69: Note the parental encouragement to whimsy, to treat reality as a plaything.*]

GAMES: Dropping bits of paper or a block off the back of the couch, then getting down, walking around the couch, and finding it. This sometimes entails considerable skill since her toy box and its attendant mess and accumulation of objects is behind the couch, so that searching, sorting and choosing has to occur for her to find the object she dropped. This she does very well. Other variations of hide-and-seek, too, as well as pushing a parent forward on the couch so she can "horsey-ride" on his or her back.

RESPONSE TO "NO!": At eight months, Debbie enjoyed a certain testing game to see how far she could go at a forbidden activity (we have very few No's here—pulling plants apart, fireplace, electric outlets and wires, and, now that she reaches for things on tables, matches, too). At nine and ten months she inhibited herself as shown by approaching a "No" object, reaching for it, and then arresting the action with a head shake and a "Nah." At eleven months she is busy re-testing again and sometimes will take a matchbook and then attempt to hide or drop it quickly before the "No" is uttered. Our enforcement procedure is mainly a verbal "No," sometimes with head shaking. If this doesn't work, we either remove her or offer a substitute, with varying success.

11 months, 22 days. November 30

VISITED by a man and his five-year-old son over the Thanksgiving weekend. Debbie exhibited much interest in watching them dress, brought the man his shoes on request, etc. She followed the boy all over the house, sat next to him, brought him all her favorite toys, tried to engage him in give-and-take games, and seemed never to forget his presence (much to his alternating pleasure and disgust!).

Which brings up the matter of Debbie's sociability as it has developed. She has never exhibited shyness thus far, for although she does not smile automatically at strangers, she usually eyes them openly and prefers to move in to study them at close

range, and in a matter of moments is willing to accept them
with or without grins. Children fascinate her and have done so
for months, particularly those who are active. She markedly
enjoys groups of children (four or six) from ages one to seven
who live in the neighborhood and whom she sees weekly or more
often. She smiles as they enter, cries when they leave, seems to
realize that the older ones will carry her or talk to her or use
her as "baby" in playing house and goes to them to join in this
activity. She tends to ignore very young and inert babies, and to
endure with some confusion the impulsive noises and actions of
a nineteen-month-old boy, but otherwise enters into the play
situation with interest, spending some time interacting, some in
watching, some in being passive "patsy." She objects, however,
to being pushed around physically and to having all her gestures
ignored by children. Until marked fatigue sets in (after 30 to 120
minutes) she does not seek out an adult. Then she comes to sit
quietly on Mother's foot while she "rests" and watches from a
distance.

1 year. December 7

Took Debbie to the doctor's office for her one-year check-up.
Weight 17 lb. 6 oz., height 28 inches. Eight teeth present. Enjoyed seeing the other children in the waiting room and went
to them to proffer whatever object was available (mitten, book,
rattle, hat). Immediately afterward took her into a large department store for the first time to buy her first pair of shoes
(has been barefoot until now while she learned to walk well).
Walked slowly and wonderingly *backward,* staring down at her
shoes for the first fifteen or twenty steps, then gaily took off forward to investigate the area with delighted parents in close
pursuit.

Debbie is one year old today (December 8). We took her to
Grandmother's for the afternoon, wearing a dress and her new
shoes of which she is already quite fond. (Until recently dressed
in more utilitarian clothes, since skirts got in the way of her
creeping and annoyed her.) Pleased to investigate the strange

apartment, not inhibited in her actions but quite happy to look at all the different items without any particular urge to touch them all. Given a telephone of red plastic, she looked over at Grandma's phone, nodded her head, then proceeded to lift and replace receiver, holding it up to her ear now and again and jabbering occasionally.

On return home she was fatigued and said "Ess," she'd like a nap. Was awakened in a moment, though, by the riotous entrance of four excited, shrieking children who announced they were going to give Debbie a birthday party. Not fully awake, Debbie watched all this with more reserve than usual, seemed distraught as they all opened the packages they had brought her (apparently she does not yet like to tear or knock down or "spoil" a thing), but fingered each toy gently as they handed it to her, and smiled at each child in turn. She tried to mimic blowing and did nearly succeed in blowing out the one candle on her cupcake. Everyone had a tiny piece. Then as if on some mysterious pre-order, they all trooped to the door to go home. Debbie stood at the door and cried a bit as they all left her, but in a minute calmed down, ate a scanty supper, and collapsed thirty minutes early for bedtime.

1 year, 12 days.   December 20

Took Debbie to the clinic Christmas party—her first time in such a large group of people crowded noisily into such a small area. She had a fine time, gave her hand to a stranger and walked about to be "introduced" to each one. Was serious in expression but showed no signs of fear or confusion, nor did she seek out her parents for solace. Soon went to work in one corner, moving purses or picking up bits of ribbon or paper to present to people, jabbering to this one or that one as she felt like it. She accepted a cookie but carried it uneaten for the duration of the party, though she did drink some fruit juice offered her by a nurse. Came to grin at Mother for a minute two or three times and then left again to go join the fun. Waved goodbye with big smiles. The rest of the day uneventful.

Summary of an average day at one year.

Awakes, cooing and jabbering happily, anywhere from 6:30 to 7 A.M. Plays contentedly in her crib until she decides it's time to get up and see people, at 8 A.M. She emits a series of whoops summoning adults, and we find her standing at the crib side grinning broadly as she greets us. She has always torn her bed quite thoroughly apart and we find her three stuffed animals scattered over the floor and her blankets and pad dumped out, too. On rare occasions when we go in before she has called us, she turns her back to us and works busily at something, glancing briefly and ruefully over her shoulder, dismissing us. [*Note 70: Such behavior can be taken as one more indicator of the development of psychological "autonomy," the ability to fend and decide for oneself, with an implied awareness of oneself as an entity.*] Once picked up, she points to or waves at all her favorite objects in the room. Her "Ss-ah?" (What's that?) has somewhat diminished as she has learned to point at things that she wants named.

Diapers changed, she walks quickly out to the dining room jabbering cheerfully and demonstrates interest in breakfast either by going to her table and banging or by hampering every kitchen activity by being eagerly underfoot.

Breakfast consists of scrambled egg, bacon, dry toast, fruit juice, fruit, and milk. She finger feeds all lumps, accepting various degrees of help from Mother. Uses her own spoon on occasion, filling it by hand or accepting some from Mother's spoon. Holds spoon pronately and is very successful at getting it to her mouth and fairly well cleaned off. She points to the cleaning tissues and, when given one, wipes her mouth and hands, very pleased with herself. Breakfast is quite leisurely and she enjoys it. At its end she stands, grabs her piece of toast and is lifted down, and walks forthrightly off to some project or other.

Play period. Sees Daddy off to work. Wanders off to her room to collect her animals and put them in some odd corner or perhaps on a chair. Back again, she repeatedly comes to the table for long draughts of her milk. Then to toy box. Picks and chooses among objects, plays with some right there, throws others in all directions to get them out of her way, carries others into various other rooms, making the entire house look like one huge playpen. Frustration if she can't do something as she wants to (stacking or pulling beads apart) results in shouts of anger, but "Help Debbie?" usually elicits a firm "Nah" and head shake. She follows Mother around the house as chores get done, but is usually busy at her own projects, in contrast to her previous concentrated help with, for instance, bed making. As Mother sits at the table for a cup of coffee, Debbie comes for the rest of her breakfast milk, brings various toys to Mother for shared "helpful" play—e.g., she fills her plastic bottle with water but needs help in shaking it empty again. She isn't strong enough to push plastic beads together, though she can line up the bump on one with the hole on the other. [*Note 71: Debbie's perception of the correct spatial relation between two locking beads can be appraised even though she cannot complete the action of locking the beads together.*] On some mornings, she brings a magazine or a book to my lap and sits there for ten to forty minutes, turning pages, looking at pictures, pointing at objects. She can find dogs and babies and noses and eyes and butter-flies and O's and a variety of other things in random advertise-ments on being asked "Where is the . . . ?" A book of baby animals pleases her and she does a fair but inconsistent job of mimicking—dog goes bow-wow, meow, peep, baaa, etc.

Fatigue is indicated by a slight but diffuse irritability at about 9:30 A.M. "Do you want a bath?" "Ess," and off she goes to the bathroom. Helps get herself undressed, dumps bath toys into the running water, wanders vaguely out and around this part of the house, then back in again. Bath time usually lasts ten to twenty minutes. She grabs wash cloth to wash face, hands, tummy, and each foot on request, drinks water from her cup with great skill and often one-handed (but still has never tried to hold her milk or juice cups—I wonder, in view of her inde-pendence in much of her motor activity and her having rejected the bottle by her eighth month, if this isn't a comforting bit of helplessness), agitates the water to make the floating toys circulate around and around her in the tub, inverts the cup to make bubbles under water, etc. Then a slowing down and a vigorous nod in response to "All done?" Dried, she cooperates in being dressed, and drowsily goes to bed at 10 or 10:15 for her morning nap.

Awake and laughing by 11:30 or 12, toys on floor again, and again she greets all the pictures, lamps, horsies. Changed, shoes and socks on with some cooperation and pleasure, down from the table and out she walks for lunch—which had better be ready and waiting.

Lunch consists of chopped or fragmented meats, two vegetables, fruit, and milk. This is a more erratic meal—eager to get it over and done with so she can go about her business. She sometimes helps feed herself but just as often brings objects to the table for a bit of manipulation as she is fed by Mother.

Afternoons are more free-form than mornings and require more alertness and ingenuity on Mother's part in order to meet Debbie's varying needs or interests. They are characterized by: (1) a greater need for sociability and for cooperative activity; (2) larger scale and more concentrated effort on projects involving related groups of big objects—such as pushing all the movable furniture in a room into a jumble, or arranging and combining all of a set of pots and lids and then putting them back or moving them all to another room, or playing house in a cupboard with three large stuffed animals, then taking them to a chair and rocking them and then to a bed or couch, etc.; (3) an indicated need for frequent changes of pace—brings a book to Mother so we "read" together for ten to thirty minutes, or initiates a bit of rough-housing, or goes to the kitchen and points to the cracker cupboard, or points to the door to go out. She most usually takes a brief nap in the afternoon now, since learning to walk.

Supper at 4:30 or 5 P.M. consists of cereal-cheese and fruit, or vegetable-meat and a custard pudding and milk. Followed by a snack of whatever she seems to indicate (apple, pear, cheese, dry cereal) she would like. This she nibbles periodically from a dish on the coffee table as she enters joint play with both parents as they talk—brings us toys, pats the dog, cuddles on a lap, etc.

Fatigue now apparent by a speeding up and a slight loss of coordination. "Nap?" "Ess," with nod and off to bed at 6 P.M. Drops off to sleep quickly and quietly and sleeps the whole night through. (We change her at 11 P.M. to forestall floods, but she rarely rouses.)

1 year, 23 days.   December 31

CHRISTMAS: Was fascinated by the tree, with much "Oohing" and pointing to various ornaments, but no attempt to touch the tree at any time. Distressed by unwrapping of packages, so we unwrapped most of them while she was asleep and left only a few out for her to encounter. When she showed signs of being overwhelmed and fatigued by so many new toys, we put some away for the future. She was immediately pleased by a new blue teddy bear, a toy xylophone (she does not like to make banging cacophony but the musical tones apparently appeal to her), a musical ball, and a plastic bottle with spools and clothespins— she fills this repeatedly, but cannot empty it. [*Note 72: From my observations of twenty babies 8–15 months old, it seems that deliberate pouring out does not occur before age one, and seven of fourteen babies past age one could still not pour out the trinkets. See Note 84.*]

Absolutely refused her "baby dinner" and demanded turkey and all the trimmings. Chewed on a bone afterward. And since then, for the past week, the sight of a baby-food jar brings on tears and rage, so we have been busy thinking up and preparing more grown-up meals for her, to her zestful pleasure.

1 year, 4 weeks.   January 5

TOOK Debbie visiting, where she found herself in a living room completely littered with toys, and containing a silent eight-month-old girl sitting contentedly in a bouncy chair, chewing a rattle. Debbie went to the baby and stooped down, hands on knees, to peer at her face and to jabber to her. Then she gently patted the baby's shoulder and stroked the baby's cheek and in a moment laid her head next to the baby's with soft cooing sounds. Baby paid no attention, so after a few more moments during which Debbie studied her speculatively, Debbie began to wander to and fro about the room collecting all sorts of toys and dolls and piling them up carefully on the tray of the chair. When the baby had nearly disappeared from view behind this pile of objects, Debbie approached her from the side and ever so carefully tried to take the rattle from the baby. Once she got it, she shook it, studied it, and then, apparently satisfied, put it on the pile of toys and left to do something else. (I was surprised at this clever use of tactics for we have not been in the habit of this kind of substitutive legerdemain with Debbie, nor have we often used toys to placate or distract her.) [*Note 73: To judge by the behavior of many children, it seems to be a perceived characteristic of younger children that they are susceptible to this kind of deception. It seems too much to say that Debbie "reasoned out" this mode of attack; rather, faced with the task of getting something out of the baby's clutches, Debbie simply transferred the clutches to something else.*]

A note on her other social activities over the past month or so. Markedly enjoys being in a group of five or six children of the neighborhood who visit her weekly (ages one and a half, two and a half, three, four and a half, six, and seven). She watches actively, follows eagerly, exchanges toys, hands them cookies, goes to the bigger ones and asks to be jiggled or carried dangling about the room, is most cooperative in their games of "playing house" and allows herself to be put to bed or told to stay in a corner as they dictate, happily but with occasional expressions of wonderment. She does NOT like to be pushed around by the four-and-a-half-year-old boy and will cry if he forces her to "go over there" (prefers to be led). She begins by approaching the sturdy one-and-a-half-year-old boy openly, but he tends to poke, prod, hit, grab, and scream, and after a while she detours around him to avoid any more trouble.

At the grocery, attention is riveted on any other baby or child in sight, with a hand out to touch or pat any close enough (particularly the three-and-a-half to seven-year-old group). She stares at adults without shyness, but rarely smiles at their blandishments and makes no sound.

13 months, 1 day.   January 9

DEBBIE cut her left lower first molar yesterday afternoon and this morning the left lower canine tooth is visible. No disturbance except for fretfulness and biting yesterday relieved by ice chips.

13 months, 10 days.   January 18

THIS is certainly an interesting period in Debbie's development, best described by a spurt in motor, imitative, and perceptual growth accompanied by signs of anger and frustration with brief but frequent flare-ups whenever things just won't do what she wants them to. A brief listing to describe each of these might help:

MOTOR CHANGES: Pivots on one foot and is beginning to run hither and yon with good balance. Does not trip over rug edges or toys. Walks with fairly straight back and feet well approximated. Makes games of walking or creeping backward for five-to-ten-foot distances. Throws ball in game of catch with good control and now also bounces balls with vigor and delight. Opens and closes magnetic-latch and sliding doors. Dances, using alternate foot balance. Bends from the waist as often as she squats. Pushes stool alongside couch and climbs up over the end-arm. [*Note 74: This use of the stool is probably not a manifestation of a general orientation to space in which one moves steppingstones from place to place as needed. It is likely that Debbie found the stool at the end of the couch one day and, having discovered the possibilities for movement that it offered, was thereafter able to reconstruct the circumstances when she so desired.*] Tries to slide down off furniture [*facing?*] forward instead of backing down. Manages spoon fairly well with elbow raising and with care to clean it well (is very neat at this and rarely dumps a spoonful). Turns herself over onto belly in the bath with caution and skill, then blows bubbles under water, bobs for floating toys and cups, successfully and with much gay laughter. On the other hand, she does not like to knock things down, to spill things, to tear a book she's "reading." Nor does she yet fill and empty cups, or invert containers to dump out the contents.

IMITATION: She brushes the floor or table with wide-flung arm motions to clean it. She scrubs herself in the tub and looks to see if "All clean?" Has decided some specks are not edible and brings various tiny bits of trash to parent for disposal or tries to put them in wastebasket. Relinquishes taboo objects she reaches (brings matches to parent) with great sense of accomplishment. Found her standing in the kitchen brushing her hair with vegetable brush. Watches parents' mouths in attempt to copy sounds of words (says "clock," "bib," "hat"). Approaches "no" objects such as electric wires—points, shakes head to herself and, finally convinced of her own inhibition, walks away. In response to "bunny rabbit" imitates nibbling action they make. Has marked interest in "reading." Has begun to develop happy delaying games of running around (increasingly nude) pre-bath and also to call us after nap and then play hide and seek from her crib as we enter the room. Some jealousy of and impatience with her dog occasionally.

PERCEPTUAL: Finds and recognizes her faint or distorted image in pot lids, car dashboards, etc., and is ecstatic over this. Spends occasional periods looking under things (stove, refrigerator, couch, etc.). Has discovered her nose and eyes, as well as the top of her head and fingernails all in the past two or three days (interesting because nose and eyes of others and in pictures have fascinated her for months but she never tried to find her own until now). Already knows her mouth, tongue, teeth, knees, foot, "piggies," ears, hair, tummy. [*Note 75: Apparently Debbie indicates the appropriate parts of her own body in response to the words. It is doubtful whether she has reached the more advanced stage of naming body parts when these are pointed to.*] Always ticklish on her chest; her sensitivity has now spread downward so that she is occasionally ticklish on tummy and vulva. Interested in the similarity of the *f* sound in fire and fish. Attempts to put on socks first, then shoes—also hats, gloves (cannot yet work zippers or buttons, to her extreme anger) but accepts help with these before frustration sets in. Smells flowers and bananas and apples with varying degrees of pleasure and displeasure (apparently doesn't like banana odor). We estimate that she recognizes and responds correctly to about eighty words and twenty simple phrases.

Her frustration tolerance threshold seems quite low this month—anger directed both against people and things, sometimes specific and at other times displayed quite diffusely. She brooks no failure in mastering a toy or performing some precise action, and soon flings the object away and hits herself in the face with anger and disappointment. Or, suddenly deciding that she does *not* want that gulp of milk after all, she strikes out vigorously at the glass and then at the offending parental hand. (Does not rely on the head shake or "Nah" these days, but hits, instead.) Occasionally approaches dog or parent with full intent to scratch or tweak or pinch as though experimentally, just to "see what will happen," and persists despite quiet admonition until a loud "Ow" (sincere, not play-acting) results. Then she appears startled, pats the injured part gently and moves in to be cuddled (and "forgiven"?).

13 months, 18 days. January 26

LUSTY and vigorous and self-assertive indeed! Still emotionally a bit labile, Debbie sometimes nonetheless concentrates contentedly on various projects. She also shows her delight in the new or surprising by coy smiles or giggling with total abandon.

Her impatience with things has subsided somewhat as she has learned to accept or reject the offer of "Mommy help?" at her own discretion, and brings the offending toy for a cooperative solution. We have attempted to reduce stimulation somewhat, and even the "play nap" in her own room has seemed soothing to her on a few occasions. Her own dismay at spilled milk has somewhat curbed her wild flinging actions, too, helped along by a speeded-up maternal withdrawal reflex and some emphasis on "More?" "No more?" "All done?" and a respect for her choice immediately she has made it and before the catastrophe occurs, we hope.

She apparently handled her urge to bite and scratch, at least on one occasion, by biting of her own arm (after biting a parent's) firmly and slowly. When it began to hurt her, she stopped, looked up at me sadly, patted my arm, and put her injured arm up to be patted. Now, "Don't hurt Debbie" or "Don't hit" seems to forestall fury until we can do something more satisfactory about her need or wish. "Wait a minute" also makes her seem more comfortable in these instances and she quiets her anger and waits with fair patience for Mama to do the right thing.

Along with all this anger, she has continued her cuddlesome and affectionate behavior, too, at intervals during each day. Pats and strokes and hugs her various stuffed animals, comes to a parent's knee and puts her head down on the lap, patting and stroking the knee as she stands there. Also, she now often brings a stuffed toy to Mother for a brief bit of round robin patting and snuggling among all three of us. As she "loves . . ." (Ollie or Red Fox or Mommy) she wears a sweet expression with a slight soft smile, and she makes low cooing sounds of endearment as she strokes and pats and is patted and hugged in return.

13 *months, 25 days.   February 2*

A FEW odds and ends: (1) Taken to visit a farmer friend ninety-two years old, she liked the sturdy old man immediately and smiled and jabbered at him; marvelously pleased with the warm, aromatic barn. She sniffed appreciatively and showed great curiosity about cows and horses and cats. Came home "Maaa"-ing in imitation of cows' moos.

(2) "Works" with her Daddy—e.g., crumples paper for the fireplace as he gathers kindling; holds screws and screwdrivers for

him as he makes her a toy box or assembles a desk, and hands them to him gaily on request. [*Note 76: Observe that Debbie is making a genuinely functional contribution and is not acting blindly. Note, too, that she can be trusted not to pop the screws into her mouth.*]

(3) She carries a piece of toast—preferably stale—about with her all day, eventually eating it after placing it carefully beside her a thousand times a day as she works on various projects. Her memory for where she last left it during her perambulations around the house extends over two or two and a half hours even for the most unlikely spots, and when asked "Where is your toast?" she thinks for a moment then trots off and goes *directly* to it.

(4) Has gotten into and back out of the bathtub unseen and unhurt on at least three occasions since November—usually to get a bath toy propped on the far edge.

(5) Two episodes of toilet and diaper play thus far. The first one, in November, was a wide-arm, random flinging of water everywhere with brief wall- and tub-scrubbing efforts, puddles and splashes everywhere! The second one yesterday entailed use of a clean diaper she took from the linen closet and dipped repeatedly into the toilet bowl, carrying it to the floor where she wrung it out with fair coordination and then "washed the floor" with it area by area. Carried this on most neatly until she had used up all the water in the bowl, then complained and threw the well-wrung diaper into the tub. Happy to see Mother get the mop and very eager to help clean the floor.

(6) Have never mentioned her BM pattern—usually one after breakfast and another between 3 and 5:30 P.M., unrelated to meals. Never diarrhea. No potty training of any sort yet, but some cheerful response to "Are you wet? Debbie need dry panty?" Is beginning to recognize the phrase "Debbie doing BM?" and joyously nods assent.

(7) A querulous "Mim? . . . Mim?" as she looks for mother if we've become separated by several rooms during chore and project time and she needs or wants something. Does not use this as a title or appellation (Maam or Mah Mah for that).

(8) Response to TV: casual interest in puppets; interrupts play to listen and "go see" if she hears children's voices; some participation in dancing to a teen-age dance program—these all for a mere moment or two at a time. But sat transfixed for nearly one full hour during a Lincoln Center program featuring the Philharmonic Symphony Orchestra (she "conducted"), ballet (she pivoted and whirled and jigged), arias from Don Giovanni, mainly bass and baritone (she hummed and sang and smiled), all with repeated sharing eye-contact with her astounded and openly pleased parents. [*Note 77: Here we must assume that Debbie's interest in the program was not altogether intrinsic, but was sustained partly by her parents' reaction to her reaction.*]

(9) Has discovered the limitless treasure of the floor-level kitchen cupboards. Works like a trained archeologist carefully uncovering layer upon layer of valuable artifacts, making neat piles of similar objects out on the kitchen floor, then reaching back into the cupboard to find the next object (does not dump things out of these either) for easy reference and further study later. Then, this perusal and investigation finally completed, she does a most adequate job of putting them all back in of her own accord.

14 months, 4 days.   February 12

A BREATHLESS week. Parents have often felt perplexed and laggardly as Debbie surged forward headlong. Developments can be mainly described in two areas:

(1) Mother was inadvertently away from home for a weekend due to a blizzard, but Debbie remained at home with dog, Daddy, and familiar Grandmother, and things went smoothly and happily to all appearances. On my return, however, Debbie started to run to the door all smiles, but as soon as she spied me she checked herself abruptly, the smile faded from her face, and she turned nonchalantly away, ignoring me. She soon was following me all about the house, but refused any eye contact or smile. Within thirty to forty-five minutes she was capable of

bringing Teddy Bear to me, and would accept my patting it
and her, but without smile or return patting. Then a brief period
of reconstituting her family during which she would coo and pat
me *if* she was secure in Daddy's arms and he patted both of us.
But for the rest of the day she had to keep reminding herself
that she was really still mad at me and would inhibit laughter
or a "conversation" or the sharing of a toy in mid-act, and again
abolish the smile from her face and pull halfheartedly away. By
the next day we were friends again and all seemed healed.

(This was quite a shock to Mother who had rather expected
either a more casual welcome or a more open show of anger
and resentment. For though I have not often left her, she has
always accommodated very well to my absence; nor has she
shown any particular signs of making specific demands on me
either at home or out among strangers. Never has come flying
to me for protection from people or new surroundings.)

(2) Feeding for many months has been a pleasant and conversational, rather face-to-face situation, with Debbie taking
over increasingly for finger and spoon feeding, though with
steadfast refusal to handle any cup or glass (except in the bathtub, where she manages with one-handed competence). In the
past week, however, she has shown some irritability at mealtimes
and one day she threw screaming rages at being put into her
chair and would only eat finger foods snack-fashion from the
coffee table. Mother at first thought some of this was an en-
capsulated residue from the separation episode described above,
and attempted to deal with it in this context, and failed. So on
February 8 at supper, when all overtures only produced more
storm, her table was pushed into the kitchen (linoleum floor here
—no door separates kitchen from living-dining room in this
modern house) and her suction plate and spoon placed on it.
Debbie came right to the table, arms uplifted. A big plastic bib
was put on her for the first time without fuss and she was left
"alone" in her table while I went about getting dinner and
setting the grown-ups' table. She immediately dove in spoon
first and managed extremely well and without mess or confusion.
A small amount of milk in her plastic bath cup was put on the

table, and then her diced pear. She picked the cup up without hesitation and drank with some slight spilling into her bib pocket. This she wanted to clean up, using tissues, and refused all help. Tried again and was distressed at her spilling, to judge from her speedy mopping activities, and her deadpan expression. Finished her meal—happy but silent, asked for "more" dessert, signaled she was done by standing up and calling to me, and was set down with her usual stale toast.

She then was completely exhilarated and joyous, prolonged her playtime past her bedtime (by an hour) and engaged in lusty crowing, shouting play with us both, proclaiming her new, powerful independence.

Since then (testing her willingness to continue this) moving her table toward its old position in the dining room results in tearful withdrawal, but with a change in course out she comes all smiling. [*Note 78: Early communication between parent and child often calls for this sort of experimentation, with the parent being regulated by affective feedback from the child.*] She prefers some "company" provided it requires no answer on her part. She manages very well, indicating by pointing that she needs a napkin or more of something. She has not attempted her own milk since her first try, but is now filling and emptying her cup in the bath, as though practicing for her next try at the table.

14 months, 18 days.   February 26

DEBBIE now has sixteen teeth. Cut four all together as is usual with her, and with no particular upset other than a slight tendency to cry easily, relieved by aspirin.

Her play pattern has taken on greater complexity in the past few weeks:

(1) She now offers her various dolls and animals bits of food at her snack times, occasionally tries to dance with one of them, rocks them in her arms, gives them piggy-back rides; and on one occasion put one in her stroller and then with great seriousness went through a pile of old magazines, selected one, and

after much laborious turning of pages, brought it to me and pointed to a half-page picture of a child's room in the corner of which was a doll in a pram-stroller. I had never pointed out this detail to her and her copying of it (a week or so after we last went through that issue) was a complete surprise to me. [*Note 79: It is hard to know whether Debbie first recalled the picture and then modeled her behavior after it or, having put her doll in the stroller, she then was reminded of the picture. In either case, it is a remarkable mnemonic feat for a fourteen-month-old. In general, of course, the behavior described in this section is exceptionally advanced.*]

(2) She attempts to hang things up—clothes on hooks, towels on rods, etc. [*Note 80: Observe the awareness of spatial relations implied in the action of hanging something up.*]

(3) She engages in "talk" over her toy telephone and over ours. Says "hello" and "goodbye" clearly in the right places. Recognizes Grandmother's and Father's voices, and also that of one neighbor.

(4) Walked about making car noises and with hands in front of her as though she were holding and steering with the wheel.

(5) Now pours water from cup to cup in the bath. [*Note 81: I find this observation interesting because age 14 months seems to be the turning point for an experimental task I have tried with sixteen babies, which requires the baby to pour a pingpong ball from cup to cup. Note that pouring from one container to another requires knowledge of a particular spatial relationship, more advanced than simple pouring out, which is not innately given. See Benjamin, 18 months, 6 days, page 148.*] Also flicks the drain-stopper lever back and forth and watches and listens with interest.

(6) Has a spindle toy with solar-spectrum-colored rings in sequence corresponding to graduations in size. Has fairly consistent success in piling these correctly on her own. [*Note 82: Logically, it would seem that Debbie could be guided by either relative size or by position on the solar spectrum, but we know that spectral relationships are not visible to babies, and indeed*

may remain invisible to educated adults even after being pointed out. A control experiment could, of course, be carried out, to test a subject's generalization to spectrum-colored rings all of the same size and to graduated rings all of the same color. On this more "abstract" task, as compared to the one of pouring from cup to cup, Debbie's behavior is far in advance of that of a sample of lower-class subjects tested by the editor, of whom only two, one age 1:2:20 and the other 1:6:9, arranged the rings in sequence, while fourteen others, ranging in age from 1:3:6 to 2:2:3, did not.] Holds two rings and studies them and usually puts the larger on first; shakes head and tries again if she makes an error. Sometimes now responds correctly to my saying "red one," "yellow one." [*Note 83: Debbie's failures on this task illustrate that a child can know that "red" and "yellow" designate colors before he knows which colors they designate.*]

(7) Plays her toy xylophone with obvious pleasure and on occasion sings along with it with fair approximation of the notes struck. On two occasions has laboriously gathered together items such as xylophone, empty cereal box, empty plastic bottle, saucepan lid, and a rattle and constructed for herself a percussion orchestra, which she played at with great seriousness and concentration.

(8) Practices standing boxes, books, cartons, cigarette packs properly on end. She asks for permission with much jargon and gesticulation, and when done puts them back without any mishandling.

(9) Spatial experiments—"headstanding" to peer between her legs, rolling on floor, pivoting neatly on one toe (has learned that she can swirl more easily on linoleum than on a rug), flings self around wide-legged and with great sense of silliness; takes sidelong steps to squeeze through narrow spaces without using hands to guide her or to hold on; walks backward "just for fun"; walks about the house with a plastic cup held in teeth and covering face, with fair ability to avoid touching furniture; turns corners through doorways, does not often stumble on a toy. (She is not clumsy, or normally a "faller" anyway, even with vision impeded, no matter how hurried or preoccupied she is.)

15 *months, 1 day.* March 9

DEBBIE decided last week to hold her own cup or glass at the table again. Her spilling has been most minimal. Usually holds *glass* with two hands, finger and thumb tips only, and empties it with movement of fingers and wrist. But holds *cup* with one hand and tilts head back to empty it.

She has discovered that if we can play "this piggy went . . ." on her toes, she and we can also play it on her parents' toes. This is obviously a humorous situation to her as she struggles to remove our slippers and to touch each toe in turn, waiting for us to supply the proper lines.

Has at last learned to up-end, shake, and empty her plastic fill-bottle. Seems quite relieved at this advance. [*Note 84: In the sample of twenty babies I tested—see Note 72—the ability to remove trinkets from a bottle by pouring them out seems to have become the rule by age 15 months. See also Benjamin, Note 24, page 138, and Ruth, Note 45, page 205.*]

Debbie is a lot of company around the house these days. She attempts to mop and to dust, asking for a cloth or a mop of her own to use as we work together. She scrubs her own tub (no mimicry here, as this was a chore not done in her presence), she washes herself at basin and in tub with considerable precision. She does not leave her crib until she straightens the pad and asks us to pick up and give her all the blankets and three dolls which she then sorts and places with great precision and speed. She spontaneously puts most of her toys and books back in place intermittently during a play period (and this is her own idea, since Mother makes no consistent effort to tidy up while Debbie is busy playing).

15 *months, 13 days.* March 21

ON THREE occasions in the past two weeks when Daddy has been delayed until 6 P.M. (fifteen to twenty minutes later than usual) Debbie has repeatedly asked "Daddy?" and been told "In a minute"; and finally she has gathered her six or seven animals and dolls one by one at the door, sitting them all up laboriously, and then sat down among them to wait for him. No pathos in this but rather gives an effect of busy acceptance. Her greeting of him on these nights is no more or less exuberant than on other nights. [*Note 85: Observe how the child develops schedules and expectations well in advance of any vocabulary of time.*]

Grandmother taught Debbie to dance "Ring around the Rosy" and a simple Kick-Kick (other foot) and Bow routine and these she repeats to music at home. She now asks me to dance with her and twirls holding onto a finger—this last at her own instigation in contrast to the "taught" tricks above.

She has discovered clocks and watches—teeters stiff-legged from foot to foot saying "tic tic" to clocks; has her dog and her dolls listen to watches too, ear down.

16 months, 1 week.   April 15

DEBBIE still requires a morning nap at around 9:30 or 10 and lasting until noon. Not always very hungry for lunch, or for afternoon snacks. Supper is at 5:30 these days and at this meal, as at others, she feeds herself, quite neatly, with right hand only, using spoon and/or fingers. Her afternoon naps are variable, but most days likes a rest of thirty to forty minutes beginning at around 3:30 P.M. Bedtime and immediate sleep come at 6:30 to 7 P.M.

This nap schedule has interfered somewhat with her playtime with other children in the neighborhood (since those nearly her age nap when she is awake, and the older children are available only from 3:30 on). However, at the arrival of any of them, she dashes to the door, attempts to open it (but cannot reach the knob), squeals and jabbers in eager anticipation. She beckons them in with hands held palms up and flexing fingers, backing up and on toward her toys as though to lead them on into the house. She indicates various toys, offers them others, and rushes into any play situation with full, happy cooperation.

Her play around the house is usually quiet, sustained, and

purposeful. She is more self-reliant than before, and asks less often for help with recalcitrant toys.

She continues to offer food to her dolls and animals. Washes their faces and hands if they are dirty. Blows their noses (does a fine job of blowing her own), brushes their hair and hers too, begins to take one or another of them about the house and, if she leaves one behind, goes back later to get it. [*Note 86: Among the developmental achievements of toddlerhood are being able to blow out through the nose, to drink through a straw, to chew gum without swallowing it, and to eat an ice cream cone—the last is best done outdoors, however.*] She has long since chosen special places for certain dolls or animals, and returns them to these places after play spontaneously (e.g., a bunny "lives" on a window sill; a dog in her table cranny; a baby on her bookshelf; a teddy bear on a bench in the entry).

She sometimes manages to stack or to fit her plastic cups and laughs, slapping her thighs at her success. She still takes great pleasure in playing with her small blocks.

She changes pace by selecting reading material—her own or ours, or even a telephone book. Tearing is rare and occasions loud complaints to us. She consistently "reads" right side up now, and has for approximately a month. [*Note 87: At earlier ages, the baby is relatively indifferent to the orientation of pictures (see Hunton, 1955) and starts a book equally well at back or front. It is quite remarkable how a baby comes to know the "right" orientation of things.*] She still studies her greeting cards and has not torn or mangled any of them, although her favorite, now four to six months old, is a bit soiled.

Not content to carry one or two items around the house, she loads arms and hands too with various objects—can hold three cups and one block in one hand and is able to release each one with good-to-fair selectivity, retaining her hold on the others in hand and arm.

Since she enjoyed her sled all this past snowy winter, we gave her a small plastic wagon with a pivoting front axle. This toy frustrates her—she wants to push it, with sorry results, and is not too pleased to pull it behind her where it is out of sight and she cannot see her riding dolls or animals, even though this works just fine.

Confronted with her first puddle of springtime, she proceeded purposefully to enjoy it to the fullest and without a second's delay—as though she knew it was created for a child's pleasure.

16 months, 20 days.   April 28

ECZEMA behind her knees necessitated severely limited diet. Debbie being eager for and even demanding widely varied fare, this restriction has caused some very slight inconvenience to both of us (no wheat, no milk or milk products, vegetables ad lib, no fish, and only pears, prunes, apple, or juice allowed). The main problem is my ability to select from such a small array and then to stick to it.

Have forgotten to mention that Debbie has suffered a major loss of words in the past two or three months. Random and rare use of a word does occur, and for two or three successive days, but she has markedly reduced her vocabulary, primarily to "dis?" or "dat?" accompanied by pointing at the object in question. Seems relieved to find her forgotten word, and repeats it joyously and with emphatic head nodding. At the same time she has developed a patternless jargon which she uses in paragraph-long explanations to us—exercising tongue and perioral muscles in an exaggerated way, as though this would somehow clarify her message. (Which it doesn't, *often!* Nor have we lapsed into the "speak slow-ly and e-nun-ci-ate clear-ly" method with her in an attempt to have her copy our speech. Her behavior is reminiscent of the American abroad who speaks his English more loudly and more emphatically, as though that would ensure comprehension.)

Given a new chair by her godfather a few weeks ago, she has decided that it belongs in the living room at the coffee table. And, further, that she will have supper and lunch here instead of at her feeding table. Also, that this particular "toy" is not a toy to be stomped on by all the other kids. "No," if it is usurped

—but still not so with other household objects or other toys of hers, all of which she happily offers to share. [*Compare Ruth, 16 months, 16 days, page 240.*]

17 months, 2 weeks.   May 22

A RELATIVELY quiet month in many ways, but with some changes in the social and motor spheres nonetheless.

SOCIAL: Always very observant of and responsive to the differentiating characteristics of people, it has been interesting to watch the development of this "trait"—her response to varying social situations in the home is instantaneous and nearly infallible. For example:

(1) With a hyperactive and chaotic four-year-old girl whose frustration tolerance is very low, Debbie retrieves her thrown toys for her, attempts to show her how things work, with added explanations in verbal jargon, pats and coos at her encouragingly when she can't do something.

(2) On the arrival of a particular house guest whom she hadn't seen since February, Debbie greeted him most seriously, calling him spontaneously by name "Jahm" (for John) and responded to him during the time of his visit with an absolute mirroring of all his salient characteristics (he is a warm but *very* quiet scholarly man with a capacity for silence and protracted sitting as well as for the subtlest of silent, nearly deadpan, kindly humor with children).

(3) With a five-year-old boy who has been consistently angelic with Debbie over the past year, she demonstrates full trust and confidence in him, calls him clearly by name, "Geoffrey," and *always* cries when they have to part company.

(4) With a grandmother who dotes on babies who are "100 per cent good," Debbie is demonstrative and about 90 per cent good.

(5) Marked interest in tiny babies—great ability to watch them without actual interference for thirty to forty minutes, providing an adult is present, ministering to the baby and acting as

Mother's helper, gently, and spontaneously as well as on request ("Debbie, hand me the powder"). Now rocks her own dolls and animals in her arms and coos softly at them the while.

(6) Resolved some of her fear of the lusty two- to two-and-a-half-year-old boy by poking back at *his* buttons or *his* shoes or *his* navel when he pokes at hers. This bit of interaction obviously pleased the boy, because instead of continuing his usual "bullying" actions, he begins to make a gay and happy "game" out of it with her for a change and without anger and confusion on his part as usually used to happen.

MOTOR: It is hard to single out any new behavior as purely motor, since everything she does has components of perceiving and thinking and remembering and imitating. For example:

(1) Gives a simulated yawn at a picture of a yawning bear in pajamas.

(2) On seeing a pair of closed pruning shears sitting idly by for the first time, she picked them up and prepared to demonstrate to me how she could clip her fingernails with them (I was surprised because the closed clippers bear very little resemblance to manicure scissors).

(3) On seeing a picture of a fish, for instance, in a book, she points to a fish mobile we have; or a bird picture, she points out a window, etc.

(4) She claps and laughs in response to clapping and laughter over the radio and at funny cartoons.

More specifically motor changes: (1) Has learned to rock herself in rocking chairs of all types and sizes and also to rock on her rocking horse, and gets up onto them all neatly and nicely.

(2) Continues to be physically in good control. Crawls under couches and cribs and backs out as usual without ever misjudging and bumping her head on the way out. Never bumps head under tables despite her increased height. Rarely falls or stumbles or loses balance and therefore has never had bruises for display, or need for comforting and bandages.

(3) She now stacks several objects (two to five of them), then stoops or squats, picks them up gently at the base of the pile, and proceeds to carry them elsewhere. Refuses, however, to have

anything to do with her small blocks, and either ignores them or flings them out of the box with fine vigor.

(4) Dissatisfied with the way a spoon works with gelatin, she reaches for a fork and manages nicely. [*Note 88: Again observe that these "more specifically motor" items involve orientation to objects and their spatial relationships.*]

Her neatness and precision persist, although now that she has gotten used to her sandbox, she can be fairly active and tolerate spilled sand or sand in her clothes more comfortably than before.

She now occasionally usurps driver's seat in the parked car and goes through an energetic mimicry of starting and driving it, with gear-shifting and horn honking, key and wheel turning, etc. She begins to do the same thing with the garden tractor (and inside the house makes differently pitched sounds for car and tractor). She expresses "No" with great irritation if I say "Is that a tractor?" when *she* knows she is making *car* noises.

18 months. June 7

DEBBIE's weight is now 19 lb. 6 oz. and her height 29 inches. Her allergic rash is improving and her diet is less restricted. We can begin to introduce all foods but eggs and milk, cautiously and with observation of results.

Great friendliness and welcoming gestures to all other children present in the doctor's office but reserved acknowledgment of the presence of adults there.

18 months, 10 days. June 18

DEBBIE is good company these days—eager to cooperate or "help" in anything we do. She works alongside me in the garden, manages to rake or use a trowel fairly well for ten or twelve strokes before her coordination begins to fail. She helps put weeds in the basket, and works along with either of us at various yard chores. In the house, she helps push the vacuum or mop, finds a sponge and "dusts" furniture, anticipates her father's needs in dressing or in building a fire in the fireplace, insists on helping to wipe spoons, "sets" the table by carrying flatware to the table and scattering it about the periphery, continues to put most toys away spontaneously, finds various bits of dog fur or other fluff on the floor and puts them either in the ashtray or a wastebasket.

She has begun to take great pleasure in bedecking herself with beads, hats, work gloves, Father's jacket, Mother's slippers, etc. Demands to have face washed as Father washes his after shaving, or powder or perfume or hair brushed as Mother dresses.

The addition of a full-length mirror in the parental bedroom two weeks ago has interested Debbie. She goes to see herself in various costumes and in various moods, either mugging extravagantly or eyeing herself detachedly and with extreme casualness. [*Note 89: Observe how this dressing up and posturing before a mirror, common in toddlers who have access to costumes and looking glasses, contributes to the definition of the self. It is reported (Baltimore City Public Schools, 1964, pp. 48–49) that some "culturally deprived" four-year-olds cannot recognize themselves in the mirror or in pictures.*]

Her father and I think we see a greater acceptance of other children close to her in age and size since she has begun this self-observation, as though she now distinguishes them as not identical to herself even if they seem so in size and behavior. Has not had any visible problem accepting older children.

18 months, 2 weeks.   June 22

FOUR days ago Debbie suddenly looked alarmed and took me by the hand. She led me to the bathroom and indicated that she wanted to sit on the toilet. This arranged, she accomplished nothing specific, but sang and jabbered and was extremely proud and euphoric. This surprised me, for we have made no attempt to toilet-train her and had only gotten to the question "Are you wet?" etc. Since then she has taken one or the other of us to the bathroom many times, but no results so far except her crowing pleasure in doing this much all on her own.

18 months, 22 days.   June 30

WARMER weather and an inviting yard lure Debbie outdoors constantly. She brings her shoes, or works angrily on the screen doors, pleading "Out, Out" as soon as breakfast is over. She does not play well outdoors completely alone, and asks for company in the yard. This is undoubtedly all to the good since our yard is ill-defined, large, and full of rock-cliffs, brooks, pools, brambles, and patches of poison ivy.

But now her father spends more time at home on a reduced summer schedule and is busy with various major yard works. And the neighborhood children, now out of school, are eager to include Debbie in their play. She is thoroughly cooperative, and sharing, and happy with any or all of them, and they all seem to understand her outlandish gibberish with perfect clarity. So things move smoothly and pleasantly.

She is still extremely quiet outside the home, except with other children. Is beginning to "flirt" with men visitors or the other fathers in the neighborhood, and to be a bit shy with strange women.

AESTHETIC SENSE: For about four months now, Debbie has been able to pick out reds and blues in all sorts of contexts and to call them by name—and happily. She does not yet identify yellows or greens at all and avoids them if asked, making us think these colors are known to her but disliked.

We have a car turn-around paved in crushed bluestone. One of her favorite outdoor occupations is to comb this large area for odd-colored stones and to line them up, with many careful re-arrangements, atop a low stone wall—yellow, shiny feldspar, black or white quartz, red and purple stones, etc. Then she stands back and admires her collection.

Flowers are "pretty," and Mother mustn't pick any, even faded blossoms, or else Debbie pulls a fake "hurt" act and puts them all back, tucking them neatly into the foliage.

EVIDENCES OF HUMOR: Plays a game of "which hand is it in" with parents, utilizing either real or imaginary objects. Also has great fun finding imaginary bits of fluff and brushing or flicking them from surface to surface; or swatting non-existent insects. All this with knowing, sidelong glances of shared make-believe of "You *know* it's not a real bug and so do I, but. . . ."

19 months. July

Now THAT the summer schedule is in full swing, with Father home a lot and a ready supply of neighborhood playmates, Debbie's routine has begun to change too, in two main ways:

(1) She has all of a sudden become a midday napper (from 12:30 or so to 2.30 or 3), having finally given up her morning nap.

(2) She completely rejects her feeding table, and insists on eating at the family table—sometimes in her new high chair, sometimes on a parent's lap, with varying degrees of independence and marked variation in demand for others' morsels in preference to her own. (Milk has now been reintroduced to her diet, but she is not overly interested in it yet.)

In the motor area, she can now pull her wagon, and gives her various dolls rides. She can get on and off her big rocking horse unassisted, and rocks it by herself. She delights in carrying, well above floor level, large objects such as footstools, small chairs, huge pillows—seems to do this only to achieve a goal or purpose, and not out of a general urge to motor activity. She gets into any empty stroller, tricycle, Irish mail, etc., that happens to be available, and, if she weren't so short, would probably take off at great speed—her leg action is good.

Has found two new jobs for herself: (1) She closes all outside doors a hundred times a day—fine, except that the July heat makes open doors welcome to adults. (2) She routinely appropriates one parcel at the grocery store and refuses to relinquish it for the cashier, the packer, or Mother—takes it into the kitchen and gives it to me with great expression of pleased pride in work completed.

LANGUAGE: Random new words appear and are in proper use for a day or two, then abruptly disappear from her vocabulary. Phrases such as "How about that?" "What's that noise?" "You're welcome," "Sit in chair," "Didn't do it," etc., appear in context, but only rarely. Begins to say "Show" and lead parent by finger. "No" for second helpings, etc.

20 months. August

STILL content to play by herself in her crib in the morning until she calls us. The only trouble is that now she has such a variety of calls that we are hard put to it to answer the right one and, if we err, are told firmly to "Go away."

Has dropped the whole potty seat business (with never a production) long since. About once every other day we ask "Are you wet?" and get a firm denial even if she is. However, the whole subject is an academic one now, since she very rarely wets or soils during her waking hours for the past four or five weeks. Diapers cause her great rage, so these days we use training pants, which she never wets. She is most cooperative in getting into and out of clothes, except for diapers and rubber pants.

Meals have altered their characteristics markedly, except for breakfast, which she still enjoys in a businesslike but leisurely fashion at the table. Otherwise, she rejects spoons or forks, preferring "finger foods." She refuses most vegetables most of the time, although if the other neighborhood children chomp away on raw carrot strips or celery bits she mimics them, and she may actually get a mouthful down before she quits. Extremely busy, she has made meals peripatetic in various ways: (1) She eats a bite from her plate on a low table every time she passes in the course of working on some project. (2) She may choose to have a quiet picnic on the porch steps or the footbridge or under a tree on the lawn. (3) She may bring to the table all the necessary equipment for the continuation of a project, and work on it (feeding a doll, or reading books, or fitting toys) while she accepts feeding absent-mindedly.

She remains neat, however—scrapes her lip with spoon, asks for or reaches for napkin, dislikes even the most minute spilling and cleans it up before going on.

MOTOR AREA: Crosses her fingers. Does a fair two-legged hop in imitation of a frog or other kids. Does a gay step, with laughter, imitative of a "giddyap horse" step we used to see when kids believed in hobby horses. (She has, in fact, made a hobby horse out of a toy, but walks sedately and with silly sidelong glances that indicate she knows it's make-believe and that she's proud of it all.) She turns "somersaults" and has all her dolls do them, too—claps at their success and praises them extravagantly. She has "played" ball with one or two adults on her own initiative for several months, but increasingly sets up the rules for each one's position and turn at rolling. At present, she prefers a game in which two adults are opposed, with Debbie in the middle being some sort of fielder, catching wild balls that are not supposed to be aimed at her. She has finally learned to walk on tip-toe, does a bent-over old man's gait which she thinks is particularly funny. She practices standing on one foot and does pretty well once in a while, and then claps or crows with glee. She kicks a ball all over the lawn using alternate feet in a rhythmic walk-and-kick routine. She's beginning to climb up onto, into, through all sorts of things—over couches, etc.—using boxes, chairs, and other things as step-stools. All cautiously and with good balance, no falls or bruises. Calls "Hup" (for "help") when she needs it, and will follow directions such as "Hold on," "Down easy," "Put the foot on the rung," from a distance and without hesitation or confusion.

LOGIC: Having found a dead moth in a door corner, she proceeded to check all analogous door corners (right lower), and then all other (left) door and window corners in the house; and then closet corners.

20 months, 1 week.   August 15

WE TOOK Debbie to Jones Beach. She did not nap during the whole day, but "rested" at frequent intervals in the car. She collected (and insisted we bring home) sea shells and stones.

She exhibited no fear of the breakers. She played either in the water or in the sand but did not mix the two areas or the two media. A happy experience.

20 months, 16 days. August 24

A TRIP to New York City by both parents, during which Debbie remained at home with her grandmother for three days. She sent us off with gay waves and welcomed both of us without resentment or upset, in contrast to her hurt at being left by Mother for a weekend six months ago.

20 months, 22 days. August 30

AN OUTING to a country fair in the company of her father and our twelve-year-old godchild. Exuberant greeting of all animals, much urge to pat and hug all baby animals, much mooing and baaing and peeping on sight of the animals (interesting only because she has refused to do this at pictures of animals for many months now). Rode a pony with balance and glee, but cried when her ride was over. Came home and reported everything to Mother with gestures and dancing and jargon interspersed with noises and names of animals. Overjoyed!

21 months, 2 days. September 10

Now THAT school has started and the informal neighborhood gatherings have diminished, we find that Debbie has definite need for children, as shown by: (1) She goes to the door often to look up the road "to see kids, Mommy," and if, luckily, she sees one, she chatters and squeals, calls "C'm here, play, Debbie," jumps up and down, and brings Mother to see him, too. (2) Has apparently learned the names of all eight or nine neighbor children and their dogs during the summer, to our surprise, and asks "Jeffy here?" (hoping he can come visit her), etc. (3) Her sharp ears pick up the distant sounds of children playing a block or more away, and as though drawn by a magnet she starts in their direction at a run, calling out as she goes. [*Note 90: Debbie's response to distant voices is probably less a matter of acute hearing than of figure-ground organization. The adult, after all, can hear the children at play once his attention has been directed thereto, just as he can hear the far-distant airplane once the toddler has said "airplane" (or his infantile equivalent).*]

She continues to play well with children of all ages (from two and a half to eight and a half), engaging fully in their activities in a highly cooperative way—everything from active marching games to playing the passive baby in elaborate ritualized dramas of domestic life. She shares automatically, it seems.

Two new abilities. Is no longer confused and upset by the disappearance of an older playmate in hide-and-seek games. Is beginning now to say a firm "No" once in a while to questions or demands from other children, particularly if the other child is being too distractible and flighty and not finishing any project or activity at a pace satisfactory to her.

She is fascinated by infants and will sit quietly, watching intently for twenty or thirty minutes, as the mother ministers to it. Talking very little, cooing at it occasionally, and once in a while reaching out to replace a lost rattle in its hand or to help cover it gently, or to hand the mother some object she asks for.

Doll play is filled with new complexities lately, putting dolls in various roles. Making them her "baby," she washes and dries their faces and hands, feeds them ("More, baby—more toast?"), puts them to bed, and covers them. As "companion," she takes them with her to the store, out to the sandbox, sits them in conversational circles and talks to them, shows them whatever delights her, reads to them, etc. And as Alter Ego, she scolds them, praises them, explains to them in a way suggestive of reinforcing for herself various parental admonitions and teachings.

On rare occasions she has thrown a doll in a show of anger that is both rather impetuous (no relation to the play situation) and also somehow theatrical (too short-lived or too shallow). These outbursts are apparently related to some anger at Mother for some oversight or failure to understand. When Mother asks, "Are you mad at Mommy?" ("Yes") and Mother says she's "Sorry —made a mistake," Debbie then accepts this and forgives both Mother and the doll eagerly.

21 months, 10 days. September 18

DEBBIE has some new sense of self that she demonstrates in two new ways: (1) She insists on taking on some responsibility for her own activities, e.g., she delights in putting her own bed in order, she begins to choose the clothes she will wear, she actively helps dress herself, begins to ask for a cookie on her own initiative, has definite food preferences, particularly as regards amounts she wants to eat, asks permission to perform new tasks (help bring up laundry, turn on the TV, bring Daddy's slippers, etc.) by saying "Debbie *dood* it!" (definite awareness of tense here). She also now goes to get the sponge or the broom on her own initiative to clean up her own spills or mistakes with great calm efficiency as opposed to her previous upset pleas for help. She asks for a tissue and blows her own nose, then puts the tissue in the wastebasket herself.

She now often refuses proffered help when some project frustrates her, and attempts to master tasks well beyond her previous limits. She kisses her own hurts without drama or tears, and asks for "medicine" if she continues to hurt for too long a time afterward. By the same token she will refuse ointment if it doesn't bother her—"No. No hurt" (or "No itch"), "Mommy."

(2) She demands some intermittent responsibility for our actions, too! A certain degree of imperious and detailed ordering of our behavior has begun, from demands that we either do or not do a given chore, such as vacuuming, to insisting that Daddy change his shoes, to meticulous outlining of exactly how and where we are to sit and exactly what game we will play and how. And she begins to order her dog verbally, too! "C'm here," "Sit, Ollie," "Down!" with varying success. She goes about all this in a cheerful mood, investing much of it with a sense of fun and usually accepts our ending the game with great good

grace. Rarely does she seem to invest it all with great serious intent or to be hurt and/or angered by our inability to remain permanently and infinitely malleable, but soon joins us happily in a routine more of our choosing.

21 months, 18 days.   September 26

LANGUAGE: "Don't want (have) any," "Debbie need cookie," "Don't see kids," "Ollie go out?" "Go play . . . sandbox," "Boom—Wow—Whee—Oh Boy!" "Easy" (as an admonition for safety's sake), "Toot, bang, bzz, ding-ding," "Go out." Beginning appearance of positional words, such as "sit down," "stand up," "in-out," "on-off," "under," "in back," "next," "over," "high," and "too high."

CONCEPTION OF TIME: Begins to distinguish "now," "hurry," "later," "in a minute," "yesterday," and "tomorrow." For instance: "Did we go to the store this morning?" ("No"), "Did we go yesterday?" ("Yes"), or "We'll do it tomorrow" and, sure enough, on the morrow she reminds me of my "promise," first thing.

(An aside: I was taken ill in August and confined to chair day and night for a month, and convalesced for another month. Household routine was little disturbed since Father was home for much of that period and, fortunately, I didn't have to be isolated or in bed. Debbie adjusted "intuitively" to this and accepted my sedentary position as well. The only sign of her awareness that things had not been quite as usual was her insistent joy in leading me again to "show" me things and her obvious delight in my ability to lift and carry her again after the month of her having to climb up into my lap.)

22 months.   October 8

A WEEK-LONG visit by her grandparents from the West, whom she hadn't seen for a year (October 28 of the previous year— age almost eleven months). Obviously remembered her grandfather and instituted the specific "bumble-bee, bzzz" game he had played with her. Also began again, at her own instigation, the specific "pocket-search" game that she invented with him last year. Eager to welcome them both, she led them all around the house offering them her favorite objects, pointing at things, "Jacket off, please." Appearance of a girl cousin two months older than Debbie from afar—greeted with exuberant glee, happy hugging and kissing at intervals, shown "Debbie's room," invited to "Play . . . toys, Debbie's . . . we do it," decided they should have supper together perched on stools with dishes on a bench. Her cousin entered into all of this gaiety with pleasure. Debbie cried when the cousin left and days later was still asking "Penelope . . . (go) . . . home?" Initially a bit timid with her grandmother, she soon found that Grandmother took jewelry and cosmetics seriously, and Debbie began to ad- mire these to her grandmother's obvious enjoyment.

Taken to a game farm—especially delighted with the giraffes, hugged and kissed a benign bactrian camel. Walked from group to group saying "Bye, bye" to each as she left to go on to the next. No sign of hyperactivity, but great watchful interest that was unflagging even when parents were worn out. Walked amidst the fallow deer as though she were one of them. Marvel- ous day—for parents, too!

22 months, 3 weeks.   October 29

A BUSY month of gradual, overlapping development, a bit hard to describe except in categories again.

SOCIAL: So glad to see children at the door that she continues to jump and squeal in greeting, but has developed a new "hostess" behavior, indicating that they come in, take jacket off, put it away, come play. Will not take a cookie unless they have one first, usually insists they have two. Begins to beckon them to participate in her activities. But now also begins to show resentment or confusion if a child engages only in isolated or parallel play, or if he monopolizes a toy, and comes to me to see if some sort of give and take or shared play can be instituted.

At the same time, Debbie is beginning to show great pleasure

in naming objects as Daddy's or Mommy's or Debbie's or
Baby's, and respects this somehow or other. When visiting, she
does not grab or usurp or turn to me for help, but, instead, asks
the mother of the house for help or permission. I marvel at this.

MOTOR: Walks contemplatively with hands clasped behind
her back, pours with precision, tries steps in adult fashion, asking now and again for help, wipes hands well with towel, rides
on the vacuum picking up various toys on the way and deposit-
ing them on chairs or tables as we go, covers herself with
blanket in bed instead of becoming entangled, uses fingers skillfully in one-handed reversal of tiny objects for fitting. In drawing, she prefers small finger-controlled or forearm action, constructs complex, smallish doodles that are specifically meant to
obliterate a printed or drawn symbol. She controls a wooden
hammer well and pounds pegs gently but accurately.

SELF-AWARENESS: All the usual facial features, with curiosity about and response to names for eyelash, eyebrow, shoulder,
chest, back, arm, elbow, leg, knee, heel, ankle, toe, foot, navel,
etc. Also begins to name articles of her and others' clothing.
Also some new awareness that "Debbie can . . . (use) . . .
spoon. Ollie no no spoon." Also now does not react to teething
with vague irritability but says "tooth hurt" or "bump lip" or
"hurt foot." Also, a new fondness for hats, new clothes, bedecking wrist in plastic beads, and some humorous dressing up in
Father's boots, Mother's gloves or jacket, etc. Goes to the mirror
to examine herself in any new or outlandish outfit, also occasionally to inflate a rather theatrical crying spell by seeing "another
baby" cry—but this always ends either in laughter or in a *real*
need for soothing and a breakdown of the false self-pity.

Also the appearance of the word "Me" to refer to herself.
[*Note 91: Toddlers characteristically have trouble with first-
and second-person pronouns, which refer to different people
depending on who is speaking.*]

SYMBOLIC INVENTIONS: At bedtime in the evening variously
indicates her readiness for bed by insisting that "shoe come off,"
or by finding a book with a picture of animals or Little Boy
Blue napping, or by putting all her huge family of animals and

dolls in proper positions. Also, on two occasions when she made a puddle on the floor, she quickly grabbed a doll and put her on a potty seat and said "Debbie no dood it." Parenthetically, Debbie still intermittently asks to be put on the seat, but is still unable to let go and produce anything, and, despite reassurances, cannot then be led back to try again until her next brave attempt.

MEMORY: (1) Guitar—either sees a striated object which reminds her of this instrument and laughingly strums it, or picks out guitar sound in music and strums one hand's fingers on the other hand's fingers, saying "Bob, Bob" (the man who twice has played for her). (2) On seeing a small snapshot of a white terrier, she immediately said "Nell" (the name of a white terrier who spent a week with us this summer). (3) Heard a radio commercial for "forty-three beans" that she hadn't heard since May, and was overjoyed to recognize it. Sang and danced, and "Mommy, hear!" (4) Still goes, at three- to four-month intervals, to find her favorite books (remnants of infantile experience between her first and fifth months) and greets them noisily and with glee, and "Mommy come see."

23 months, 6 days.   November 14

BUSY baby! Debbie has been upsetting old patterns in some areas as she proceeds along her merry way and goes in straight-line progression in other areas—and all with just enough inconsistency and unpredictability to afford Mother considerable surprise, and confusion, too.

In straight-line progression we have such things as these:

LANGUAGE: "Dropped it," "Picked it up," "Fix it, Mommy," "Get it" and "Got it," "Debbie put it way," ". . . (Go) way, Mommy," "Broke it!" (usually with tears). Also "Dear, oh dear, oh dear" and "Tch, tch."

PLAY AND MOTOR ABILITY: (1) Tries and sometimes really accomplishes a good somersault. (2) Now enjoys real rough-house with her father in the evening. (3) Drawing (with pencil) is bolder in action now with circular and straight lines—still asks

Mother to draw in alternation with her on the pad and asks by name for the object she wants her to draw ("flower," "horse," "star"), indicates where she wants it on the page, and then Debbie draws. (4) Interest in and some facility with screw toys and bottle caps. Would turn door knobs if she were taller. (5) To the best of our knowledge, Debbie had never tried to climb out of her crib, but yesterday she got out twice and called "Open door, Mommy!" all cheerfully as she stood proudly in the middle of the room. (6) After many months of refusing to play with small blocks, Debbie now seeks them out, says "Sit floor. Play blocks, Mommy," and proceeds to stack them (twelve to fourteen of the one-inch size) in a hasty, slap-dash fashion several times over. She occasionally gets so exuberant at this that she jabbers at, slaps, and blows on each block in turn. Reminiscent of the ritual crapshooters go through with their dice, though where she learned it I haven't any notion! Then she begins to line them all up with great precision and to push the row about, saying, "Train. Goes choo-choo."

In other areas, however, lability and change are the words these weeks:

(1) Apparently has decided she needs to see more of Daddy, so suddenly has decided to call for him to "Open door" at 7 A.M., wastes no time with diaper change, but proceeds to dog his heels, prompting him and imitating shaving and toothbrushing, helping him dress (holds pant legs, gets shoes, helps with shoe horn, etc.). And now eats breakfast in his lap, with smug satisfaction, begrudging him every single bite and flirting with him. Also has reconciled herself to his leaving, tells him "Go work, bye-bye" as she leaves his lap to begin her own projects. In the evening, greetings are nonchalant until he is settled, and then she monopolizes him in all sorts of activity, after telling Mommy to "Go way." [*Note 92: Debbie and Ruth (21 months, 25 days) both show Electra-complex-like behavior at a very early age.*]

(2) So quick to familiarize herself with new books that she seems bored by them even as she brings them to us. Will not name objects for Mother, but points and waits for me to name

the picture; but does just the opposite with her Daddy. Has converted all suggestions in the books into action—picture of bear, dashes into another room to get bear and show it its picture; a second's glance again at a girl dancing or jumping and Debbie is out dancing or jumping wildly for a moment, then back to the book. [*Note 93: Here, and earlier, Debbie is not merely identifying the objects in pictures, but also the activities in which they are engaged, a more difficult task. It is likely, too, that she could recognize pictured facial expressions indicative of simple emotions.*]

(3) But one day took my finger and pointed it to words to read. This was not enough, so she pointed to letters and seemed happier at words spelled out. We came to the word "P-L-A-Y, play" at which she flicked hastily through the book and found two other words "play" and pointed them out to me proudly, and then was off and away, "Playing, Mommy." [*Note 94: Here we see further shreds of evidence that instruction in reading can be started at an early age, and in literature-minded homes usually is. It should perhaps be added, lest overeager parents try to force their offspring into early reading, that such instruction must be adapted to the child's own pace and shifting interests.*]

(4) Lability reflected these days in shorter attention spans, but a greater associational wealth (as with books), mercurial switching on of wails and tears, an inability to tolerate any variant of "No," an insistence some days on going from one previously accepted taboo object (matches, fireplace, Daddy's pipes) to another, under great pressure—seems relieved when all of them are proved still to be "No's" and then is all relaxed and busy again in a happier mood.

(5) Lability is reflected also in sudden and brief interludes of rest and withdrawal from concentration. For example: (a) Now stops without warning while working on a project that is not going as she wants it to, and silently jabs thumb in mouth for a second or two while she thinks it all over. She always refuses help in these situations, and shortly goes back to work on

the same task, often with success. (b) Announces "Debbie nap, couch (or floor)" and stretches out for a few seconds of relaxation.

(6) Rejection of and anger at some parental action now expressed in a good show of temper and some tantrum-like behavior, occurring suddenly and without warning amidst what had seemed to this parent to be perfectly acceptable behavior on her part (wrongly so, of course, according to Debbie). She also now begins to show some destructive and angry actions toward her dog and her various dolls, and gives them a good thwacky thump or a tweak now and again. Then she repeats her old apologetic behavior (that she used formerly when she dropped or knocked over a toy), and clutches the offended object to her with loud and patently false protestations of "sorry, bear," with none of the old empathy and shared hurt.

(7) Now begins to show, at intervals, real shyness with some adults and also with strange children—much use of sidelong glances and back-turning. This can occur at home or elsewhere, and is usually fairly brief in duration. [*Note 95: The reader should be aware that all these varied emotional reactions are included in an account of cognitive development because they represent the child's increasingly variegated sensitivity to the properties of situations and of his own standing in relation to them—including, of course, his ability to manipulate situations by means of emotional displays.*] Is also now beginning to color her long-standing preferences for males with a flirtatious parody of shyness, and then catapults herself into an utter abandon of blandishment and coy flirtation and a wild proffering of toys. Kisses and wiggles.

(8) Clothes now a source of very feminine vanity and she has begun to insist on having her mother put on lotion and perfume and "Wipstick, too, Mommy," seriously and urgently (quite in contrast to her gay participation in Daddy's shaving ritual).

(9) Alternates refusal to play alone with imperious insistence on privacy and solitude. Some breakdown, at last, in her "specific place for things" orderliness. Seems to thrive in a room completely disordered, with toys strewn everywhere, and insists that

they "stay there, Mommy. No pick up, Debbie no do it," even when no maternal notice is paid to it at all.

Now an aside of sorts. Her new insistence on having everything out and in use at once, coupled with her boredom with it all, has resulted in her remembering suddenly that one specific closet holds other things that she hasn't seen since last December, and she now demands occasionally that all these objects be added to her collected hoard of inventoried but no longer stimulating "Debbie's things." She is beginning to have difficulty sharing, and imperiously asserts her ownership. Mother finds that substitution or duplication seldom works, but that the toy which is the bone of contention is best removed for a while.

As antidotes, Debbie thrives on a complete change of scene now and again and more than welcomes a brief play session at another child's house or an all-day visit with Grandma. She asks for these explicitly and with great insistence about once a week, and we try hard to arrange it for her a bit oftener. (She sees no particular fun as yet in shopping or in just riding around in a car.) She responds to outings with great joy—gathers and tries to select her clothes and helps in dressing, saying, "Hurry, hurrry," and on arrival says "Jacket off! Bye-bye, Mommy." She frequently turns her back with a quiet "No" when I reappear, and denies my presence totally; but in a few minutes she relents with a "Go home" and brings me a hat or a mitten. Visiting, she is a totally "exemplary" child, according to casual comments from disparate sources, and after being away she seems overjoyed to return home for a day or more.

Also, she begins to ask for the TV. Watches "Captain Kangaroo" about two out of five mornings and delights especially in the Dancing Bear (cries when he leaves), some of the slower animations, which she laughs at and mimics, and all the music-making and small animals. On dull afternoons she asks for "Dance" [*presumably a teen-age dance party on television*] and enjoys it—the "Kids, Kids." Demands to watch a program with real children on one channel. She sings "Happy to you, happy to you" with them and waves and makes overtures to certain children. She is most firm about "Turn off!" when she is tired of watching, which nearly coincides with the end (pre-commercial) of a given program. She mimics the twist, is completely absorbed in watching any musicians performing, and on occasion will go get her tambourine to accompany a drummer, or her toy xylophone to play softly along with the pianist or xylophonist. She ignores commercials (unless she is drawn back hastily for a quick look if she hears children's or "cartoon" voices), and utilizes the time for various activities of her own—runs to complete a project, or talk to me about something, or to look at her book for a moment.

23 months, 3 weeks

On Thanksgiving, spied the turkey all stuffed and ready for the oven, and somehow or other recognized this bald, headless, footless object lying on its back as "Bird, oh dear, *poor* birdie." She was most interested in having me check up on it during its stay in the oven, and would lead me to the stove at intervals. At dinner she was so concerned for "Poor birdie, oh dear, oh dear," so insistent on patting and trying to reassure it that eating was of no importance whatsoever. Seemed pleased to know it was a "turtie" (turkey) and not upset over its being carved and eaten, which she simply paid no attention to. (Debbie was not served any turkey.)

23 months, 25 days.   December 3

VISIT to pediatrician's office. Weight 20 lb. 3 oz., height 32½ inches. In the doctor's waiting room: quiet but contented behavior, approached several mothers with infants to observe them, and also several solitary and shy girls standing at their mothers' knees—with a hand out and a bit of greeting. Watched with interest an active group of older children noisily playing at a table but did not approach them. In the office was very comfortable, adequately interested in all persons and activities, but contained and quiet. After examination all but flew off the table into the doctor's arms and was very pleased to hug him and be hugged and talked to by him. (A note on the state of her allergies: no further skin flare-ups, provided she does not eat citrus fruits, apricots, pineapple, or plums in any form. We introduce small tastes of these every few weeks one at a time, and though her sensitivity is diminishing, she still reacts to them.)

2 years. December 8

SECOND birthday. Debbie was absolutely delighted with all small signs of celebration, glowing with pleasure and filled with hugs and proudly announced "Debbie's *two*" to everyone who asked.

Mother and Debbie went to Grandmother's house on the evening before for a quiet supper (to dilute the excitement, if any were to arise the next day). She was proud of her new dress and twirled to show it off for Nana on request. All in most ladylike fashion. Was utterly silent but beaming when a tiny cake with two candles was brought to the table. Having been expert for two months now at blowing out matches, she chose to prolong this "pretty thing, Nana" by leaning on her elbows and blowing many small puffs of air through pursed lips to hold on to the flame. When, as happened a few times, one accidentally blew out, she would ask "Light it, please" and begin again. When she was finally satisfied, there were only nubbins of candle left, and she was joyous to have "Cake to eat, Mommy!" Given her present, she asked the donor to "Ope it, Nana," and hugged her new pajamas to her with great warmth and affection for them: "So soft." And got into Nana's lap eagerly to show them to her.

On her true birthday (today), she was visited at unexpected intervals by various children and was most hostessy and gracious and smilingly pleased with all overtures and greetings. Welcomed each gift with warmth and thank-you's, all spontaneous, and with eagerness to have each child enjoy and share it too. By evening when her father came home, Debbie was a bit wound up and greeted him with a great burst of exuberance and energy, showed him everything new, then, putting all that behind her,

seemed eager to return to her usual playtime with him uncolored
by the events of this extraordinary day.

2 years, 8 days.   December 16

RESIDUE of birthday: sings "Happy to you, Debbie two" with
the TV children, accompanied by a sort of hop-skip of excitement. Now recognizes pictures of cake (has never had any except on her second birthday) and asks "Debbie blow? Debbie
two?" Gave her greeting cards brief hugs, then took them to
introduce them to her collection of cards from her first birthday
and last Christmas, which she had finally tucked away at the
back of her book cubby several months ago. Greeted each old
card with "Hello, baby. See? New birdie" or "Hi, horsie" with
all the happy recognition of seeing an old friend again. [*Note
96: Debbie's behavior toward the cards themselves can be interpreted as animism, whereas her treatment of the pictures is an
example of picture realism, which, like animism, seems to be
founded in a more general way of viewing the world which has
been dubbed dynamism, seeing the world as held together and
activated by an all-pervasive but undefined energy.*] So pleased
with her new pajamas that she likes to breakfast and play a
while in them and at last is put into day clothes only over loud
protests. Chooses the "Nana ones" with great feeling.

2 years, 3 weeks.   December 29

A SUMMARY of the Christmas holidays. We made an effort to
keep Debbie from involvement in all the outside cultural doings
(no long excursions to shows, etc.) but she noticed and was
pleased by the new decorations in the small local shops we
visit routinely. She exhibited no grabbiness at stores, although
she enjoyed looking at all the dolls and toys and whatnot. Play
situations deteriorated a bit, much to her confusion and disappointment, due to the high level of tension and over-excite-
ment in her playmates.

She spent one day of the week before Christmas, as usual, at her grandmother's, and was so pleased at seeing the decorated tree that she was transfixed in the doorway. Said often during the day, "Just look. Pretty, Nana." She was given a tiny tinsel tree, with glass balls attached, to examine, and carried it about all day with no damage at all.

We planned the large family dinner for the Saturday before Christmas, with only our outdoor tree lighted and no indoor decorations. She enjoyed it all thoroughly—ate a bit of turkey this time (though she was still very concerned about "poor bird"). A few of her packages were presented on that day, and she was pleased at the wrappings, helped pile them up and accepted our "we'll open them later" with ease. At opening time, she went to each adult in rotation (her own idea) for "help ope it" and was full of *oohs* and *aahs* as she saw each gift, then spent several moments examining and using each one in a leisurely fashion before going to get the next package.

Sunday was a quiet day of ordinary routine, planned so in order to allow respite for this alert and involved child.

On Christmas, our tree was up and she was almost beside herself with surprise and glee—"Come, Mommy, Debbie *show!*" She reverently asked permission to poke gently at some of the decorations, spent much time just looking: "Oh pretty, *pretty!*" She ate a leisurely breakfast, then asked to open a package, which was a small wooden apple filled with tiny bowl, two wooden cups and saucers, a teapot with lid, sugar bowl, all half-inch to one inch in size. She immediately set them up, with great delicacy and finesse, on the seat of a dining room chair and proceeded for forty-five minutes to conduct a completely credible "foffee" party for herself and two dolls, asking, "More foffee, baby?" to which she would reply, "Okay, more," pouring and refilling and sipping and proffering ever so nicely. She began then to bring us into it and shortly thereafter was finished with this game and asked to open another package. She paced her packages throughout the entire day, was grave and smilingly delighted by turns; and when Nana arrived, Debbie bestowed all the gifts on her (as guest) to "Help ope, please."

We had thought to prevent any overexcitement and overwhelming fatigue in her so that she could enjoy the holidays freely, by our dilution of stimuli over several days. But we were entirely unprepared for her graciousness, her elfin warmth of appreciation, her wisdom in pacing her day so beautifully, her ability to share in others' pleasure in their own gifts, her delight in introducing new toys to her old family of dolls. This was an unforgettable experience for us indeed—if adults could retain just a fraction of this open-heartedness, what a different world this would be!

During the days following Christmas, neighbor children dropped in at intervals to inventory her gifts. She shared them all gaily, and on visits to others' homes was no more aggressive with all their displays than she was with her own.

The occurrence of so many special events in December has interfered with the description of Debbie's general, non-festive undercurrent of growth. Will attempt a summary of it here for convenience and an indication of who she is at age two and how she lives her days. This will be a bit difficult, for we've been through another one of those periods of extreme flux as she readies herself for the next Giant Step in development, and though she has stabilized again now, she has made so many changes in so many areas that we have a chore in even organizing our thoughts.

To describe the tumultuous six weeks of pre-Giant-Step Behavior.

Normally a sunny child with a comfortable range of emotions to appropriate stimuli, a joyful intensity for all her projects, a surprising patience with reality, a need for neat balance between independence and interaction with others, a sustained affection for things and persons, Debbie threw all this topsy-turvy for a period, in a distressing (even to her) lability and inconsistency— a sort of impelling urge to re-test every old familiar boundary and landmark for its validity. At the same time she literally pushed herself into the future, trying new experiments in every dimension at once. During this period her world and her conception of herself in it must have seemed full of surprise, heartbreak, sheer intoxication, and perhaps even the terror of being caught in quicksand.

Not all of her days, not even all of many single days, were so chaotic during this period. On most days she floated into new territory with a sort of real ease and instant mastery. For example, having had a miserable morning in which nothing, but *nothing,* could reduce her frustration and relieve her tense unhappiness, I introduced a completely new set of plastic beads for stringing and arranged them on the floor in the living room at random so as to surprise her on awaking from her nap. Debbie found them, said "Oh" in a matter-of-fact tone, sat down and proceeded to string them quickly and with facility, matching colors and naming them absolutely without demonstration or help on my part. When done, she asked me to "tie bow," put them on with no expression at all, and went about her business as though nothing had occurred at all, and related to all old patterns with familiarity. But on a second's notice all this could change, every pattern shattered, emotions inexplicably rampant, a complete deterioration of old manual skills, the whole world suddenly hostile to her and beyond her comprehension, language reduced to a shambles of "uh-uh-uh's" as she groped for words that had fled her in her time of need. Comforting became a complex and harrowing task, demanding every resource and technique I could dredge out of myself. And then, miraculously, all would be well again with Debbie.

Through it all, Debbie was achieving a whole new mastery on a much higher plane of integration that we could catch glimpses of now and again, and she has now just begun to crystallize into a perceptible new pattern—roomy enough for challenge but already comfortable to her and familiar again. (Whether or not this kind of *sudden* step-wise growth pattern is typical I don't know, but it has been characteristic of Debbie all along—and also her need to leave behind earlier patterns with never a backward look or resumption-and-regression once she's made the transition; e.g., her weaning herself first from the breast and then from the bottle.) [*Note 97: It seems to be true of all three babies described in this volume, and perhaps of babies in general, that the emergence of major developments is signaled by a period of disruption and turbulence. Thus, the early years seem to consist of eras of calm and consolidation alternating with periods of stress. It is important to recognize that there are qualitative discontinuities in organization, both in these years and later, so that the person who emerges from a time of rapid growth is not the same person he was at the beginning. This point is obvious when we compare childhood with baby-hood, adolescence with childhood, and so forth. But it is also true for changes that take place over much briefer spans of time.*]

To describe these changes by area.

COMPETENCES: Quite straight-backed; tummy protuberant mainly when she is fatigued. Capable of marked pace change, turns and twirls, does a fair run with very little arm flailing, enters into TV children's games with fair mimicry and rhythm, hops, bounces, walks on knees (upright trunk), on tip-toe, tries to jump, tries to stand on one foot with occasional success. Very expressive face with new expressions of wrinkled nose for dis-taste, of sidelong and from under eyelash pleading or flirting, of open defiance. Initiates and invites whoever is present to "March," "London Bridge," and "Ring-Around," and sets up a rotation of turn-taking by each participant. She sings songs, some of the words to the music, and in marching sees to it that rhythm noises are made by each marcher, either with the instru-ments she provides or by clapping or counting: "You clap, Mommy"; "Daddy count, Debbie toot." Much interest in faucets (distinguishes hot and cold by position), light switches, door knobs, wind-up toys, and toys with mechanical on-and-off switches. Likes simple puzzle fitting and hammering and fitting tiny pegs in holes—has good precision for these until fatigue sets in. Beginning to be especially fond of tiny objects and makes up certain relationships between them which she insists on pre-serving (e.g., a rubber band, a small screw, and a tiny plastic bit "belong here—stay in box"). Much interest in moving stools, chairs, etc., for climbing purposes, and practices falling (has always been so sure-footed that the occasional clumsinesses she experienced during her transition period were shocking to her). She practices doll-dropping and rescues them for a while by way of reassurance. Her one real fall took place on our sidewalk as she was running to help a two-and-a-half-year-old retrieve his boat. She bumped her mouth and as a consequence has one dead upper incisor tooth despite no visible bleeding at the time. Frequently gets up from being seated on the floor by rising, trunk erect, onto one knee and then directly on one foot.

LANGUAGE: In direct verbal mimicry Debbie is poor and inconsistent as always, but words appear spontaneously with perfect clarity whenever she chooses and with a sudden increase in frequency, in perfect context even for a surprising number of words that we had no idea she could have learned (e.g., "suck it" when she saw a lollipop in the store). Phrases are common, and four-, five-, and six-word sentences are appearing. She has word-lapses still, and now when she makes up sentences, she fills the spaces where a word she knows (or wishes she knew) should go with "uh's," and this increases with fatigue or excitement. She has long since used "Debbie . . ." (or the possessive form) in phrases, but last month began to use "Me," and now uses "I need . . ." or "Give it to *me*" or "My blocks" with increasing frequency.

A word list now indicates a speaking vocabulary of about 750–800 words.

In the past week she has begun to count things, though she has never shown much interest in parroting the one-two-threes. So she surprised us by putting up two fingers for "Debbie, two years," by reporting off-handedly "Debbie dropped four Cheerios" (and, by gosh, she had!), or saying "Ladder. Three steps," with ladder in question out of sight.

Yesterday she saw a picture of a toadstool. To the best of my recollection the word "mushroom" was mentioned only on one afternoon in the garden last summer. When she saw the picture, though, she said "ushroom" without prompting.

Occasional sing-song, two-note repetitive rhyming word use

while playing, such as "fi-sh, di-sh, bi-sh" or reiterative "Ol-lie, Ol-lie, Ol-lie" (her dog's name) idly as she strings beads.

SOCIAL: Remains especially attached to one five-and-a-half-year-old boy whom she trusts implicitly (and with good reason, for he is most "good" with her) and obeys willingly.

However, she is now beginning to "schedule" her days in a most interesting fashion. She starts a day off by naming any one of the neighbor children (Patty, Richard, Geoffrey [the five-and-a-half-year-old], Vicky, Jamey) and either indicates with unswerving finality whether she is to go "Play Patty's house" or "Patty come home—play my house." And she rotates these in loose fashion (never Patty on two days in a row) and with near alternation of visiting or being visited. She skips some days and demands "store" or "Nana" on others. Seems quite a nice awareness of need for variety to me.

She again entertains or visits with great stability now. Shares well, though with an occasional squawk of "No—it's for me" and also begins to look on my "Let Richard do it (or have it) now" with a new turn-taking awareness. Does not grab objects from other children, but begins once in a while to assert her right to a given toy or for "my turn." Her intermittent shyness of the transition month is now nearly gone and also her previous tearful heartbreak at a child's leaving after an hour or two of play. She now begins for the first time a bit of parallel play and does not demand interaction with children. [*Note 98: Debbie's beginning with true social play instead of parallel play is not a departure from the standard developmental sequence, since the primacy of parallel play applies only to play with others of the same age, whereas Debbie's playmates were older.*] At departure time, she sometimes will "Help, jacket on" with the other child in a maternal, responsible way, and go find their mittens or boots for them.

PROPERTY RIGHTS, DOMESTIC DUTIES, USE OF SPECIFIC TOYS: Having gone through the proud repetitive process of assigning ownership, she then went through a nearly defiant denial of it all, intermittently during the transition period, with tearful insistence that it was Debbie's pipe, Debbie's shovel, Debbie's anything-that-wasn't-Debbie's, no matter how far-fetched it might be (as "Debbie's baby" for any infant in carriage she passed while in a car a block away). Now she has again stabilized but with a new complexity—"store's toys," "Geoffrey's hat," and is upset if he tries to put it on *her,* and goes to get her own instead. On the other hand, the ability to say "Debbie's tractor" has renewed her ability to press it on a child visitor and to anticipate the pleasure of watching her, patiently and with a quiet smile, play with it.

The imperious ordering of every parental routine in all details has passed and she accepts the usual fluidity again. She puts most things back in their accustomed place, unless it's something of hers. She still likes to have all of her toys out where she can find them or stumble over them for momentary use (which she began during the chaos of the transition period), but now begins to sort and arrange them by groups according to frequency or association of usage and has begun to put certain toys into a cupboard in which she sometimes plays Cave or House, so that she has them in reserve, as it were, for a bored moment and can go get them.

HOUSEHOLD ROUTINES: She is again occasionally very good company. Helps or watches us shave or dress, participates sporadically in dishwashing or drying, table-setting, bed-making, dusting, mopping, vacuuming. She will get a mop or sponge to clean up localized areas of "mess" or "dirty" or "dusty" that she runs across all on her own, and puts the tools away afterward. She will run errands and follow complex orders ("Go get the *blue* cup on the table in the living room and take it to the shelf in the playroom"), delights in clearing her table, passing needed objects, and has the routine of starting a fire in the fireplace down pat. Even in a one-time job like making and installing a shoe rack she soon knew all the cues (hold stick, ruler, pencil, drill, change to countersink, sandpaper; then nail, hammer, put nail down, now screw and screwdriver) and was holding and handing each object to her Daddy without being asked to do so long before the project was finished. She was a veritable one-girl assembly line.

USE OF SPECIFIC TOYS AND MATERIALS: First of all, it should be mentioned that Debbie began to "move into" her own room, transferring various toys and belongings from the larger general house area, in October and November, so that she goes to "my room" to play or, increasingly, invites others there. And now she is capable of quite a lot of real solitary play at various tasks, coming only occasionally for real "help, hurry" or to ask Mother to *see, look,* or *watch* something she wants to share.

Received a set of colored, medium-sized construction blocks for Christmas—does quite a lot of color and/or shape matching, and also announces that she will make "house for bear" and then tries to do so, with door, but usually needs a lot of help in carrying it out.

Dolls and animals—has begun both to tell us that "Baby no use poon, Debbie does," but also to try to help dolls walk and wave bye-bye, etc., as well as to read to them and try to dress them in rubber pants, shoes, her sweaters and hats. Formerly used to offer them real food, but now has removed it one step and offers imaginary food, in a real though early make-believe situation. Takes them for rides in wagons and buggies. Bids them goodbye on her departure, shows them their counterparts in books or on TV. [*Note 99: Notice that Debbie's animism is partial and limited. We are probably witnessing here the separate operation of thought and feeling—while Debbie feels (or at some level believes) that her dolls are alive, she knows that they are not.*]

Draws with chalk or pencil, announces "I draw star" and proceeds to make something resembling a tangle of string with a couple of star points protruding. Then says, "More" and repeats the process. If off by herself drawing, comes excitedly to get Mother, "Come see—look, Debbie drawed it." With another child, shares or takes turns with the drawing surface.

WATER: Fond of water, she helps shave, washes plastic dishes, imitates doing hand laundry. A need for the sandbox now buried under snow—she resolves this by working in the vermiculite of a planter box for thirty to sixty minutes, silent (to avoid adult attention and reprimand), but without any damage to plants, despite use of spoons, cups, etc.

MUSIC: Recognizes songs and tunes not heard for several months. Still likes syncopated or Latin rhythms and beginning to like marches. Joins in group singing (even on TV) with fair melodic accuracy. Will watch, entranced, anyone playing any instrument, is interested in mimicking such, even guitar (two hands, plus flamencan slapping) or clarinet (fingers keys, blows with pouched cheeks). Likes Mother to make up simple, song-like but spontaneous accounts of daily activities. Bored with "old hat" things such as "this little piggy" for several months now, she is beginning to repeat the last word of each line with interested glee.

BOOKS: The extreme translation-into-action phase has passed and been replaced by verbal associations to a picture or a word. She begins to enjoy going through books by herself with a monologue of chatter as she "reads" aloud. She often reads to one of her dolls or animals, choosing sometimes a book about a bear to read to a bear, and the like. She apparently is extremely familiar with the details of each book's contents, for she can go find any specific book and turn pages until she comes to the one item that she needs to illustrate some association she had during a conversation or while playing or watching TV. [*Note 100: Note Debbie's powerful eidetic capacity. Parents can often use their small children as a mnemonic storage unit, since the children can many times recall names, the details of clothing, and other minutiae lost to the adult. Obviously, certain components of situations never existed for the child and cannot be recalled, or the higher-order circumstances may fade; thus, the four-year-old may recall that, six months earlier while driving past a certain spot, a companion "cried and cried," but forget that they were on their way to go swimming.*] Also, she now begins to linger on a given page and to ask for detailed elaboration and some repetition, a somewhat story-like enlargement of the pictures, with special emphasis on babies, with her comments, too (e.g., "Babies no use poon; Debbie do it!"). She firmly corrects Mother if Mother says she thinks "that's a dog, maybe" with "No—a cat!" and also sometimes objects if I change a word in a story being read. Though at this point, the few words per page do not satisfy her need for elaboration about the picture and so, more often than not, she is impatient with the literal word-for-word reading. She has at last begun to answer with the word to parent's asking, "What's this?"

PEOPLE: Now uses words "boy," "girl," "man," "lady," "baby." Has begun to differentiate neighbor families, knows which house who lives in and can say, "Go Betty's house— Richard. Geoffrey—and Mike" (their dog). "I play with Richard now." She's beginning to say "Jennie, Vicky's Mommy—lady," though not always. However, all gray-haired women are still "Nanas" and all gray-haired men are "Papas."

OTHER ABSTRACT CONCEPTS: Appearance of words like "high" and "too high," "far," "heavy," "big," "little," "full," "empty"; "later" and "tomorrow," "after supper," "dark" and "too dark," "need light—no see it." Differentiates between "Betty's house" and Betty is "home," etc. Uses words descriptive of texture such as "smooth," "rough," "shiny," "soft" (but not "hard"), "slippery."

Begins to try to relate significant items to her grandmother over the phone, to try to tell her that she had such-and-such for breakfast, or that she saw a bird on the porch, etc. Listens and answers and has sense of closure of a phone conversation with "bye-bye" and a kiss noise into the mouthpiece of the receiver.

CHANGES OF ACTIVITY: During the chaotic period, any transition at all was likely to be fraught with ambivalence, delay, anger, and refusal or tears (prior to that she made them all cheerfully and quickly). Now she has a much more stable response, but with a wide variety of responses with which she seems comfortable. Choices offered her sometimes have to be reduced, or put into some such context as "After supper, then . . . ," to enable her to go more easily from one thing to another. But Debbie increasingly states the choice *she* has made (not one imposed on her) and is able to act on it promptly and eagerly, performing on her own initiative all the preparatory steps in fair order and busily convinced she needs no help (not usually true, however) though she will accept help more easily than she did during that weird transition phase. She still dawdles, although less consistently than in the transition phase, using patent delaying tactics to ease her tension, but for the most part now pats various objects on her way out with a bye-bye instead of either trying to drag them all with her or to stay in with them in security. She now uses an increasingly emphatic "No" to any suggestions or alternatives offered, as though she were denying the whole idea of choice and decision; but this is often sharply halted when Mother says (after a whole succession of "No's!") "Can Debbie say yes?" and she will say "Yes" and begin to grin as she realizes that she's got herself off her own hook and is then free to make the choice easily.

TOILET TRAINING: This is and always has been a self-deter-mined area by necessity, since Debbie will brook no hint or suggestion, and indicates she wants no help. The transition phase was characterized by a return to waking-hour wetting (but BM still during nap), by anger and hurt feelings at any necessary diaper change during the day, and a pathetic, repeti-tive "All dry, all dry. No wet" under the drippiest, most un-comfortable circumstances. Since then, she has again resumed her intermittent hopefulness about the whole situation—asks "Go wee-wee? OK?" and marches in forthrightly. She ignores the potty seat (puts dolls on it), and refuses the child's attachable seat, tries to get clothes off, climbs laboriously up onto the toilet "*No* help—(Mommy) sit there" (edge of tub) and perches pre-cariously. So far no success in production, but she takes pride in showing off to her doll family and seems less disappointed in her failure, as evidenced by her increased frequency of attempt. On some days she insists on training pants and is so hurt when she makes a puddle that it requires much reassurance and comforting to soothe her. She is curious about others' perform-ances, announces to all present that "Mommy (or Daddy, etc.) go wee-wee," as though she understood and had mastered the whole problem long since, which seems very reassuring to her.

APPETITE AND EATING: Always a relatively light eater, but a good one providing she is offered a great variety of food. She began to lose interest in the whole thing, however, when the doctor put her on a diagnostic elimination diet for her mild eczema, and she sought to make such monotony more tolerable by becoming a peripatetic eater this past summer. During the stressful period of transition, her appetite was minimal and her food choice capricious and unpredictable. Now, suddenly, things have changed and for the first time she evinces real interest in food preparation, often orders what she wants, says she is "hungry" or "thirsty," climbs eagerly into her chair and settles herself to eat, using spoon and/or fork with silent gusto. Remarks "hot" or "tastes good," asks for "more juice" (or meat, or whatever), uses spoon to wipe lower lip, and napkin, too, spontaneously. Remains a neat eater, but not rigid as to setting and arrangement. Often tries to read a book or continue a project during the meal and most frequently sees to it that she has the company of two or three dolls whom she talks to as she eats.

Typical day's schedule.

Awakes cheerfully at 7 A.M., calls, "Daddy, c'm'here. Open door." Waits until we arrive in her room to get out of the crib under her own power, greets whoever shows up with a "Hi," "Hello," or "Morning." Goes immediately to check up on a toy or room area, then walks to parents' room where she crawls into our bed for a quiet moment. Then, "Get up." Watches Daddy shave and participates in it all with mimicry. Goes to kitchen to check up on breakfast.

Breakfast remains her most enjoyable and leisurely meal, much sociability. She sees her father off with "Bye, Daddy. Go work. Kiss Debbie," and waves to him until car is out of sight.

Various activities follow. Sometimes requests, "Roo—Dancing Bear" (The "Captain Kangaroo" program mentioned earlier) on TV and, with permission, turns on the set and watches intermittently. On some mornings she wants to read with Mother and to draw or do puzzles; on others she wants to "Clean floors?" "Dishes, huh? OK," and sets the pace for the housework. Increasingly now, though, for the first time she is capable of solitary play in and out of her room at will, with smooth and natural transitions from dramatic play with dolls to reading to blocks, or whatever.

At about 10:30 she announces her plans for the rest of the morning, clearly and emphatically. "Raisin" (or "drink milk," or "cracker") snacks are rare these days, but she knows what she would like and asks for it, in contrast to earlier acceptance of anything offered. Then firm insistence on "Vicky here, Debbie's house, we play," or "Go see Patty, play." "Out" means out and away in the car to "Store. See birds" (or "fish"). "Outdoors" means play in the yard. She sometimes accepts substitutions if Mother can't arrange to do what she "needs" (she never says "I want" but "I *need* . . .") but whatever has been denied then crops up again later in the day.

Playtime ends about 11:30, with great variability in the mood with which she accepts it. If the termination has been difficult, she asks for "kids" and watches "Romper Room" on TV for ten or fifteen minutes with much copying of their games and singing, thus smoothing the transition.

Lunch has just moved up to 12 or 12:30, and she is most inconsistent as to interest and intake.

Nap follows immediately at her request, but is suddenly much briefer (one-half to one and a half hours). If she sleeps at all, she goes to sleep immediately, but about once a week she has a happy play period in her crib instead. She often awakes gradually, but by the time she calls "Debbie up!" she is gaily and nonchalantly standing at the foot corner of the crib waiting to get out.

Dressing both now and in the morning is delayed awhile until she can put up with the idea. She insists on standing up for all of it (even diaper with pins), is usually eager to help both in dressing and undressing (though occasionally she is negativistic to an extreme), tries to zip zippers, work snaps (not strong enough), helps with socks, manages slippers and shoes well.

She picks her outfit and is happy with no other, and then is off and busy on her own, refusing a snack.

Her behavior at suppertime is erratic and this is often a rather unpleasant meal, since, though she may be hungry, anticipation of the day's end forces her into such a frenzy of interested, multiple activity that she simply cannot pay attention to eating. We do, however, allow (because we have to) as much variation as seems feasible, but lately she has begun to respond to a very firm admonition to "Eat your *supper first!*" with evident relief that the choice has been made for her. Eats with hurried enjoyment, orders "fruit" or "ice cream" or, hopefully, "pie?" for dessert and helps get it; and then is off again. Has just begun at last to ask for celery or raw carrot (having disliked all vegetables but cooked carrots and beets for many months). Also, at last, announces "All done" or "All through" or "All gone" when finished.

Evening is a riot of activity, mostly with her father—roughhousing, "piggy-back" or "horsie" rides, reading, block play in her room, "showing" Daddy various results of the day's projects, or asking him to "show (her) how" things work. But she demands his participation in marching or music-making (tambourine, xylophone, whistle), or circle games. She then withdraws to the kitchen, ordering Mother to go "sit on couch" and engages in dishwashing or cooking (stirs the air in a pan with a spoon, shakes imaginary salt, onion, seasonings in and repeatedly tastes her imaginary concoction, or gets all the various tools out—flour sifter, eggbeaters, and the like—for a thorough performance. She gets the dog dish, helps in calling Ollie, watches and tries to help (but only succeeds in interfering) with his eating.

Then, about every other night, "Bath, now" and off to tubside, where she tugs at overalls, throws shoes off, pulls shirt halfway off. In the tub, can still do a very creditable job of washing herself, but begins to be more interested in sliding on her belly, etc. Repetition of "All done" finally ends in her opening the drain, trying to scrub the tub, and putting the slippery soap and all the cups and other bath toys up onto the narrow ledge. Drying off is less of an ordeal now that she has a terrycloth robe.

Sometimes, recently, after her bath she begins to bring in blocks or toys, requires one or the other of us to stay in the bathroom, opens and closes the door, coming and going with noisy busyness.

A drink of water and all eager to be carried to bed. She now lays herself down, but has just begun to ask for one or more of her innumerable dolls and animals to be put in the crib, too. Wants a kiss, sometimes orders us to kiss a doll in the buggy, and settles down. Door closed, lights off at 7 to 7:30 and Debbie is usually entirely quiet immediately, although once in a great while she may jabber a bit to her bedmates about some one of the day's problems (e.g., "Baby! Eat! No? All done? OK." or "Help bear? Go potty. Do wee-wee, OK?" "OK. All done. Get down. Help bear?") for five or ten minutes.

She sleeps all through the night. We change her at midnight (usually wet), offer her a drink, and she goes right back to sleep, after a warm smile for us.

References

Baltimore City Public Schools. *An Early School Admissions Project: Progress Report 1963–1964*. Baltimore: Baltimore City Public Schools, 1964.

Bayley, Nancy. A study of the crying of infants during mental and physical tests. *Journal of Genetic Psychology*, 1932, 40:306–329.

Gibson, E. J., and Walk, R. D. The "visual cliff." *Scientific American*, April, 1960, 64–71.

Hunton, V. D. The recognition of inverted pictures by children. *Journal of Genetic Psychology*, 1955, 86:281–288.

Spears, W. C. Assessment of visual preference and discrimination in the four-month-old infant. *Journal of Comparative and Physiological Psychology*, 1964, 57:381–386.

Staples, Ruth. The responses of infants to color. *Journal of Experimental Psychology*, 1932, 15:119–141.

Valentine, C. W. The colour perception and colour preferences of an infant during its fourth and eighth months. *British Journal of Psychology*, 1913–14, 6:363–386.

White, B. L. The development of perception during the first six months of life. Paper read at meetings of the American Association for the Advancement of Science, 1963.

Wolff, P. H. Observations on newborn infants. *Psychosomatic Medicine,* 1959, 21:110–111.

Woodworth, R. S. *Experimental Psychology.* New York: Holt, 1938, pp. 576–577.

PART II

BENJAMIN

❖❖❖❖❖❖❖❖

BENJAMIN, *born a day later than Debbie, was, like her, an unplanned late arrival in his family. At the time of his birth, he had a seventeen-year-old brother, Frank, and a fourteen-year-old sister, Janet. (Since Frank was away at board-ing school much of the time, he played a relatively small role in Benjy's early development.) Benjamin's father, who was in his early fifties when Benjy was born, is a college professor, and his mother, a college graduate who was in her early forties at the time of Benjy's birth, works in a semi-executive capacity in an office.*

As the records show, Benjy's mother returned to work part time shortly after his birth, leaving him for part of the day in the care of a housekeeper. Some of her work could be done at home. Benjamin's father travels a good deal as a consultant. Both father and mother are extremely conscientious, humane, and playful parents. The father is tender, thoughtful, and whim-sical in manner, the mother somewhat more crisp and mock efficient.

As will become evident, Benjamin's mother could not keep

records as regularly as the other two mothers, but her observations are acute and precise, and include a larger proportion of specific anecdotes than those on Debbie.

The family home is a large, somewhat old-fashioned house with generous grounds in a middle-class neighborhood in a small town.

Benjy at age four was described by his nursery-school teacher in somewhat the following terms:

He began his second year at nursery school in a turbulent, demanding, variable mood which has shifted steadily and gradually to one of pleasant, relaxed enjoyment of daily events. Bit by bit he has become less mercurial and more settled, predictable, and self-contained, and so less of a trial to himself and others. He increasingly tolerates disappointment, delay, and even discomfort with ease and patience.

He is extremely sensitive to sounds, which both helps and hinders him, and seems to be a key factor in his approach to life. When he is feeling gay, his vividly phrased and lengthy conversations with adults or children are carried out in lilting accents. When he is under strain, the ordinary clamor of other children's voices irritates or even antagonizes him, so that he seeks out a secluded corner in which to be alone with a book, or it may even drive him to tearful complaints of hunger or fatigue.

He is fascinated by and full of factual information about things mechanical, and speaks knowingly about drive shafts and back-hoes and the progress of construction in Main Street. He also takes delight in a wide range of school activities: painting, carpentry, listening to stories, and sailing boats. When he does something, he does it with a well-defined outcome in mind and with avid concentration.

Benjy is a captivating child whom everybody likes very much, and whose simple gestures of affection for teachers and children are gentle, direct, and patently sincere.

To this account his mother added that he was alert, curious, active, and strong-willed, and sometimes screamed with fury when thwarted. He was less shy than formerly, especially when he was allowed to make the advances. He was healthy, although his likings in foodstuffs were narrow, and slept well, taking a short nap on most days. He had a fine sense of humor and laughed uproariously and infectiously when things struck him as funny. In short, said his mother, a delightful, charming, exasperating, verbal, frustrating, fascinating handful of a boy.

BIOGRAPHY

BENJAMIN was born on December 9th.

1 month, 25 days.   February 3

UP to six and a half weeks, Benjamin was either completely or (toward the end of this period) partially breast fed. Then he got only bottles. For a while, he continued to turn toward me when lying on my lap to be fed, but today, just eight weeks old, he apparently caught on to the fact that food was now in the bottle. As I held it against my cheek, testing the warmth, he opened his mouth and strained his whole self upward toward it. [*Note 1: Note that two items of learning are included here: first, Benjamin has learned the location of his mother's breast; second, he has learned to recognize the bottle visually, before the nipple makes contact with his mouth. Preliminary findings from the study I am making of infantile cognition suggest, however, that after the baby has begun to react to the bottle on the basis of vision he has to go through a further period of learning to distinguish between the bottle and other, more or less bottle-like, forms. See also Werner, 1948, page 68.*]

1 month, 4 weeks.   February 6

A FRIEND of Benjamin's older sister, Janet, was here, who had not seen Benjamin before. I had Benjy over my shoulder, and she came up to see him. She has very dark hair, a rather pale face, and wears glasses with rather thick black frames. He stared fixedly at her for several seconds. Was he aware that this was an unfamiliar face?

2 months. *February 8*

MORE and more Benjamin is really *looking* at things—lights, faces, and now the butterfly mobile over his crib. If he is turned sideways in his crib so that the mobile is in sight when he looks toward the window, he stares at the slowly turning butterflies for several seconds at a time.

He is showing satisfaction at motion—he likes to ride in his carriage and doesn't seem to mind being jolted around as we go up and down the curbs or over snow bumps. He also lies very quietly and contentedly in one's arms, and will at least temporarily forget he's hungry, if one dances around with him in time to music. [*Note 2: The preference for motion over stasis is a general characteristic of infancy, even when the baby is not hungry. The baby out for an airing in his carriage stirs, awakens, and begins to cry if the carriage stops rolling for more than a few seconds—note the back-and-forth movement of two mothers having a conversation in the park. See Ruth, page 172.*]

He waves his arms around often when nursing and occasionally pushes the bottle away from his face. I suspect that this is still quite accidental, but am not sure.

Up until now Benjamin has shown a decided aversion to being bathed. Until about a week ago he would begin to cry as soon as he was completely undressed, and by the time he had been in and out of the bath was howling his head off. During this period, I didn't put him in the bath every day, but often just washed him in my lap—which he disliked, but less vehemently. A couple of weeks ago, I tried putting him in the big bathtub. This he didn't object to as long as he was on his stomach (and as long as I managed to keep him from dipping his face in) but as soon as he was on his back he'd begin to yell.

The yelling has each time begun by sounding more fearful than angry, but has ended up pure rage. When on his back, either in the round plastic dishpan which has served for a tub, or in the big bath, he has seemed afraid—has clutched frantically at my hand (or the side of the bowl) even though he was resting solidly on the bottom. He showed no such fear when turned over. What brought this on I don't know. The nurse we had gave him his first two baths and he yelled even then. Whether he was startled by something the first time or two, or was too cold or too hot, I don't know.

Today (February 8) for the first time he didn't cry. I put him in the big tub, face down, and he made pushing motions with his feet and legs while I washed his back and legs. When I turned him over, he let out a few mild yips when I washed his hair, but very little ones, and was reasonably calm when I got him out and into his bath towel.

2 months, 1 week.   February 16

BEHAVIOR in the bath continues to be erratic. Some days he's quite calm and others very noisy. Several days ago I'm sure the trouble was that he was hungry and resented the delay. By the time I got him out of the water—and it was a mighty short bath—he was yelling in a sharply rhythmic yaa-yaa-yaa that is apparently an anger cry rather than anything else.

He is smiling more and more. I think it was on the day he was seven weeks old that we were sure the smile was a smile and not a grimace. Now he smiles often—sometimes sort of to himself, that is, when he is looking at something other than a person, sometimes directly at the person holding or bending over him. Yesterday (February 15) he was lying on the cot in his room, well-fed, and I was bending over him. He smiled several times, very gaily, and I began saying "Hi" to him, over and over, opening my mouth quite wide each time. I'm sure he started to try to imitate me. He kept opening his mouth and once or twice made a little sound as if trying to imitate the sound also. [*Note 3: Benjamin's father told the editor that Benjamin imitated tongue-protrusion within the first few weeks.*]

He started on cereal on February 11 (two months, two days)

and seems to take to it quite well. At least he certainly gives no signs of disliking either the taste or the new consistency.

He is getting increasingly active—can push his chest up off the bed for several seconds and rolls from side to side until several times he has very nearly gone over from front to back. Being more active by day, he is at last sleeping longer at night. [*Note 4: It is questionable that Benjamin's daytime activity has any great effect on his nighttime sleeping. It is more likely that his physiological rhythms are stabilizing according to family patterns.*] Seems to be beginning to settle down to sleeping from about 11 or 12 P.M. until 6 or 7 A.M. This morning I woke him a little after 6 A.M., just because it's more convenient to feed him at 6 than at 7.

Last night he showed his first definite fear reaction to a sound. He was in my arms, in the dining room just after supper. Sam (our dog) suddenly barked not four feet away from him. Benjamin not only started quite violently, as I think I did, but his face crumpled up and he began to whimper—a very different sound and facial expression from the one he usually makes when crying. [*Note 5: Let us again make the point that emotional differentiation such as this implies cognitive differentiation, a new way of apprehending self and world.*] Incidentally, he produces a few tears now when crying, but more from the left eye than the right.

2 months, 25 days. March 6

ACTIVITY increasing at a terrific rate. In the last few days, Benjamin has begun to kick, one leg after the other, with much vigor—a change from the way he used to upfling both legs together. His arms are much more active, too, and he is awake a great deal more. [*Note 6: Note the change from symmetrical to asymmetrical movement, implying a differentiation of control over the body.*]

He "talks." Many new sounds have appeared and he burbles, coos, and occasionally lets out little shouts. He smiles a great deal—almost laughs sometimes, and is *most* responsive to talk and to singing. [*See Deborah, 2–3 months, page 9, and Ruth, Note 5, page 168.*]

He stops crying as soon as anyone enters his room, but doesn't yet turn his head toward the sound of a voice or other noise.

The last couple of weeks he has slept quite consistently from 11 or 12 at night until 6 A.M.; except for last night, when he elected to wake up at 3 A.M., very playful and full of smiles and not really awfully hungry.

2 months, 26 days.   March 7

THIS new-found delight in "talking" and grinning and kicking has its disadvantages! Again this morning Benjy woke early, this time at 4 A.M., full of merriment. Would take only about two ounces of his bottle, so it certainly wasn't hunger that woke him. Played around for a while and then went back to sleep until 6 A.M., when he took most of the rest of the bottle and went off to sleep again. Certainly in the last few days he has slept much less in the daytime than he had a week or two ago.

3 months, 9 days.   March 18

THE pattern of life is changing. Benjamin this morning woke about 6:15, took a few ounces and spat up most of it. The last few days he has been less and less interested in that 6 A.M. feeding, and I doubt if he really needs it. He was awake most of the time—perfectly happy—until 9 A.M. when he had his bath, and then was very hungry for his breakfast. He is eating more solids: cereal at 9:30 (more or less), meat at lunch time, and cereal and fruit about 5 P.M. He usually is awake from about 4 until 6:30 or 7. At 10 or 11 P.M. I wake him and he takes about three or four ounces and sleeps through the rest of the night.

Several times last week, when he was less interested in solid foods than he now is, he had huge quantities of milk at supper time (twelve ounces one night) and then slept through from about 8 P.M. until 6 A.M., but I don't think he is ready to do this permanently. The 6 A.M. feeding is dropping out instead of the 10 P.M.

He watches things more and more; people's faces, anything that moves or is light in color. He is very responsive to voices talking or singing to him. He watches closely and very often "talks" back, and grins with a most wonderful expression of glee.

This morning, Janet gave him a small rattle, putting it into his hand. Always before he has immediately dropped it, but this time he hung onto it for several minutes, waving his arms around and watching the rattle with great fascination.

Early last week, he turned himself over once, but as it hasn't happened again I guess it was just accidental.

When being fed from a spoon, he is still rather resistant to the first few mouthfuls, but, especially with fruit, after that he is more receptive. Doesn't yet open his mouth when he sees the spoon coming, but does often open up and strain upward when he sees the bottle coming. [*Note 7: See Note 1. Benjy has apparently learned to discriminate visually beween spoon and bottle.*]

3 months, 18 days.   March 27

INCREASED activity of hands and arms. Can get his fist, or rather first two fingers, into his mouth after only a few tries. Is increasingly aware of his own hands as they wave around. When an "interesting" object is held in front of him, his hands and arms often wave more vigorously, but he makes no real attempt to grasp an object yet.

He sucks his fingers quite often, particularly when falling asleep or just waking up.

Is very unpredictable about eating solid foods—it may depend upon how hungry and how tired he is, with greater desire for the bottle with greater hunger and/or greater fatigue. Has been very weepy over his supper the last couple of nights, but cheers up if held against any shoulder or put in his bed.

4 months.   *April 8*

A WEEK ago, I had Benjamin in the living room lying on a blanket on the floor. He had been playing with his rattle (which he can now hang on to for several minutes at a time) but had dropped it. He was on his back and the rattle dropped near his outflung arm. I went upstairs to get something and when I came back, he had picked up the rattle again. This is the first time I have known him to pick up an object, though I'm sure he did it because his fingers happened on it, not because he saw it. But he did pick it up and hang on. That same afternoon he produced his first definite consonant, somewhere between a *t* and a *d,* and it has happened once or twice since then. He has also produced a real laugh a couple of times—a lovely chuckle— but it's still rare and more often he grins and/or squeals or shouts.

He has a big rattle, a dumbbell shape with transparent ends containing little beads. He has learned to shake it—it's quite noisy—and watch the little beads roll around.

When holding any of his rattles or one's finger he often spends a minute or two clasping and unclasping his fingers. He usually tightens them before the object slips out, then relaxes again.

Benjamin's father thinks he is beginning to notice color, that he picks out the brightest-colored objects to stare at. [*Note 8: This observation agrees with experimental studies of infants' color preferences. See Staples, 1932, and Valentine, 1913–14, cited in Deborah's biography.*]

He also is beginning to respond with grins and obvious pleasure to being gently poked, chucked under the chin, or what not.

He uses his hands much more about his body—rubs his head, feels his ears, sometimes pokes himself in the eye. Also sometimes puts his hands on the bottle when sucking it.

His hatred of the bath evaporated as soon as I got hold of a bathinette. Now he loves it and doesn't want to get out, and is kicking happily. (Fortunately, he hasn't learned to kick *down* on the water, only *in* it, so I'm still dry!)

He shows a noticeable preference for his right hand. (His father doubts this.) He can hold a rattle in either hand but I, at least, think he is more apt to *shake* it with the right hand.

4 months, 20 days. April 29

As I remarked before, Benjamin is, and has been for many weeks, very responsive to being talked and sung to. I sing to him a good deal, and he *very* often reacts by cooing—or crooning, if you prefer. Lately, he has taken to grinning or even laughing at particular phrases. Several days ago, I started telling him about Dr. Doolittle and all his household pets, and the name of "Gubgub the Pig" brought on a real laugh, not once, but again and again. After many repetitions it isn't quite so comical but he will still grin as I go through the list of names.

At least four weeks ago, maybe more, I started telling him about "The Three Bears," with the *ee* sound very long drawn out. When *I* mention them now it may or may not provoke a smile, but almost invariably when his father asks him, "How are the Threeeeeeee Bears?" Benjamin will grin at him. There are several other songs and bits of stories which almost always will bring a smile. [*Note 9: Such humorous, as contrasted with social, smiling implies that the baby has a sense of the familiar so that he can recognize the incongruous. We have no way of specifying which incongruities will produce amusement and which terror, but we know that adults' attempts to entertain an infant sometimes have a contrary result. Incongruity implies novelty, and we know that novelty is a potent dimension of stimulation, to the point where it can produce psychogenic abortion in newly impregnated mice. (Eleftheriou, Bronson, and Zarrow, 1962.) See also Notes 11, 12, and 13.*]

His mouth is pretty active—sometimes apparently sucking on his gums or blowing spit bubbles which he sometimes does with apparent amusement. He will open his mouth for spoon or bottle *if* he wants either one. Will push out the bottle with his tongue when he doesn't want it, but has discovered that when he doesn't want solid food it is much more effective to clamp his mouth shut than to cry a protest. An open mouth sometimes means the spoon slips in! He can now shut his mouth very tight. [*Note 10: According to conventional theories of learning, Benjamin would be said to learn to keep his mouth shut because of the reward value of avoiding the disagreeable experience of having food put in.*]

He can communicate quite a lot now, in various ways: "I don't want the bottle"—pushes nipple out with tongue. "I don't want my meat and/or vegetables" (he likes cereals and fruit but is less enthusiastic about meat and vegetables)—either closes mouth or pushes food out with tongue, or yells with mouth full. "I want my bottle *first*"—when put in his chair for a meal he will at once begin to cry if he wants the bottle first. If he doesn't cry, I know I can start with the spoon. "I'm tired and sleepy and want to be turned over" (always sleeps on face)—a particular tone of cry. "I'm lonely and bored; where is everybody?"—an entirely different cry, higher, more tentative. Anger—a very loud, rhythmic *bellow!* Satisfaction—a soft cooing which can come in the middle of a meal, when being sung to, or almost any time. More vigorous pleasure—a happy little shout, heard often when kicking in his bed early in the morning, or in the bath and most often associated with vigorous physical movement.

He has found his "other" hand—twines the fingers of both hands together and watches them with great interest. He rubs his head, explores an ear, and very often sucks two fingers. In fact once or twice he has put his fingers so far into his mouth that he has gagged himself, with regrettable results.

Two or three weeks ago, I held him up to the mirror. Then and several times since, until yesterday (April 28) he seemed to see me, but not himself. That is, he looked right at me—our eyes met—he seemed quite interested and even smiled once. But yesterday he looked at himself. He stared and stared and finally gave himself a tentative little smile. I suppose this indicates he was recognizing the face he had been seeing previously in the mirror—I'm obviously not suggesting he recognized *himself.*

Benjamin *hates* being gotten into a long-sleeved slipover shirt (polo shirt type). The first arm goes in all right, but as the shirts aren't any too large, getting the second arm in is rather a struggle, and several times he has been crying angrily when I finally got him in. This morning he began to cry the instant I got the shirt over his head, before I even started to put the first arm in! And he kept it up in spite of the fact that I had rolled the sleeves up so there really was almost no struggle necessary!

Not much to say about space perception. He watches things—the butterflies above his crib, the figures printed on the bumper around the crib, people, smoke, lots of things. Several times he has become aware of Sam (the dog) and once of another dog, and has laughed and laughed—goodness knows why! [*Note 11: It is possible that the two dogs contain the kind of incongruity or novelty that produces amusement rather than fear. See Notes 9, 12, and 13.*]

Benjamin can wait, without much distress, for his meal to be ready, so long as he is in the kitchen with me and can see me. But, as mentioned above, the minute he is put in his chair, he'll begin to fuss, *if* he is very hungry and wants his bottle first.

His daily schedule has changed this week. For several nights he took none of his late evening feeding and sometimes not much of the 6 A.M. one. So this week I tried a three-meal-and-one-bottle schedule and it seems to be working. He wakes at 6:30 or 7, has bottle, cereal, and fruit at 7:30 or 7:45, lunch (bottle, meat, and vegetable) at noon, and supper (bottle, cereal, and fruit) about 5. Goes to sleep about 6:30 or 7 and we wake him at 10:30 or 11 for another bottle.

RANGE OF AWARENESS: I have no evidence that Benjamin is aware of smells. He is certainly aware of many sounds, but only if they are close to him. If Sam barks in the house, he jumps (but hasn't cried since the time mentioned earlier). He was quite unaware of a recent thunderstorm, but I think he was aware, and not very happily, of Janet practicing scales one night when he was having supper. [*See Deborah, Note 24.*]

He certainly has some food preferences—likes cereals, applesauce, pears or pears-and-pineapple, applesauce-and-apricots. Did *not* like his first (so far only) experience with fresh bananas. Of meats he seems to prefer chicken and lamb to beef and pork, but isn't too keen on any of them. Of vegetables, he prefers sweet potatoes to the others, but again he's not too fond of any of them yet.

Benjamin weighed 5 lb. 8 oz. at birth and measured 19 inches long. On our last visit to the doctor at four months he weighed 14 lb. 8 oz. and was (I think) a little over 23 inches. Although he has had the first two of his four quadruple-vaccine shots, he hadn't (last time) associated the doctor's office with pain. He goes again May 11th.

One day last week, I went out about noon. A friend of mine came to stay with Benjamin, bringing her two-year-old boy, and later her four-year-old boy arrived, too. They came just in time to give Benjamin his lunch. Janet was at home with a cold, was up in her room but could hear what went on. Benjamin was apparently upset and weepy, presumably because of the strange person feeding him plus the noise of the two boys. When he was put in bed for his nap, Janet says he was crying quite hard, so when he was alone she slipped into his room, wound up his music-box rabbit, patted him a little, and closed the door when she left. She says he quieted down almost immediately. [*Note 12: Here is an instance in which a slight amount of contact with the familiar—his sister and his music box—fortifies the baby against the onslaught of the strange and disturbing. See Notes 9, 11, and 13.*]

5 *months, 6 days.   May 17*

A COUPLE of weeks ago I was taking Benjamin downstairs for his breakfast when his father happened to come out of the bathroom with a good deal of shaving cream still on his face. He spoke to Benjamin who looked at him hard and then his lower lip thrust out and he would have burst into tears if I hadn't carted him off downstairs. [*Note 13: Here is one more example of the baby's reaction to the incongruous and novel. In the present case, we cannot know whether Benjamin's distress was caused by perceiving his father as an unprecedented object or by the unprecedented deformation of something familiar. See Notes 9, 11, and 12.*]

He is using his hands much more now, grasping at anything his fingers encounter such as his bib, pajamas, or anything else. He very often latches on to my finger when I'm putting the pins in his diaper—such a help! He has discovered his feet but hasn't yet managed to get hold of them. He grabs for them but so far has only succeeded in getting hold of his pajama pants or overall legs and hiking these up toward his face.

He can't crawl, but is at least trying to do *something* when on his stomach. He humps up his rear and reaches forward with his hands, but can't begin to get his torso off the ground yet.

He likes being outdoors and will usually quiet down (if he's been fussing) if I put him in his carriage where he can watch the leaves on the trees.

He has developed a new noise in the last week or so—a sort of fretful rumbling in the throat which can go on for quite a while before it erupts into a roar. It seems to mean a vague distress, not an acute one—something like boredom or frustration.

He shows some degree of insensitivity to heat and cold, and pain in some areas. Benjamin has drunk milk from his bottle that I would have thought was *much* too hot. He yells plenty when he has his shots and once when I accidentally pricked him with a pin. But one day recently I pressed a pimple on his chin (it had quite a head on it and was ready to pop) and he seemed quite unaware that I was doing anything at all.

Response to sounds is a funny thing. Benjamin seems totally unaware of noises outside the house if he's inside. He is getting used to Sam's barking and is less apt to jump when he hears it. Has given no evidence of hearing Sam's occasional howls. But

he'll jump if someone sneezes or coughs in the same room; yet
he beams with pleasure if I clap my hands and say "Bang!"

5 months, 23 days.   June 1

FRANK (Benjy's older brother) has been home now for three
weeks and I am wondering whether it is only coincidence that
Benjamin has seemed a little more sensitive and easily tired.
It's hard to tell whether the increased activity and sound and
movement of an extra person in the environment, plus a certain
amount of extra tension while we establish new routines, have
affected Benjamin's behavior or whether it is merely teething or
something else. Anyway, whatever the reason, Benjamin *has*
been a little more jumpy and occasionally fretful than he had
been. About two and a half hours is usually the most he can be
"up and around" before he begins to show signs of needing to go
back to sleep in his own room.

He is teething—no doubt of it. His hands or the end of his
rattle are frequently in his mouth, and he uses the end of the
rattle to really *bite* on.

Greatly increased large arm movements now and much greater
precision at getting whatever he holds into his mouth. He now
likes to lie in his crib holding the big noisy rattle and slam it
down on the mattress above his head, often kicking vigorously
at the same time.

Still can't do anything in the way of progressing forward, but
sometimes goes backward. Several times lately I've found him
down at the foot of the crib, once or twice with the blanket
over his head.

One of his favorite amusements these days is watching the
dog. I hold Benjamin in my lap and toss dog biscuits to Sam,
who chases them or jumps for them. This can go on for five
or ten minutes and Benjamin sits fascinated, often grinning if
Sam jumps for a piece quite close to him.

The department's majors (all female) were here for a picnic
last night, and Benjamin was out in the yard with us for about
an hour and a half. Part of the time he was in his carriage, part

of the time on various laps, some familiar, some not. I don't think he made a sound the whole time—just sat and *looked*. Finally, he began to nod on a faculty wife's shoulder and I carried him off to bed.

6 months, 11 days.   June 20

MY apologies for the long gap!

Benjamin has acquired two lower teeth, as of June 9, his six-months birthday. From the amount of finger sucking and drooling that is still going on, the uppers must be on their way, too. I bought some teething biscuits for him, but he isn't at all interested. (The dog thinks they're lovely.)

In the last few days, Benjamin has managed twice to turn from stomach to back, unfortunately during his nap both times, so we have seen only the result, not the action. He hasn't yet rolled from back to front, though he gets as far as rolling way over on his side. What he seems most interested in trying to do is to stand up. He can keep his knees straight and be fairly steady for about ten seconds now before he buckles, and he wants to do it again right away.

This noon he became nearly hysterical with glee. He was in his little chair and his father was sitting near him. His father covered his face with his hands, then took them away and said "Bang!" Benjamin began to laugh and continued to react with the greatest glee as his father repeated the action again and again. Finally, Benjamin got so wound up that his laughter turned into crying—either because the "Bangs" got louder or he had just had more excitement than he could take.

He is much more used to and interested in solid foods than he was a few weeks ago. Likes most things that he has tried except rennet pudding and cottage cheese. I suspect the latter of being too lumpy for him. For breakfast he has cereal, fruit, and his bottle, and usually finishes all of them. Likes all fruits he has had except strained peaches. For lunch, meat and vegetable or sweet potato—doesn't care much for peas as yet. I've been trying gelatin lately. It's hard to get it into his mouth, but once there he'll swallow some of it. Supper same as breakfast. It varies from meal to meal whether he wants a lot of milk before the solids or whether he'll take most or all of the solids first.

His reaction to the bottle we give him late in the evening is unpredictable. One night he'll drain it, then for several nights he'll take very little of it. Last night he was more wakeful in the afternoon and evening than usual and wanted most of his "night" bottle about 7:30—then slept through until 6:15 this morning.

His internal clock seems to be beginning to regulate his hunger. That is, the intervals between feeling hungry are beginning to conform to the hour of the day rather than the length of time since the last meal. Today, for instance, he had his breakfast at a quarter of seven. Yesterday, it was 7:30 or later—but both days he was equally ready for lunch at 12, but didn't demand it earlier than that. It is still true, however, that the hungrier he is, the more apt he is to want his bottle before the solid foods.

If I have him in the kitchen while I am fixing his meal, he usually waits pretty patiently. But the minute I bring him into the dining room and put him in his chair, he begins to fuss and can hardly wait till I get his bib on and reach for the food. [*Note 14: Note the goal-gradient effect. Compare Deborah, Note 16, page 13.*]

He loves to be outdoors, either on the playpen pad or in his carriage. It may be partly my own feelings, but it seems to me that he is much more cheerful and easy to take care of on sunny days, when we can go out, than on rainy days.

6 months, 26 days. July 5

SINCE the last entry, Benjamin has mastered turning over from both prone and supine, and happily does so. This afternoon he was outdoors on a blanket and he rolled over and over from one end to the other; would have kept on going but I stopped him. He is trying hard to creep. His rear end humps up but not quite far enough to get his knees really pushing, so his feet slide right back again. Often when I hold him with his head over my shoulder he bounces up and down with tremendous vigor and enthusiasm.

Sitting up is still pretty unsteady. He's fine for the few seconds that he stays still, but when he begins to wave his arms or kick his feet, he topples. He loves to be held up on his feet. He beams all over, and tries to get back up as soon as he sits down.

The biggest change in the last week has been in the kinds of sounds he makes. He forms many consonants and the sounds are word-like rather than long strings of vowels hung together. Now it's "Da-da-da" and "Ba-ba-ba" and *m* sounds, and the general effect is much more like an attempt to imitate speech than anything we've heard before.

The other night when I got him up for his bottle (he was very uncertain whether he wanted it or not), he was half asleep and rather unhappy for several minutes, and the sounds he made were exactly like the muffled, half-asleep murmurs of an older child; it was hard to believe he wasn't really talking. [*Note 15: Benjamin may be showing early evidence of "phonetic drift," the alteration of the universal sounds of early babbling in the direction of the particular intonations of the mother tongue.*]

Naps are getting a little shorter, and I think that last night's performance of sleeping right through from about 6:30 till 6:15 this morning will soon become a regular pattern.

More solid foods by day and much less demand for milk. Except for rennet pudding, he has liked everything lately, even gelatin, once you can get the rubbery stuff all the way into his mouth!

7 months, 3 days.   July 12

LAST Friday, I took Benjamin for the last of his four shots and a regular check-up. He was perfectly cheerful as we went in and sat down in the waiting room. Pretty soon another mother came in with a little boy perhaps three years old. He had come for a polio shot and was very apprehensive. At first, he simply whimpered and fussed, and Benjamin watched him, looking increasingly solemn himself. Finally, when the other boy's mother picked him up to take him in to the nurse, the youngster really began to cry—whereupon Benjamin let out one big wail, too. The mother tried hard to quiet the child, telling him not to "upset the baby" and Benjamin did quiet down and remained calm until after he had been undressed and measured. But when the nurse weighed him he began to yell and kept on yelling until everything was completed and he was dressed again. He weighed 16 lb. 5 oz. and was 27 inches long.

He is now getting equal parts of evaporated milk and water instead of the canned formula he had been having. Whether he is still objecting somewhat to the change, or whether the heat and humidity (causing some prickly heat) are bothering him, or whether his upper teeth trying to erupt are very uncomfortable, *something* has been making him exceptionally fretful the last few days. He has never cried very much except for fairly obvious causes, but since Friday he has yelled a good deal, had very short naps, had a hard time going to sleep at night, and has been most unwilling to be anywhere except in his carriage or on someone's lap. Probably it's heat plus teeth.

The thing that makes teething harder, in a way, is that unlike most babies of this age, Benjamin does *not* put everything possible into his mouth—so no teething biscuits, pacifiers, cold things, or what have you, are of any use. The only thing he will suck on, aside from his bottle, are his fingers—usually the two middle ones of his right hand. Along with this, he won't have anything to do with a cup. He clamps his lips shut and jerks his head away as soon as he sees it coming. It will be interesting to see whether there is a change in some of this behavior once the upper teeth erupt.

His hands are constantly active, fingers flexing and stretching. He will reach for things sometimes and can hang on to an object for some time, but almost never does he pick up something and put it right in his mouth.

One of his greatest joys is still "bouncing" when held against one's shoulder. If he could do lying flat on his stomach what he can do held upright he'd be all over the place. The other day

I was lying in a lawn chair outside with him on top of me. He got his knees up under him and his weight on his hands and rocked back and forth at a great rate. But he hasn't yet managed this on the floor.

While he isn't as interested in toys and objects and investigating things with his mouth, he seems to us to be slightly more aware of other people than some babies his age. Sunday we had him up at Debbie's parents' house. Debbie was in her playpen with various toys and we put Benjamin in with her. They lay and stared at each other for a moment and then she rolled over and reached for him. He objected to having his nose and hair investigated and we took him out. Whereupon he sat in his little chair and watched the many other people and kids, while Debbie was creeping around her pen and playing with various things. Later, in the house, Debbie's mother had Benjamin on her lap while I went to dress [*after swimming*]. She reported that he looked quite concerned while I was gone, and upon spotting me on my return, beamed all over and began to bounce.

7 months, 15 days.   July 24

JUST in the last few days Benjamin has discovered that putting things in his mouth may be quite interesting—things other than his fingers, that is. Given a cracker or cookie, he shoves it in his mouth right away, or tries to, though he's apt to hit himself in the cheek first. [*Note 16: Observe again the ambiguity of early localization of unseen parts of the baby's own body. Observe, too, that grasping something and putting it into one's mouth is a more advanced operation than simply putting one's fingers into one's mouth, since the shape, size, orientation, and location of the extraneous thing are not given directly to the senses in the way that fingers are.*] He doesn't retain his interest in the object very long, usually, but he's experimenting anyway. He's put his toes in and tried their taste. Also his blanket. And sometimes he will take a few swallows from a cup or glass.

His attempts at creeping are showing progress. He can occasionally get up on all fours for a few seconds but collapses before he can move anywhere. He rolls over easily and often. He sits up better and better. He can stay upright for a couple of minutes at a time before he topples sideways. He hasn't attempted to get into a sitting position by himself, except to try to sit up straighter when he's in his sort of lounge chair.

He laughs more and more often, sometimes at funny noises, or noises that seem funny to him. These include a choice little song:

> Benjy is a creepie-peepie
> Benjy is a creepie-peepie
> Benjy is a creepie-peepie
> Bang, bang, bang, bang, bang.

(Real hilarious!)

Sources of laughter also include little games of peek-a-boo, or sometimes watching Sam's antics. He's very merry most of the time—is always gay and bouncy when he wakes up unless he is wakened suddenly.

7 months, 18 days. July 27

THE sounds Benjamin makes are becoming more and more differentiated. We have noticed that the only times he makes a "mum-mum-mum" sound is when he is distressed or unhappy, particularly if he is wakened suddenly or half-rouses in the middle of the night. It does not express boredom or frustration, only some sort of unhappiness. Whether this "mm" sound will turn out to be attached to Mama remains to be observed.

Occasionally he lets loose with what sounds like a whole paragraph—a long babble of syllables and inflections. Noises indicating boredom, as when he has been left alone or there is nothing moving around him to look at, or frustration, as when he tries to sit up from the semi-reclining position of his chair, are quite different from the wail, accompanied often by rubbing his eyes, which indicates fatigue and a need for bed—and both are very different from the squeals and shouts of delight.

He is more and more interested in his feet, though only once or twice have I seen him put his toes in his mouth. And he still often spends minutes gazing at his fingers as they fold, wiggle, and bend. He finds his ears every so often and explores them as best he can.

A few days ago Benjamin was in his crib while I changed his diaper. The window was open and a fire engine went by with siren screaming. His face puckered up and he gave a few wails of unhappiness and alarm. This is the first time I have known him to react to that sort of external-to-his-immediate-surroundings sound. When our roof was replaced a month ago, he was apparently quite oblivious to the pounding and other noises, although a certain amount of it was directly above him.

8 months, 8 days.   August 17

BENJAMIN continues to show alarm at certain loud noises close to him—his father's cough (not mine), too loud a squeal or other noise from Janet. But he no longer gets alarmed at Sam's barks, even sudden loud ones very close by.

I am quite sure that Benjamin's "ma-ma-ma" sounds are reserved for times of distress, and I'm pretty sure that they're beginning to mean he wants *me*. For weeks now I've listened to his increasingly frequent babbles and gabbles, but there are *no* "m" sounds except when something is making him really unhappy and he wants comforting. The "ma-ma" sounds aren't yet attached to me in any real "naming" sense; he doesn't call out "Mama" when he sees me, but this seems to be a precursor. [*Note 17: Such sounds seem to have a linguistic status intermediate between babble and word. See Church, 1961, pages 61–62.*]

In the last few days, he has begun to resist, muscularly and vocally, if something is taken away from him when he's playing with it. Yesterday his father was holding Benjamin on his lap at the dining room table, and Benjamin got hold of the place mat and started flapping it around, bending it, etc. It was time for his nap, so I removed the mat from his hands and started to pick him up. He clutched at the mat, wailed protestingly, and stretched to reach it again. This has happened several times with this and other objects. He will occasionally make protesting noises if he drops something and wants it back, but this behavior is less frequent.

He continues to be fascinated by his own hands. He spends minutes moving his right hand and forearm in the kind of rotary motion one uses to turn a doorknob—back and forth, back and forth, almost always with the right hand. He still enjoys hanging on to his feet, but spends more time trying to creep, which he still hasn't mastered. He can get up on all fours easily, and even though he can't make much forward progress, he still loves to try!

One pastime which Benjamin has recently discovered and enjoys doing is looking out the window of his room. During the hot weather his crib is right against the window and often when I come in after his daytime nap I find he has wriggled his way around sideways and is peering over the top of the bumper pad. I suppose the movement of the leaves and branches is what he mostly sees—possibly occasionally a passerby on the sidewalk beyond the next house, or a person or a dog in the next yard.

One of his upper teeth cut through the gum today and maybe he feels better for it, as he has been very merry and full of chatter all day.

9 months, 3 days.　September 12

SORRY for the long lapse but various things have combined to make recording difficult, and there have been few sharp changes anyway.

Now that Benjy has two upper teeth, he is much more interested in putting things in his mouth—crackers, toast, spoons, or his parents' fingers or such parts of the rest of their anatomy as he can get his teeth on. He will also bite hard on the nipple of his bottle once he has had all he wants to drink.

He continues to do a good deal of chattering and babbling, but I can't be sure that certain sounds have become firmly attached to specific things. He makes very clear "Ma-ma" and

"Da-da" sounds as well as something approaching "goggie," which will probably come to mean the dog, but nothing has quite jelled yet.

We left him for overnight (about two weeks ago) with our cleaning woman, of whom he is very fond. He got along fine with her except at meal times, when he refused *any* spooned food, and would only take his bottle. Since then both his father and Janet have fed him and we'll continue to switch around so he doesn't get too dependent on me. He now has a feeding table and meals have become a lot easier for both of us.

A few days ago he was out in the back yard and Sam was, as usual, lying very near him. A neighbor's dog, black, came wandering over and sat nearby. Benjamin watched him and I said, "There's another doggie," and repeated "Doggie" when he looked first at one dog and then the other. He seemed faintly puzzled that the same name was attached to two rather different-looking creatures.

As far as asking for things is concerned, the clearest instance is the demand for his bottle. Our usual practice is to give him several ounces of milk and then feed him some solids. He will take from two to a dozen spoonfuls and then begin to wail for the bottle. The wail is accompanied by turning his head vehemently away if the spoon is presented. If he seems to want *very* little solid food, he can sometimes be coaxed or diverted into taking more by singing to him, but this is becoming rather less effective.

He does a lot of laughing—sometimes at new sounds, or old sounds said to him accompanied by one's own laughter, sometimes at nothing that one can see, sometimes at things that we can't see the humor of. He went into gales one day watching (and hearing) Janet cut up a stalk of celery. He often laughs at the dog's scratching himself.

Going back to eating again, he is having quite a time learning how to hold an object so as to get it into his mouth. This is particularly evident with crackers. Sometimes he tries to put it in at right angles to his mouth so that his teeth just scrape the narrow edge; or if he bites off a piece, the remainder is often so small that it doesn't stick out of his hand far enough for him to get his teeth on it. If you offer him a cracker, he is more apt to open his mouth for it than to reach out his hand, and sometimes he will refuse to take it in his hand, wanting you to put it in his mouth. If you won't comply but instead put the cracker down in front of him, he will then pick it up and try to eat it.

He is much better than before about drinking from a glass or cup, but he wants you to hold it for him. He will seldom put his hands on the cup as long as you are holding it, unless he doesn't want to drink, in which case he will turn his head away and also sometimes try to grasp the edge of the cup so he can play with it. He is often interested in drinking something that we are drinking; he has reached for, and sampled, beer, iced coffee, and martinis; the first two he seemed to find quite pleasant.

AUTONOMY: Benjamin can "resist" vigorously when he chooses. He hates to have to lie still on his back while his diapers are changed; it's more fun to turn over, bounce, sit up, or kick. He resists the spoon when he wants his bottle. Sometimes, he protests about going to bed, though not often. He resists sitting down, or rather being put down, when he'd rather be on his feet. In the latter instance a verbal resistance is coupled with an arched back and stiffened knees—and they're very stiff.

9 *months, 6 days.   September 15*

Took Benjamin to the doctor yesterday for his regular check-up and vaccination. He measures 28¼ inches and weighs 18 lb.

The doctor's waiting room hasn't acquired any evil connotations. Benjamin was perfectly happy for the ten minutes or so we waited, and when we went into the examination room he continued cheerful until he began to be undressed. Then he yelled miserably until all was over and he was dressed when, as usual, he quieted down.

I was supposed to give him his first egg yolk today, so I mixed a little into his cereal tonight. With the first mouthful, although he swallowed it, he yelled like fury, and would have no more solids except a few spoonfuls of fruit and some pieces of bread crust. I have never before seen him show such a violent negative reaction to any food.

He is more and more vocal and vigorous in his awareness of people he knows; he bounces and grins and babbles when any member of the family or the cleaning woman comes into his room or comes near him if he is elsewhere by himself. He exhibits the same eager reactions to the dog, turning around or leaning toward the edge of his feeding table if Sam comes along. Recently he has also become much more conscious of the presence or passage of the cat.

9 months, 13 days.   September 22

I STARTED work again this week and, if all goes well, will work four mornings a week. On two of these, Benjamin will be with Sarah, our cleaning woman, who knows and loves him and who will have very little trouble with him. On Wednesday of this week, he spent the morning (at our house) with a friend of ours, Marion, and her two-year-old, and she will have him the other two mornings. He hasn't seen them recently enough to remember them and I was unable to have Marion visit to get them reacquainted before I left them together.

The first morning wasn't too successful. Being looked after by a stranger (who is a pretty matter-of-fact person and apparently not given to much in the way of demonstrations of affection—hugging, cuddling, etc.) and some small upset from his recent vaccination weren't too good a combination and apparently Benjamin yelled most of the time except when he was in his bath and when Marion took him outdoors for a while.

9 months, 27 days.   October 6

BENJAMIN has settled down very well to the new routine. After the difficult first morning, Marion dropped by a couple of afternoons later and just sat around and chatted while Benjamin first played around outdoors and then had his supper. The next time Marion took over, Benjamin was less fussy, and since then he has gotten along fine.

After spending *weeks* attempting to creep and getting nowhere, all of a sudden the whole process meshed and literally within twenty-four hours he could navigate all over the place—and did! He seems much happier now that he can go places, and he is 100 per cent active. We have now introduced him to the playpen and he seems to enjoy it—at least if not left alone too long.

Before he learned to creep he was very eager to stand up, but had to be held under the arms as he seems to have no notion of hanging on to anything with his hands. Now that he can creep he has lost most of his interest in standing. He used to love to stand on our laps; now he wants to get down on the floor and "get moving."

He "talks" and "sings" more and more—long strings of babbling or cooing but still nothing definitely intelligible. In the last few days he has been making little smacking noises with his lips. Sometimes these have followed his being kissed several times and suggest an imitation of a kissing sound. Yesterday his father said Benjamin seemed really to try to kiss him—laid his lips right against his father's cheek, and didn't nip with his teeth as he has done with me!

There is, I think, now no doubt that he is right-handed. *Almost* always if an object is held out to him he will reach for it with the right hand. He is getting increasingly adept at handling very small objects—such as putting pieces of dry cereal or small bits of toast or cracker into his mouth. He doesn't always succeed, by any means, but is improving steadily. [*Note 18: Benjamin's mother does not say whether he grasps bits of food pincers-fashion or with his whole hand. Many babies begin feeding themselves by clenching the food in their fist, raising fist to mouth, opening the fingers against the mouth, and pushing the food in with the palm.*]

Perhaps along with this he shows a greater interest in eating things he can put in his mouth himself—toast, crackers, etc.—and is eating noticeably less of other things, except for his beloved bottle. At the moment, he will usually take strained fruit, but I never know how much of anything he'll eat. Except for the fruit, he seems usually now to prefer junior foods to the strained, but one can't predict from meal to meal.

10 months, 9 days.   October 18

WE seem to have settled down to a new period, doubtless temporary, of comparative peace and relaxation. By which I mean that Benjamin is eating and sleeping better and fussing less. For a couple of weeks he more often than not woke anywhere from 5 to 6 A.M., yelled if you offered him a spoon, no matter what was in it, and was generally rather touchy. For several days now he has slept well and seems in excellent spirits practically all the time. [*Note 19: See Deborah, 9 months, 3 weeks, page 38. In general, children seem to show a pattern of periods of active development separated by plateaus of consolidation and enjoyment.*]

His new favorite foods are a particular brand of dry cereal and animal crackers; he is a little less passionate than formerly about his bottle and will eat at least a few spoonfuls of other foods.

He has taken to imitating us. It started with imitating us when we imitated him. In other words, he'd do something and then we'd do it, and then he'd do it again, all of which he found great fun. There are now three things which we can get him to do by doing them ourselves—all of them things he originally did first and we copied. (1) If we wrinkle up our noses, bringing the lips as close as possible to the nose, and sniffing hard and noisily, he will do the same thing. (2) If we make kissing or lip-smacking sounds, he will often copy them. (3) If we first make "ma" sounds silently and then vocalize them, he will copy us—in gales of laughter.

We had a long game of peek-a-boo this afternoon and each time I popped out at him from behind a pillow I'd make a different sound—and each time he laughed so hard he nearly fell over.

He responds occasionally to suggestions that he "wave bye-bye" or "play pat-a-cake"—by no means always, but often enough for it to be apparent that he is responding to specific words. [*See Deborah, Note 63, page 42, and Ruth, 10 months, 1 day, page 209.*]

A couple of days ago, his father reported that Benjamin discovered how to cough voluntarily. He said Benjamin did partly choke on a crumb and coughed several times; that he then sat and screwed up his face and with great effort produced a fake cough—and was delighted with himself. He has done it several times since and always looks around at us with a very pleased and impish look on his face. [*Note 20: It is essential in describing a response to include such emotional components as these as an index of intelligent action versus blind or random movement.*]

11 months, 5 days.   November 14

THE "peace and relaxation" were temporary! A couple of weeks ago he ran an unexplained fever for a day or so, which made him very unhappy, and ten days ago he caught his first cold. He has been cranky and irritable a good deal of the time and is again sleeping and eating very erratically. He has a decided temper and can yell till his face breaks out in red spots.

We have been fascinated to watch his gradual learning about his own body. A few days ago on two occasions I hung a little straw bracelet of Janet's over one of his ears. Both times he reached up to the other ear, then finally to the right one. The third time I tried it, a day or so later, he reached up with *both* hands at once and so got the bracelet off more quickly. [*Note 21: Apparently Benjamin realized that the bracelet was on one of his ears but, at this stage of body schematization, could not tell which.*]

He responds more and more often to specific words, such as "Open your mouth." This isn't to say he always does it—more often than not he doesn't—but when he's not in one of his "I don't care what's in the spoon, I don't want it" moods, he will often bring his attention back from elsewhere and open up if asked to. [*Note 22: Observe again how the behavioral context supplements the verbal instruction. It is unlikely that Benjamin could obey an arbitrary request that he open his mouth.*]

He is also more and more responsive to music. If I am holding him in my arms in the living room, he will often lean down to the phonograph and, while seldom vocalizing his desire, make it plain what he wants. He loves to be held and danced around the room to music—it will usually quiet him down, especially at bedtime. If he's sitting on the floor when a record is on, he will usually sit very quietly and listen, often bouncing up and down if the music is lively.

11 months, 3 weeks.   November 30

BENJAMIN gets increasingly fond of music. There are four or five records which he has heard very often, and several of them are particularly good for "dancing"—holding him while I dance around the room. One is "South Pacific." A couple of days ago he was on the floor in the dining room while his father and I were having coffee. The radio was on and a singer sang one of the "South Pacific" songs. Benjamin scrambled right over to me, climbed up to my knees and held up his arms, making frantic little noises, indicating quite plainly that he knew the music and wanted to dance. [*Note 23: Note that recognition is indicated not by repeating some previous response but by initiating a new and appropriate action. In other words, Benjamin does not "dance" to the music, but invites his mother to pick him up and dance with him. See Ruth, 8 months, page 200.*]

He now responds to several spoken phrases, such as "Give it to Mommy (or Daddy)," "Pat, pat," which will make him slap the pen rail, chair, or whatever, "Bouncy-bouncy," which gets him to bounce up and down, either standing or sitting, and, since yesterday, he will produce his wonderful fake cough if you ask him if he has a bad cough.

He also is beginning to know what "No, no" means, though

he is not, of course, very obedient to it! [*See Deborah, Note 37, page 22, and Ruth, 8 months, page 201.*]

If he wants something and is refused it—most often if he wants to be picked up and we won't do it—he is apt to fling himself down with a loud wail of rage. This is usually, fortunately, of brief duration!

He has all sorts of little games now. He loves to throw or drop things out of the playpen and laughs with glee at the mock scolding which follows. He likes to hide small objects under the living room couch, returning after a few minutes, or even the next day, to see what he can find under there. [*See Deborah, Note 39, page 25.*]

His space perceptions have improved noticeably. He is much less apt to bump his head on corners of things he plays near; he can flatten out and crawl under low furniture, and squeeze through fairly small spaces. He is getting quite adept at putting small objects into things, such as bits of dry cereal into his mouth, a milk bottle cap into a small can, etc., and has also learned to fold his fingers together in order to put his hand into the small can and get something out of it. [*Note 24: Observe that the baby tries to reach into a jar for something before he learns that he can simply pour it out. It is also an interesting fact that the baby can remove things from an opaque container before he can take them out of a transparent one. My tests of thirty-five subjects indicate that, up to the age of about ten months, babies try to grasp a lure directly through the side of a transparent container and are unable to see the jar mouth as a means of access to the interior. See Deborah, Note 84, page 65, and Ruth, Note 45, page 205.*]

Benjy is beginning to notice more things through a window —will watch birds and squirrels on the feeder in the back yard. Likes to look at himself in the mirror, and in the top of the aluminum garbage can in the kitchen. Knows that there is a big mirror on the back of our bedroom door and will often try, either by himself or when being carried, to push the door closed so he can look in the mirror.

He is making more and more sounds. "Dada" and "Mama"

and "dog" are very nearly established, and he said a quite distinct "hello" a couple of times but hasn't done it since, so I'm not sure that that one is definite yet. Very frequently lately he has made a short definite response to our saying a word—and while, except for the three mentioned above, they are not accurate imitations, it is clear that he is beginning to *try* to imitate words.

The particular gibberish that he murmurs to himself at play will vary from day to day. For several days it was mostly "g" sounds. Another day it was lots of "th" sounds. Today and yesterday it has been mostly of the "chookachookachook" variety—lots of experimentation with sound and use of the lips and tongue.

He is much too active now to be willing to play in his feeding table. Once he has had his milk and whatever is being spooned into him (at the moment the spoon is more acceptable than it was a couple of days ago) he is standing up in the chair and must be moved, if only for safety's sake, to the floor or the play pen. He will play pretty well in the pen either if we are busy about the room (cleaning, for instance) or if he is sitting with his back to us and absorbed in something. Once he loses interest in his toy, or notices that we are watching him, he wants OUT, unless we play a game of some sort, such as picking up an ejected toy, putting it back with mock scolding so he can throw it out again, etc.

Going back to space perception—it was several weeks ago that I noticed him one evening standing on one side of the bench in front of the sofa. He had some small object in his hand. He leaned way over the bench and dropped the thing. He looked at it for a moment, then got down on the floor, crawled around the bench to get it, crawled back to where he had been before, stood up, leaned over, and dropped the object again, crawled around after it, and this time shoved it under the sofa and left it there. [*Note 25: Compare the behavior of another boy, age 11 months: "Trying to lift pot from potty-chair through hole in seat. Can approach only from the front. When, accidentally, he finds himself beside chair, with pot in plain view, returns to front and resumes trying to get pot through hole." Apparently in the two cases there is a "correct" route to the desired object. While, as we know, Benjamin is perfectly capable of creeping under the bench, the way to get something on the far side of the bench is to go around. This kind of behavior illustrates primitive rigidity.*]

A couple of days ago his father was carrying him on the second floor. For the first time, Benjamin really *saw* a large photograph of the dog, on top of a bookcase. He gave a sort of squeal as of recognition and lunged forward to try to touch it— the first instance we've seen of recognition of a pictured object. He likes to look at pictures in magazines but hasn't reacted to anything specific before.

1 year, 25 days.   January 3

Too long a lapse of time, but December was a very busy month!

He stands unaided quite frequently now and on a couple of occasions has ventured a step or two before lowering himself to the safety of all fours.

For his birthday we gave him a color cone—a toy consisting of colored wooden rings, graduated in size, which fit over a peg. He was soon able to get them off but it was about ten days later that he managed to put them back on again. They still don't go on in the "right" order and I've never seen him put all six rings on. He usually puts one or two on and then takes them off again. For Christmas he got a wooden truck with various take-apart parts and he has a lot of pleasure out of taking everything out of the truck and then trying to put some of the sticks into their holes again. Another of his favorite games involves all sorts of play with marbles—putting a marble on the "marble track" so it can roll down the several inclines, putting marbles into any object that will hold them (and some that won't), putting them in his mouth and chuckling when told to take them out, dropping them down the register, etc. From watching him with another toy he has, it is clear that he doesn't yet understand how intentionally to move something horizontally—he can lift it or push it down, but he hasn't grasped yet how to shove something on a track, or to close a sliding door.

He is trying harder and harder to communicate. "Dog" is still his most used word, plus "bow-wow-wow." Also once in a while "Mama" and rather frequently "Dada." "Ball" is next, I think, and "baa" for bath.

His eating habits continue to swing back and forth from spoon to no spoon. It seems to be about two weeks of tolerance for foods from a spoon followed by a couple of weeks of almost nothing except what he can eat with his fingers, plus his bottle which I begin to wonder if he'll *ever* give up! He is responding more and more to the spoken word. The other day when I got him up from his nap he had pulled off both his socks. I said to him, "Where's your sock?" and he turned around, flopped down on all fours and went off to the other end of the bed and got the sock and threw it on the floor!

He loves to knock down piles of blocks and is imitating our sound of "aaaah" when he does so—a mock scolding sound which he now applies to himself and thinks is very funny.

13 months, 2 days.   January 11

BENJAMIN is trying harder and harder to talk. In addition to the above-mentioned, he has definitely recognizable, if not very accurate, sounds for "cracker," "cookie," "marble," and "good-bye" (actually just "bye").

This morning he discovered he could climb all the way upstairs, and was delighted with himself—promptly tried to get down but this is harder as Mama refuses to allow the head-first approach!

Yesterday afternoon he had his bunny (a stuffed creature with music-box inside which is usually in his crib) downstairs with him. I picked it up and held it against my cheek and said, "Nice bunny, nice bunny" in a cooing sort of tone. Benjamin came over and took it, held it against his cheek, and sort of cooed to it and then flopped down flat on the floor with the bunny as if going to sleep. He stayed down a couple of seconds, got up and crawled a little way, and then repeated the process.

Size perception is still uncertain. He can with considerable skill drop marbles or cereal bits into bottles, but will try hard to put some large piece of paper into a bottle. [*Note 26: Even though Benjy has learned pragmatically, through experience, that marbles and cereal bits will go into a bottle, he may not have learned to see the size relationships involved, and so has to find out by trial and error that the piece of paper will not fit.*]

15 months, 6 days.   March 15

APOLOGIES for the long gap!

Benjamin is now walking most of the time—has been for several weeks. He seems to get a considerable amount of satisfaction out of it, and toots around at a great rate, looking very pleased with himself. He has passed through the hands-up-in-the-air stage and can now walk with hands no higher than waist level, and can carry objects about with him, and get back on his feet from a crouch or sit without dropping what he has in his hands.

A few additions to his vocabulary: "mee-ow" for both the cat *and* the cat sound, and—a most overworked word—"dis," apparently meaning "this" and usually accompanied by an imperious pointing of outstretched forefinger. His favorite word still seems to be "doggie."

He understands quite a few spoken phrases now, such as "Where's your ball?" or "Where are your socks?" He responds by looking around, or sometimes going off to get the object if he knows where it is. He waves goodbye—will start as soon as anyone puts on a coat or hat. He understands "Let's go out" or "Let's go in the car" (says "car") and certainly understands "No," whether he obeys it or not.

His eating is still very limited. He clings to his bottle for milk but will take other liquids (including cocktails!) from a glass or cup. The only foods he will accept from a spoon are gelatin and applesauce—otherwise either he takes it in his fingers or he doesn't eat it. Still he seems to thrive, aside from two mild bouts of intestinal flu.

He is passionately attached to the phonograph and we have records on a good deal of his waking time. He now knows the record jackets of most of his favorites and can indicate the one he wants. [*Note 27: Note that each record envelope has its own distinctive physiognomy which the baby comes to know very rapidly.*] Often he will bounce up and down to the music—for some particular pieces he demands to be held while the grown-up dances—particularly a couple of the louder, more vigorous songs from "South Pacific." He is beginning to be able to follow a pointing finger and the instruction "Look, Benjamin, there is
. . ." (your ball, the dog, etc.). [*Note 28: The baby's first reaction to a pointing forefinger is to look at the tip. Somewhat later, a pointing finger is a signal to look around for the designated object. It is usually not until about age three that the child can look in the specific direction that the finger is pointing.*]

He has various little games he has invented. One is to crawl out of sight behind a chair and wait till we have said "Where is Benjamin?" about a dozen times before he crawls out, beaming, then back in again to repeat the performance. Another (very dull!) is to go into the pantry, indicate that all four frying pans are to be taken from their hooks and put on the floor, nested one within the next, and then return them to us, one by one, to be hung up again. He is, of course, into every cupboard and drawer he can reach, pulling things out and then, often, putting them back again.

He is quite adept at stairs now, still on all fours, and we no longer insist on trailing up and down with him. He has made no attempt to go down the stairs standing up.

He likes to look at magazines and often brings one that has pictures of dogs. I am still not sure, however, that he really sees the pictures as dogs. I suspect he likes to have us point to the spot and say "doggie" but, given a picture of a dog in a previously unknown book, I am quite doubtful that he would recognize the dog as such. He does not yet recognize pictures of himself or us.

One of his favorite occupations is pushing the vacuum cleaner wand and brush around. Inevitably, this leads to frustration when the brush gets caught on a chair or under the bed, and he protests violently. He has quite a temper—will bite my shoulder or try to bite my finger if I insist he do or stop doing something, or if I refuse to do something he wants to do at that moment. But he is also easily diverted and is sunny again in a few minutes, provided *my* temper can hold out, which is not always the case.

He shows fear very seldom—or the sort of distress which could indicate fear. Sometimes a loud sound very close to him, such as his bottle getting knocked over, or a sneeze, can make him cry, but not always. Recently I had him at a friend's house where there are two Siamese cats. Benjamin had seen them several times and was quite used to them. He was eating a cracker, and one of the cats came over, stood on his hind legs with his forelegs against Benjamin's chest, and investigated the cracker. Our hostess spoke loudly and sternly to the cat, and Benjamin burst into tears. It was quite clear that he thought he was being scolded. I'm sure it was the voice he reacted to, not the cat.

15 months, 25 days.   April 3

BENJAMIN's vocabulary is growing steadily. It now includes "All gone," "this" (no longer "dis"), "car," a sort of "jat" which means the phonograph record jacket, and "down."

His familiarity with the record of "South Pacific" (by far his favorite) is now so complete that in the few seconds before the band with "Bloody Mary" he begins to bounce in anticipation, that being his favorite part of the record.

He is gradually beginning to part with his bottle—at least on several occasions in the last week we have managed to get through a meal with just a glass or cup.

He has a very hot temper and if he doesn't get what he

wants, he will lash out with his hands, catching at my glasses or even trying to bite. I can't remember either of the other two being quite this fervent in their protests, but my memory may have failed over the years!

16 months, 1 day.   April 10

BENJAMIN is getting more adept at conveying or communicating his desires. For instance, if the parts of the vacuum cleaner (with which he plays constantly) come apart, he will now bring one or both parts to one of us and hold them up, making little noises of request for action. If he wants something in the kitchen and we are in the living room he will come to us, grab a hand or indicate that he wants to be picked up, and then point (or pull us) to the kitchen.

He now knows not only what record is in the jacket, but which *side* of the record he wants. In both "South Pacific" and "The King and I" he prefers the side which does *not* start with the overture, and if we start with the wrong one, he will reach over from my arms, waving his hands and making protesting noises. When the record is removed he grabs at it and tries to turn it over.

I think he is beginning to realize the approximate time I come home from work (about noon), that is, if he is inside the house. I'm told he begins to look out the window and to say "Mama" just before I drive up.

He is one of the busiest kids I ever saw—always involved in some little project. It may be moving all the empty soda bottles from the kitchen to the stair landing and back, or taking all the pots and pans out of the cupboard, or dropping marbles down the register. It's always *something!*

16 months, 4 weeks.   May 7

WORDS are appearing as well as other kinds of communication. "All gone," and "oh-geh" (for O.K., we assume) are in frequent use. Benjamin uses practically no final consonants but the meaning is pretty clear. He understands quite a lot of spoken language now: "Sit down," "Bring me your shoes," "Bring me the jacket" (for the record), "Let's go upstairs. Time for bath," etc. He usually seems to respond to his name, especially if he is wandering off somewhere outdoors and is called back.

Although he can use some words, he also comes out with long sentences of sounds that sound intelligible until you try to decipher them.

He doesn't seem to have much awareness of some parts of his body yet. He likes to look at his toes and clap the soles of his feet together—he looks to see his hands come through the sleeves, but sometimes he tries to pick up his legs with his hands (while standing up) to place the feet on the steps!

He likes to pull off his socks, and is just beginning to try to put them on—also shoes and rubbers.

While we have made no real efforts to toilet train him, if he is dry after a nap or before bed I take him in the bathroom and ask him if he wants to "make peepee in the pot." This he thinks is great fun. He knows exactly what I mean and want, and tries hard to produce. If he can't, he seems to know he can't and pushes the pot aside. He is rather pleased with himself when he succeeds. We've got nowhere with bowel-training yet. He seems to have very little real regularity and most of what there is occurs in his sleep. Big help!

Space perception seems rather mixed. He can crawl around things, squeeze under something without bumping his head, romp all over the yard, but I caught him a week or ten days ago just about ready to step off the back porch steps into space. He would never do this with the stairs inside the house, but there was apparently no relationship between the stairs he was familiar with and these other steps.

He has just learned to fit together a set of plastic beads—he still can't get them apart. A small projection on one end of each bead fits into a hole in the next bead. A couple of days ago he was working away at this—he could snap two beads together, but when he started to add a third bead, he was holding bead A rather than bead B as he tried to add bead

C. I said to him over and over again, "Move your hand, Benjy" and would move his left hand from A to B. Today I discovered that he has grasped the idea. As he starts to add each new bead, the left hand moves up to the bead on the end of the string.

He can still be startled or disturbed by some loud noises and quite unconcerned by others. I was in the attic with him today and Janet called me from downstairs. I called back, in a voice certainly louder than usual but less than a shout, and Benjy cried with alarm for a minute or two. But a prolonged thunderstorm a couple of weeks ago didn't wake him, although he did whimper occasionally in his sleep.

18 months, 6 days.   June 15

HE showed a week ago the first sign of what might be interpreted as color discrimination. He has a truck, the front end of which is made of three blocks which fit over two pegs. The lower two blocks are blue, the top one white. There are other colored blocks that help make up the truck, two of them white. Having, with some help, fitted the blue blocks over the pegs, he looked around for the top one, which was not immediately in sight. He picked up one of the *other* white blocks but realized it wasn't the right one—ignored all the red, yellow, and green blocks and hunted around till he found the correct white one. Color? Or just form? [*Or brightness?*]

His vocabulary grows bit by bit—phrases such as "Oh dear," "All gone," "Whass dat?" The latter is particularly frequent—sometimes he seems to use it as a real question but more often he says it over and over again, apparently enjoying the sense of communication which the response brings.

He sometimes responds to his name but not always. If you tap his chest and ask him, "Who's this?" he will often answer "Be'-jee" but the word "Be'-jee" seems to be a nice word which will do for other people, too. If, having got him to say that *he* was Be'jee, I put my finger on *myself* and say, "Who's this?" he's just as apt to repeat "Be'jee" as to say Mommy.

He has learned the whereabouts and names of his ears and nose but doesn't know about eyes yet. He will show you his fingers and toes, but uses no words for them yet.

When the hot weather came recently, he spent a great deal of time in the back yard with a watering can full of water and several cups. Sometimes he would empty the filled cup back into the can; sometimes on the grass, driveway, or elsewhere. Sometimes he poured it from one cup to the other and back. [*See Deborah, Note 81, page 63.*] This necessitated a good deal of passing cups from his hands to mine. He would first fill a cup from the can with his right hand and pour the water into the other cup, held in the left. But he couldn't *pour* with the left hand, so he would give me the full cup, move the empty one to the left hand, take the full one back from me and start over again. If an extra set of hands isn't available, he'll set the full cup down on the ground or table.

The outdoors absorbs so much of his attention that his former indoor pursuits have lost much of their appeal. He hasn't asked for a record to be put on the phonograph for weeks—he's usually either on his way out the back door or pounding on it if it's closed. He wants to play in the water if allowed—or to walk, usually either pushing his stroller or some one of his push-toys. Sometimes he will indicate he wants to ride in the car by beating on the car door.

19 months, 20 days.   July 29

INCREASINGLY, Benjamin is trying to say back the words we say to him. The results are usually far from perfect, but he is *trying*. For the first time a day or two ago he said [*a babyish rendition of his sister's name*], the first time he has called her anything at all. His latest additions are approximations of juice, lawn-mower, kitty-cat, blanket, outdoors, and cherries (of which he is passionately fond). This morning when he was throwing cherries on the floor, I finally told him to quit it, that "enough is enough." Promptly came the response, "enuss enuss."

We have been telling him (over and over again) the stories of *The Three Little Pigs, The Three Bears,* and *Little Red Riding Hood.* He knows them so well now that he can respond at appropriate moments with words ("calf," "pig," etc.) or gestures (he always beats on the floor, the table, or his tummy at the words "knocked on the door"). He seems to love to have the stories repeated and one can usually divert him from anger or irritability or frustration just by starting with "Once upon a time. . . ."

He spends a great deal of time outdoors pouring water, and sometimes sand, from one container to another. He has sometimes six or seven containers of various sizes in use at once. Has as yet no realization of different sizes—that to overfill a small can means a great deal of water is lost. Also he'll still try to fit a large can inside a small one.

He has abandoned his bottle altogether—and has pretty much abandoned milk along with it. Sometimes he will drink a few swallows of milk from his cup; at other times he'll feed himself milk with a spoon, but his total intake is very small. He eats gelatin with a spoon fairly competently, but does most of his eating with his fingers.

He is *very* aware of what "hot" means and will shy violently away from anything that we say is hot. As a matter of fact, he is pretty wary of eating anything he thinks *may* be hot, even when it isn't.

He can be very hot-tempered, especially with me. If I won't let him do something, or won't do something he wants me to (currently he gets angry when I won't get out the lawnmower), and if I have to pick him up to remove him to another spot, he will pull my hair or grab at my glasses. He usually gets his fingers slapped, but a good strong "No, no, Benjy" seems to be rather more effective.

I have wondered if he has begun to have some sort of dreams. Several times in the last month he has cried out and when I went in, he just wanted to be cuddled and held for a few minutes—didn't want food or play or anything but a little love.

One night I was sure he must have had some sort of bad dream: when I went in he was crying in a frantic sort of way and when I picked him up he grabbed at me as if angry, and slapped rather wildly. I finally spoke rather sharply and said "Stop it, Benjy, wake up!" He stopped abruptly as if he'd just realized that I was I and that he was safe, settled down in my arms, and in a few minutes was perfectly willing to be put back to bed.

Going in the car is very satisfying—but going with me is quite different from going with Daddy. If I take him, he seems to assume we are going somewhere ordinary, such as to the store or to the college. But a ride with Daddy is special—it means an outing to the airport or some such. No matter how upset he may be about something, an offer of "a ride in the car" with Daddy brightens the world, but the same offer from me isn't very effective.

19 months, 27 days.   August 5

SEVERAL days ago in his bath, Benjamin had a bowl of water perched on the taps. It was full and about to overflow, so I poured some of it back into the tub. This angered him, so he picked up a smaller bowl, filled it and deliberately poured it out of the tub on the floor. I spoke rather sharply to him. He stood silently for a minute, looking first at me and then at the wet spot—then reached over and got the sponge and handed it to me so I could mop up!

He is now indicating his desire for a story by saying "So," since all the stories seem to be punctuated with this word.

He has rediscovered the phonograph, but is less willing than before to listen to a complete long-playing record—listens for a few minutes, and then wants something different—and is seldom sure any more which record it is he really wants. [*Note 29: At this age, many children take pleasure in a simple phonograph which they themselves can operate and in records that play for no more than five minutes per side.*]

20 months, 4 days.   August 13

CAPE COD—We are spending three weeks here in a small cottage on a lake.

Benjamin and I came up together, by bus and airplane, the others having driven up. The bus trip wasn't too bad but he got very restless and cranky, as he has never been confined to a tiny space for so long. We had to wait in the airport for over an hour and he was intermittently full of gaiety and full of rage and frustration. But the plane trip was the worst, at least for about half an hour. When, after many delays, the motors were finally warmed up and the plane began to taxi down the runway, Benjamin was terrified. He clutched me with all his might and as the plane left the ground he screamed and began to tremble all over. For the next twenty or thirty minutes he was pretty miserable—alternately clinging to me and trying to get down on the floor, which I couldn't allow as long as the seat-belts light was still on. Finally he quieted down and sat limply in my lap —and only cried out a couple of times as the plane came down. Once on the ground he was fine—very happy and gay, but very wound up. He had slept only about fifteen minutes all day, but it was eight o'clock before he finally gave up and went to sleep.

Two rather interesting sequels to our flight: (1) a day or so later we were on the beach when a large helicopter came over, quite low. He clutched at me and cried out, but only briefly, and since then has shown no special disturbance at passing planes; (2) there is an old flat-bottomed tub of a sailboat on our beach here at the lake. It had water in it and the first day he played around in it quite happily. But the next day Janet was sitting in the stern of it, too, and she moved, causing it to lurch sideways. He let out a screech and wanted *out,* and won't go anywhere near the boat now. There seems to be something very frightening about having the floor under his feet suddenly disappear or shift! I shall be interested (and apprehensive) to see what happens on the return flight.

Aside from these episodes, he seems to be enjoying it up here. He enjoys wading and splashing around in the shallow water of the lake, and playing with sand and pebbles on the salt-water beaches. He is eating a little more than he used to, and will occasionally drink milk—which he pretty much gave up when he gave up his bottle.

He is trying out more and more words—can put two together sometimes, as in "All gone juice" (or toast or whatever) and something that apparently means "Want to get down." More and more often he tries to repeat the name of something or someone. His final consonants are mostly non-existent—"hah" for hot, "baa" for bath—but he can get them sometimes as in "pigs," "dooce" (juice), "mook" (milk). He can't cope with any initial double consonants—glasses are "gass" and the same sound does for grass. Bricks are "bicks"—but he can manage *sticks* with double consonants on both ends.

22 months, 11 days.   October 20

To go back to the airplane episode. For the trip home, we gave Benjamin a sedative, which may have had some calming effect. He began to cry as soon as the plane came up to where we were waiting, and he objected to boarding it. But once we got started, he was less panicky than on the trip up. He clutched me, and spent the whole hour curled up tight in my lap like a baby monkey. He cried a little sometimes, but never screamed. He made no effort to get down, just stayed put, rather miserable but not violent the way he was on the first trip.

He has, somewhere, acquired a vehement dislike of the bath-tub. There was no tub in our cottage, so we made do with sponge baths. One day I took him over to my mother's (she had a place nearby) to give him a bath, thinking this would be a treat. But he yelled and would *not* stay in the tub—and he is still, two months later, unwilling to get in the tub. A few times he has consented to stay in it long enough for me to wash him, but he won't sit down and he gets no pleasure from an experience which he used to love. We bought him a toy boat, hoping this would help, but it didn't.

Speech continues to develop at a great rate. He strings four or five words together now—as "All gone Frank bicycle" (meaning Frank on his bicycle); "Benjy go upstairs sleep." He tries more and more often to imitate things we say—and the ability to do so correctly is improving. He called Frank "Fanky" for several weeks but he now has mastered the "Frank." He asks questions such as "Where's Benjy's tractor?" and "Where's ball?" He can name the majority of the objects in the trading-stamp catalogue—his favorite book—and is trying to count, by which I mean only saying the words in order, not actually counting objects.

Plurals are beginning to appear. No verb tenses other than the present, and not too many verbs yet—"go," "eat," "come," "get." The only possible reference to the future is in "See you tomorrow" or "See you wāter" (later). He can distinguish pretty well now between "up" and "down"—for a while he used only down, no matter which he meant. He speaks of "ou'doors" and "in," and says "Go home" or "Go Benjy's house" specifically at those times when we've been out driving and we go on past our house rather than turning in.

He has, I think, some idea of "two"—two cookies, particularly —but he doesn't yet know about two eyes, two ears, and the rest.

He has discovered the word "pretty" and uses it often, especially about music. His only descriptions of himself are "rascal boy" and "tough guy"—both of which he likes to say.

He is very self-assertive and can raise hell if crossed or made to do something he objects to (such as going upstairs to have his diapers changed). He can also yell and get quite cranky over (so far as one can see) nothing—and this temporary irritability is often accompanied by throwing whatever he has in his hand —even if it's something he has just asked for.

His space perception has developed to the point where he can, quite safely, go up and down stairs on two feet rather than all fours, and he loves going up and down a small stepladder. He uses the words "big" and "little," and I think that "big," at least as applied to cars, has a real meaning to him. [*Benjy's family had two cars, of two distinct sizes.*]

He can distinguish the footsteps of members of the family—can usually tell who is coming upstairs or is walking around downstairs.

The last time he went to the doctor's was in early October—the first time since April. Height 33½ inches, weight 22½ lb. He began to yell the minute we got inside the door—which he has not done before—and kept it up while he was undressed and examined. He calmed down only when all his clothes were back on.

22 months, 2 weeks.   October 23

LONGEST connected string of words to date: Sam had got hold of Benjamin's ball, and Benjamin said to him, "No, no, Sam—Benjy's ball—quit it!"

2 years, 9 days.   December 18

MY APOLOGIES—but I just can't keep up with Benjamin's changes!

SPEECH: He is now talking a great deal. He can cope with most consonants except *l* which is still mostly *w*. The *j* sound is gradually becoming distinct; it was *d* for a long time, but now it's a rather *dj* mixture. *Sh* is still mostly *s*.

He is parroting phrases right and left—bits of commercials from the TV, bits of stories and nursery rhymes, things he hears clerks say in stores, etc. He loves numbers and counting. Though, of course, he still leaves out several here and there if he tries to count consecutively. He grasps the idea of "two" and is beginning, sometimes, to understand about "three." For a couple of weeks recently we had three cars (a friend left hers with us while away) and he would look out the window and say, "Three cars—big car, tinky car, Tant's car." (Tinky car is our very small foreign car—we don't know whether "tinky" came from "dinky" or just where.)

Routine is playing an increasing role—things must be done

just a certain way and no other. Lights must be on in the dining room at meals, no matter how sunny it is. He must go to sleep on his stomach with one blanket over him and his two cotton blankets beside him. We must have a cocktail before dinner, mixed at the same time with him sitting in the same place, reaching for the ice-breaker, dropping the ice cubes into the shaker, etc., etc.

2 years, 1 month.   January 9

A SUDDEN consuming interest in being read to has developed in the last couple of weeks. He has about a dozen books, most of them dreadful little stories about wild animals he's never seen (the three prime favorites are the "rosserus," the "hittopotamus," and the "goriwwa"), and these we read four or five times through at a sitting—or as many times as the reader's patience holds out. Of course he knows them almost by heart and if you pause in the reading will provide the next three or four words.

He has also developed a passionate attachment to his father, who has some difficulty getting out of his sight, except when I take Benjamin out in the car or when it's time for bed or some such activity which he associates with me.

His favorite activity is still playing in the kitchen sink—pouring water in and out of cups and any other receptacle available. This is one of the few things which he will do for any length of time by himself—mostly he wants someone around to play with him.

His vocabulary grows and grows. He is attempting to use "my" but still confuses it with "your." He occasionally uses "the" now and is beginning to say "no" but hasn't discovered "yes." He is beginning to repeat our admonitions to himself. If he is crying about something, he'll often bury his head in the sofa and say through his tears, "What's-a trouble, Benjy? It's all right, Benjy. Don't cry any more—don't cry, Benjy" until one can't decide whether to laugh or cry with him, he sounds so pathetic!

27 months, 17 days.   March 26

I'LL TRY to bring this as up to date as possible and then give it up!

LANGUAGE: While Benjy's speech is, doubtless, less comprehensible to others than to his family, we can communicate with him and he with us to a quite considerable degree. He is able to express most of his wishes adequately and is gradually getting it through his head that yelling for something is less effective than asking for it and saying "Please?" (His sister is *most* particular about the "Please!") He is still thoroughly confused about possessive pronouns—uses "my" to mean "your" or "my" indiscriminately, and hasn't discovered "mine" at all. He sometimes uses "I" or "you" but is still more apt to use his name or ours. He can, if he feels like it, follow simple directions or requests, such as "Please bring me an ash tray" or "Put the diaper in the pail." He can tell you which book or record he wants, and has recently discovered "No." He occasionally obviously means "Yes," but mostly he *knows* he means no—often very vehemently indeed.

Past tenses are beginning to creep in—"went," "said"—I suspect these come more from his books than from us. He is beginning to have some idea of the immediate future—says "See you tomorrow" to his daily sitter, or "First have breakfast, then play vacuum cleaner." (The latter is one of his favorite playthings.) He is pretty clear on "up" and "down" now, less so about "on" and "under."

He is crazy about being read to and knows many of his books virtually by heart. He is picking up television commercials (worse luck) and will rush in from the kitchen to "see Brue Cross" (he still can't cope with "l" or "sh"). Sometimes we hear him telling his stories to himself, but more often he'll fill in the next few words if we pause while reading.

He picks up expressions of ours and uses them in a manner that can convulse us or make us all but weep. Recently, when

I had him in the car, we were held up in traffic and Benjamin suddenly called out, "Come on, wady, move!" Or today, when I was, as usual, getting nowhere with conveying the idea that the toilet was the best place for a bowel movement, I muttered to myself, "I wonder if you're ever going to learn." The next time I took his wet pants off, he said to himself, "Wonder if ever goin' to wearn."

His only type of question to date is of the "where" variety— "Where's big car?" "Where's Daddy?" etc. [*Note 30: Oddly enough, no one has ever attempted to plot a developmental sequence of children's questions, even though the child's questions should be extremely revealing of his cognitive status and what he can think about.*]

SELF-AWARENESS: He knows pretty well all the larger parts of his anatomy and can find them on his animals, doll, parents, etc. He has taken a renewed interest in looking at himself in the mirror.

He sometimes will spank himself and say, "Benjy spank" or "Mommy spank" but this is usually when he seems to realize he is cranky and that he *may* get spanked, rather than as result or follow-up of any particular action. He sometimes gets down on all fours and crawls around, but doesn't indicate verbally or otherwise whether he is pretending to be the dog.

The phase of "highly vocal independence" is with us with a vengeance. When I put him to bed tonight he bellowed at the top of his lungs for a good five minutes from sheer rage that I wouldn't let him get down on the floor and go on playing with his car. What he wants and doesn't want he can be *very* noisy about—but he can also obviously be rather confused as to what he *does* want. This is especially true in the afternoon after his nap. He may wake up demanding a ride or a walk. By the time he gets downstairs, it has switched to "Want to pway bwocks." And if you suggest that we go out, he may do quite a bit of fussing until you have settled for him what is going to be done, and then he usually seems to decide that's really what he did want, after all. He delights in running anywhere when I tell him it's bedtime, and I'm afraid I often turn his playful negativism into genuine opposition by clamping down too hard and too soon. (Damn it all, one is *not* as patient at forty-five as one was at twenty-five—not with small kids!)

SPACE PERCEPTION: He loves to look at pictures of himself— and of all sorts of cars, trucks and airplanes, kitchen utensils, household objects of any sort, and *fireplaces.* He has a real "thing" about fireplaces, maybe because we don't have one, and the few he has seen, especially with fires in them, are most fascinating. For a while this winter, every time we passed a certain friend's house where he had seen a fire in the fireplace, he would ask to "go see fire," and when I said no, not today, he would rather sadly reply, "No fire—too bad—some day!"

He learned several months ago that when his ball rolled under the desk or sofa, Daddy would go get the umbrella to poke it out. It was pretty funny to watch Daddy poking—but now he rushes off himself for the umbrella and does his own poking, sometimes successfully, sometimes not.

He seems far more aware of form than of color. Several times he has called [*a particular make of*] station wagon "Betty's car" because a friend has such a car, but not the same color as the ones he has remarked on. Yesterday when we were out driving, he said, "Like Ann's car" (his sitter) of about fifty different cars, every one of which was of the same general shape but which were of many different colors. He has a set of parquet blocks, and he can do a pretty good job of superimposing the right block on the outline shown on the diagram, but it may or may not be the right color. [*Note 31: Two different processes seem to be at work here. Benjy's recognition of cars is probably on the basis of the global physiognomy shared by cars from the same manufacturer. His matching of geometrical forms, however, is a more "analytical" operation and is probably made possible by his manipulation of the blocks.*]

TIME: As noted before, "tomorrow," "after supper," "after breakfast" are appearing and once he used "yesterday"—but only once so far. He uses "new" but sometimes it means something he likes very much (i.e., something that was particularly pleasing when it *was* new, so it's *still* "new") and at other times it *does* mean "new." No use of "old" or "young" except as they are learned parts of a story.

SENSORY ORGANIZATION: The foods he'll eat are still appallingly limited—and just as we think he's at last added one new food to his meager variety, he'll turn against it again. I don't think this can be caused by our attitudes—he usually shows little interest in what we eat, no matter how enthusiastic we may be about it. The meals he seems to enjoy most are Saturday and Sunday breakfast when we always have bacon and some sort of rolls or biscuits. He will have nothing to do with eggs, but will eat as much bacon as he can get. He obviously is attracted by certain smells—frying onions will always bring him running to the kitchen, and he will hang around and watch all sorts of things being cooked and help whenever he is allowed to. But most of the time he has *no* interest in eating the results (bacon, muffins, and biscuits are the exceptions here).

His bedtime rituals are changing but still evident. He must be read to—as many books as the reader will stand for—and his music-box bear must be wound up. And I don't think he knows it's even possible to sleep any way except on the stomach. But he doesn't ask for his three old favorite stories to be *told* to him anymore (thank heaven) and he doesn't always ask to be sung to—sometimes he wants one of three or four particular songs, but by no means always.

He still screams bloody murder at the doctor's. He starts the minute the nurse comes in and I start to take off his clothes, and pretty much keeps it up till he's dressed and out of the examining room. The doctor herself seems far less alarming than the examining room and the being undressed. When I talk to her afterward in her office, he plays around quite placidly.

2 years, 10 months.   October 2

I'M REALLY going to finish it off this time.

Benjamin started nursery school this morning and from this point on his teachers will know more about him than I do!

He has grown and changed a lot in six months. We have just

come back from the doctor's—height 37 inches, weight 28½ lb. He was tired when we went, as it was past his naptime, and this gave him a few extra excuses for yelling. But for the first time, he did more or less calm down while she examined him and talked to her a little bit.

He has been doing quite a lot of dancing lately—especially to some old jazz records that have no vocals. When in the car, he now works the gear shift lever, turns the wheel and really imitates driving procedures.

He talks a great deal—to himself or to anyone else he knows except women (men are all right, or girls Janet's age, but he seems to regard women as potential mother-substitutes). He can express his needs and wants. Has lately discovered "Yes" and is using "No" less frequently. Past tenses are now fairly common, and the distinction between "yesterday," "today," and "tomorrow" is fairly clear, though he is much more apt to say "tonight" than "today." He can still confuse the personal pronouns, but "I" is fairly frequent now, and the distinctions between "himself" and "herself," "his" and "hers" are clearer. He still pretty consistently says "Benjy's" rather than "mine."

It is possible now to explain ahead of time what is going to happen during a period of some hours. First we go to school, then we come home to lunch, then we have a nap, etc. And he can tell us what he has done during a morning when we weren't together.

For a while, he was quite likely to use a question rather than a statement to tell us something, although this is less frequent now. Some weeks ago he came howling into the house having apparently gotten stung—at least that's the way we interpreted it when he got coherent enough to say, "Didja bump your toe on a fwy (fly)?" [*Note 32: Notice the generalization of already available terms ("bump your toe") to a state of affairs for which Benjamin lacks the standard labels. "Bump your toe" seems to refer to both the cause (the sting) and the effect (the pain). Another two-year-old used "bang" in much the same way.*] The other day he let out a great sneeze and then announced proudly,

"I sneezed my nose." After the evening news on Wednesdays, the TV is sometimes left on long enough for the next program to come on, "Death Valley Days," which is introduced by the familiar twenty-mule team pulling a covered wagon. When Benjy sees it now he sings out, "Horsies pulling a mixer-truck."

He now handles his body better than he used to—has just learned really to jump—and delights in doing so on the bed or couch, or down the stairs. He hasn't quite mastered his tricycle yet. He will push down hard with the right foot and go a little way, but the smooth alternation of thrusts with both feet hasn't quite clicked.

He likes to play a ball game up and down the stairs using two tennis balls and three rubber balls of different sizes. He sits on the landing with all the balls and a parent stands at the foot of the stairs. He then asks, "Which ball you want?" and one has to answer either "Tennis ball" or "Big ball" or "Middle-sized ball" or "Tiny ball"—and if one fails to add "please," he will repeat your answer with a firm "please" after it—and then usually throw you the one you wanted. Or he'll suddenly send all five down at once with great shouts of glee.

Ritualism at bedtime is relaxing a little. He usually has a bath and then I read one or two stories but seldom need to sing. For a couple of weeks recently he went on a real jag and yelled like fury after he'd been put in bed—but this seems to have been a temporary thing and has died down again. If he is too slow about getting out of the bath, usually I only have to say, "Will you take out the plug or shall I?" and out it comes. Similarly, if he is still pushing cars around or demanding another story, usually one question is enough: "Can you pull down the side of your bed and climb in, or shall I put you in?"

References

Church, J. *Language and the Discovery of Reality.* New York: Random House, 1961.

Eleftheriou, B., Bronson, F. H., and Zarrow, M. X. Interaction of olfactory and other environmental stimuli on implantation in the deer mouse. *Science*, 1962, 137:764.

Werner, H. *Comparative Psychology of Mental Development*. Chicago: Follett, 1948.

PART III

RUTH

✦✦✦✦✦✦✦✦✦

Ruth *is the first child of parents living in a suburb of a large midwestern city. Her father, who was twenty-five when she was born, is a liberal-arts graduate, with a major in social and behavioral science. He holds a master's degree in business administration and works long hours in his family's retail business. Ruth's mother, who was twenty-two when Ruth was born, is also a liberal-arts graduate, with a major in child development. She is an intense, dynamic young woman, who characteristically finished her four-year college course in three years. Even after Ruth's birth, her mother found time to take courses, to be an amateur painter, and to do volunteer work. The parents, as the records show, are devout Jews who follow religious traditions very faithfully. They are sociable and do a good deal of entertaining and visiting. Ruth's paternal grandparents live nearby and provide a second home, especially for a time as regards outdoor play space, which she lacked in the apartment in which she first lived. There is considerable coming and going of relatives as well as friends. Ruth's maternal grandparents live in a city in the Northeast, but visits there are not uncommon, and Ruth stayed with her mother's family for six weeks while her parents were in Europe. There is a maid in Ruth's home, something of an old family retainer, but she was seldom asked to take care of Ruth. The other significant member of her family is her brother, Gabriel, born when she was two and a half, so that the last months of this account were written during Ruth's mother's second pregnancy.*

According to her mother, Ruth was with adults a great deal. She saw other children only intermittently, in the course of visits. As the records show, she was an object of warm adoration. Her mother notes that Ruth was perhaps excessively petted and pampered during her early months, when she suffered from colic, so that she would not cry and disturb the elderly downstairs neighbors. Her mother reports that it was only at age eight months, during a three-week vacation well away from neighbors, that Ruth was allowed to cry herself to sleep, putting an end to her somewhat tyrannical ways at bedtime. She was overprotected as well as indulged, in spite of which she was plagued with respiratory infections for her first one and a half years.

Notwithstanding the love, indulgence, and stimulation with which she was showered by her extended family, Ruth's early life was lived within a framework of rather strict expectations. Among the values explicitly emphasized by Ruth's parents are: intelligence, creativity, mastery, resourcefulness, self-reliance, self-esteem, physical safety and good hygiene, foresight, discipline, justice, esthetic appreciation, and flexibility. According to her mother, Ruth was bowel-trained, largely on her own initiative, at age sixteen months and completely toilet-trained by twenty months, with due allowance for occasional accidents. It will be seen that Ruth is remarkably precocious in many spheres, and particularly as regards expressive-linguistic functions. She began very early to play with words and ideas and human feelings, to make jokes and to tease, and to make believe.

Her mother described Ruth at almost age three as imaginative, humorous, verbal, and possessed of a fantastic memory; as spoiled and volatile and prone to tantrums; as consciously and manipulatively charming; oriented to people rather than inanimate things and abstract relationships; selfish with her belongings; overly tense and excitable, although capable of peaceful, self-sufficient play when not overstimulated; melodramatic in self-expression; and often impatient and given to whining. She was sensitive to emotional atmospheres, and major family events that cause tension in the adults—moving into a new house, her mother's going to the hospital to have Gabriel— produced vomiting and fever.

Much of what seemed Ruth's fixed temperament disappeared, however, at about age four when it was discovered that Ruth was sensitive to a whole host of allergens. When treatment was given, Ruth stopped whining, lost her tenseness and overexcitability, became able to tolerate frustration, ceased having tantrums, and, without losing her humor or a powerful sense of logic, became a sweet and well-modulated child.

Ruth's mother began by classifying her observations according to the guide I had provided, which limited the scope of her observations, but thereafter, at my request, changed to anecdotal reporting. This will account for the repetitions in the first few pages of this report. Thereafter, the reader should find a rich fund of observations on a charming and highly individual little girl.

BIOGRAPHY

RUTH was born on July 19.

Birth to 2 months, 6 days.
July 19–September 25

I. *Imitation*

Tongue protrusion at two weeks. Imitates mouth movements and makes strained sounds at four weeks. Strains with her body and mouth to make sounds at seven weeks.

At seven to eight weeks, Ruth started making noises. Her first sounds were sighs. Looked as if she were going to sneeze—drew long breath, opened her mouth, long sigh. First had to push sound out, much strain—sounded like a grunt. By two months, sounds come forth freely and have a sing-song quality. "Converses," i.e., when someone talks or sings to her she "coos" in response. Can do this for ten to fifteen minutes at a time. Enjoys this. Responds only to person talking to her. Doesn't coo to things except lamb (toy).

Ruth smacks her lips at two months. She smacks her lips *only* when eating foods, and then only fruits.

At nine and a half weeks, she was crooning to music. Ruth makes sing-songy noises in response to human voices and music, but not really crooning. She does need noise or music in order to sleep, however.

II. Communication and language

At first, Ruth's only "communication" was her crying—when wet, hungry, etc. She would hold tightly to the person holding or feeding her, or would get a grip on them by pinching their arm or neck.

At six to eight weeks I first noticed she had different cries: high and whiny when she was tired and was trying to fall asleep; a lower, distressed cry when she was hungry; and a loud, angry cry (face red) when she was put in her crib or if she wanted to be picked up. Ruth could accomplish her outraged cry by pulling her hair hard. The nurse oiled Ruth's hair and it slipped through her fingers (she only pulled it when agitated) and she could not yank it. After several tries, she twisted it around her fingers, pulled, and screamed. [*Note 1: We should not attribute too much significance to this technique for producing a cry, remarkable though it indubitably is. It seems a means of expression rather than of communication—that is, we should not assume that Ruth knows that by performing such and such acts she will produce this kind of response in an adult listener.*]

Her parents communicate with her by talking to her, rocking her smilingly, tickling her, moving her arms and legs, singing to her, and she responds (since six weeks) by smiling and cooing. (She first smiled at three and a half or four weeks, although infrequently.) She smiles now (at two months) with her whole body. Her hands and feet are lifted up close to her body—it is not only her lips that move. She responds especially to our calling her "pretty girl," to our songs, tickling, and "baby talk." At the age of nine weeks, she had a long "conversation" in "ahhs" and "eh-ehs" and "hms" with my husband which lasted ten uninterrupted minutes.

Ruth likes movement and is happiest when someone carries her about. [*Note 2: Note that in real life the variables of move-*

ment and human contact are hopelessly confounded in what Harlow (1958) has called "contact comfort."]

It is hard to attract Ruth's attention to anything. Her eyes, at random, find an interesting object (usually one which is very bright—a light, something which is moving, like a mobile, or something which makes noise, like a person speaking or a musical lamb). In order for Ruth's attention to be fixed on anything else, it must first be put in her line of vision and then she follows it with her eyes and her head for a little bit (this occurred at six weeks). [*Note 3: My observations of thirty-two babies from one to seven months old suggest that most babies do not orient to most sounds until age four months. I have, however, observed several babies turn to the sound of their mothers' voice at as early as two months of age. See Deborah, 1 month, 8 days, page 9.*] She has been seeing since age five weeks, I think. [*Note 4: Ruth's mother is apparently assuming that vision begins with tracking a moving target. See Fantz (1963) for evidence of pattern vision immediately following birth.*] At two months, if a person talks to Ruth and then walks away, she follows that person with her eyes and her head.

Also at two months, Ruth stops crying if someone claps his hands. She watches the hands.

Ruth makes cooing noises, but only when she is being played with and spoken to, and on these occasions only when she is comfortable, happy, and very engrossed in the person playing with her. Ruth has to work herself up before she coos. First she has to be totally engrossed in the person talking to her, then she smiles, then she strains her mouth, head, and body, opens her mouth soundlessly several times, and then, finally, coos. The later coos come easier and closer together. She has to "warm up" to vocalize. [*Note 5: See Deborah, 2–3 months, page 9, and Benjamin, 2 months, 1 week, page 112, and 2 months, 25 days, page 113. It is my conviction that these reciprocal vocalizations between adult and infant are an important foundation for learning to speak.*]

She makes a grunting sound and then cries if you take away her bottle before she has finished.

She stops crying when she hears footsteps beside her crib; even when she seemed sound asleep, she would open one eye. She was attentive to the slightest sound from the time she came home from the hospital. [*Note 6: Although otologists prefer not to make a diagnosis of impaired hearing until babies are five or six months old, most babies give clear evidence of hearing virtually from birth. See Wertheimer, 1961.*]

III. Self-awareness

At first, Ruth seemed aware only of distress—hunger, wet or dirty diaper, etc.—and she cried. She also seemed aware of being handled. As early as two weeks, she stopped crying when picked up, rocked, patted, etc.

Ruth did not "root" for her bottle, although starting from one or two weeks when she wanted her bottle she opened her mouth and made sucking motions, sticking out her tongue.

At two months, Ruth will hold tightly to the hand holding the bottle, or she will "hold" the bottle. She strains toward the nipple, lifting her head and opening her mouth if the nipple is held a few inches from her mouth, and she makes grunting sounds. [*Note 7: See Benjamin, Note 1, page 110. Ruth is reacting to the bottle as visually given. Comparison of Ruth with the other two babies is hard because both Debbie and Benjamin were breast fed at the beginning.*] She cries if the nipple isn't put in her mouth. Also at two months, Ruth watches the bottle when being given her solids. Her hands cup the bottle when she wants more milk. Now "holding" the bottle seems intentional, not reflexive as it did previously.

Ruth, at birth, seemed to enjoy swaddling. However, from age two or three weeks, she could not sleep with a cover on her. She would turn in her crib until she was out from under it. [*See Deborah, Note 7, page 8.*] However, since age four weeks, Ruth has seemed to like the security of feeling closed in. She either sleeps crosswise in the crib, sleeps flat against the crib bumper, in a corner, or sleeps with one arm between the mattress and the carriage side in her buggy. [*Note 8: The widespread use of bassinets as sleeping places for very young babies undoubtedly is based in part on the security the baby feels in being enclosed. The disadvantage of the bassinet is that the change to a crib, made necessary by the baby's growth, may prove disturbing.*]

In the hospital, Ruth liked to have her hands and arms free. She cried when they were pinned down or wrapped inside a blanket (she scratched herself). She struggled to free them.

Since birth, Ruth had occasionally held her bottle. When she was one day old she sucked the back of her hand and all her fingers; at two days of age, she was sucking her thumb—first sucking many fingers and then only her thumb. It seemed accidental that she could find her thumb, but she was always sucking it nevertheless.

At seven or eight weeks, Ruth seems interested in her hands (although it seems early). She holds them in front of her eyes, stares at them, makes a fist, moves her fingers, sticks out her thumb, and then tries to put it in her mouth—hitting her eye, cheeks, etc. [*Note 9: Note once again the problem of localizing unseen regions of the body.*]

At night, Ruth needs her thumb to fall asleep. She can sleep only on her stomach, and since the age of one month she has been finding her thumb and goes to sleep with it in her mouth. At six to eight weeks, Ruth seems to find her thumb by kin-esthetically given position and seeing. Prone, she brings her hands up toward her face, and opens her mouth, straining, long before the thumb finds its way to her mouth. Since age six weeks, her fingers curl around her nose and stroke it.

Ruth has grasped my finger with amazing strength. Since she was born she never grasped or attempted to grasp any object other than a finger. At four weeks a small rattle was put near her hand and her fingers closed around it, but only for a second. Then she let it go. Holding the rattle seemed accidental. Grasping a finger, or cloth, or flesh, or the edge of her mattress, seems intentional.

Ruth at two months has good control over her hands—can suck her thumb all night (finding it without too much random movement). Although at seven to eight weeks Ruth examines her hands visually (as noted above), I doubt if she knows they are hers. They're just something she wants to put in her mouth.

IV. *Space perception*

Ruth from birth did not like the feeling of empty space. At first (up to two weeks) she liked to be swaddled and since then sleeps against something—crib bumper, etc. She moves until she feels something solid against her body.

Ruth did not seem to have any visual awareness of space at all until seven weeks, when she started staring at objects and looked about a room until her eyes fixed on something.

Ruth rarely sleeps in the "usual" sleeping position in her crib—always either crossways or with her head at the foot, and always with her head toward the window. Will sleep only on her stomach since ten days old.

From the age of two or three weeks, Ruth did not like being held up in the air, even when firmly supported. Now, at two months, she much prefers being held *against* something (preferably someone) in a burping position rather than in the crook of my arm.

At first, Ruth did not follow moving objects with her eyes. She began to follow them with her eyes at seven weeks. At nine weeks her head also turns to follow moving objects, but if they move out of her range of vision, she does not look for them. They seem no longer to exist.

At two months, Ruth responds to both two- and three-dimensional objects. She watches, focuses her eyes for several minutes on such things as lights on ceiling (six feet away) or design on sheet (a few inches away).

At three weeks Ruth turned over from stomach to back. She got frightened and screamed, arms and legs thrashing.

V. *Time*

Ruth may not be aware of time, but she stops crying when she is picked up to be fed, and she stops crying when she is put in the feeding position and the "burp" cloth is put under her chin. She is beginning to sense, at age two months, that she will be fed.

She is developing a biological clock and has put herself (demand feeding) on a perfect four-hour schedule, sleeping through the night from 9 P.M. to 7 A.M.

VI. *Responsiveness*

Ruth pays attention to her bottle, her mobile, people, lights, curtains, cut-outs on her wall, designs on her crib bumper, her musical lamb, designs on dresses, shiny objects, voices, etc. She must hear noise—voices, radio, music—to fall alseep. If she's crying (eight weeks) and she hears a music-box lullabye, she stops and listens. She seems unaware of telephone bells, doorbells, and thunderstorms, but is aware of doors closing, footsteps, and voices. [*Note 10: Note again the meaningful selectiveness with which she responds, and the difference in responsiveness to near and distant sounds.*]

Ruth has been very much aware of movement since the age of two or three weeks. She is content when she is in a moving car or carriage, but when it stops she cries or wakes up if she is sleeping. [*See Benjamin, Note 2, page 111.*]

Ruth is attentive to sounds—looks about to follow and find voice or music. She does not respond to odors. [*Note 11: Since we know that malodorous chemicals at strong concentrations produce distress reactions in neonates (See Pratt, 1954; Engen, Lipsitt, and Kaye, 1963), we interpret this statement to mean that Ruth takes for granted the odors of familiar things, although these probably play a part in her knowledge of them. Many older infants approach new foodstuffs by first smelling them.*]

VII. *Sensory organization*

Ruth will fix eyes on an object and stare at it constantly for five, ten, or fifteen minutes at a time. She listens to voices and music, turning her head to find the source. She seems to like our saying "ah-ah-baby" and stops crying to listen to her musical lamb. She has been attentive to noises since the age of ten days.

Since the age of two and a half weeks, Ruth has liked the tub part of her bath, when her body is in the water. She does not like being soaped or sponged.

Since age four to six weeks, Ruth has stopped crying when she hears footsteps approaching. At six weeks, she stopped crying when she saw a face approach her. At two and a half weeks, Ruth looked directly at the person talking to her. Since age two weeks, she opened one eye while sleeping when someone approached her crib. At ten days, Ruth liked being patted and caressed.

Ruth already has food preferences. She was given cereal at two or three weeks and she ate it. At four or five weeks she was given fruits and vegetables. She seemed to like them equally well. At eight weeks, however, she no longer likes cereal. She accepts a few spoonfuls, then makes a face, cries, won't open her mouth, and if I sneak a spoonful in, she "gags." I don't think she *really* gags, for as soon as I offer her fruit or milk, she is fine. She adores fruit, eating it very fast. She cries if there's a minute's delay between spoonfuls, and smacks her lips, and opens her mouth and strains toward the spoon. She seems to like banana best. Ruth likes vegetables, beets especially, but does not like squash and cries so she won't have to eat it. She prefers her bottle to everything, fruits included.

At nine weeks, Ruth likes cereal again. I have to add a pinch of sugar to it.

VIII. *Rituals*

I have not noticed rituals as yet, although Ruth always finds her thumb the same way—curls hands around head, opens mouth, sticks out thumb, moves thumb to mouth.

IX. *Growth pattern*

Birth—7 lb. 12 oz., 21 inches;
4 weeks—9 lb. 8 oz., 21¼ inches;
8 weeks—11 lb. 8 oz., 22⅜ inches.
Ruth cried when the doctor gave her her four-week checkup. When the doctor checked her at eight weeks, she really enjoyed

it—she loved the company and cooed and smiled at him during the examination. [*Note 12: Ruth's four-week and eight-week examinations were given at home, and she did not receive any immunizing injections. Such injections play an important part in babies' feelings about doctors.*]

2 months, 1 week.   September 26

RUTH began exploring with her fingers. She touched her fuzzy stuffed lamb in her crib and stroked the crib bumper with her fingers.

2 months, 9 days.   September 28

RUTH is content to lie in her crib or playpen looking at her toys —rattles, animals, etc.—for as long as an hour without crying.

She now holds her bottle almost every feeding with her two hands. She grasps it "correctly."

2 months, 10 days.   September 29

RUTH was in my lap beside a table with candies on it. I put her hand on the candy. After a few minutes, *she* touched the candy, grasped it and opened her mouth, making sucking noises, but had no idea how to get the objects into her mouth.

2 months, 11 days.   September 30

RUTH smiles at faces, even when people do not speak to her. She is greatly interested in people—she can follow a person around a room, turning her head to keep him in sight. She smiles instantly when someone talks to her.

She is beginning to use her hands for holding and clinging, her thumb in opposition. She constantly holds her kimono, blanket, etc.

Ruth was bathed in a sink for the first time, sitting up (no hammock). She enjoyed her bath more than ever before. She seems secure propped in a sitting position rather than lying down in a sling.

2 months, 13 days.   October 2

RUTH was in her crib watching her mobile. My husband went in and stood by her crib—didn't talk. Suddenly she noticed him, jumped, and started to cry.

The first time Ruth was put in her playpen, she must have felt strange or afraid. She just lay there rigid, not moving at all.

2 months, 2 weeks.   October 3

RUTH handles more objects in her playpen. There is a doughnut-shaped plastic rattle hanging by a ribbon on the side of the playpen. Her hand brushed it accidentally and it moved. She stared at it, then touched it, grasped it, held on with her hand several times.

Ruth is very interested in the side of her carriage. She strokes it with her fingers. She has begun to feel everything she is put in contact with. [*Note 13: The reader will notice a stronger tactual-textural component in Ruth's exploration of her surroundings than in that of the other two babies.*]

For the past week, when Ruth is finished with her bottle she "bites" hard on the nipple in the side of her mouth and it is very difficult to remove.

Ruth recognizes her family, I think, or certainly takes pleasure in our presence. She smiles when she sees us near the crib, before we even speak, and she doesn't take her eyes off us.

Ruth is much more interested in the netting that forms the sides of her playpen than in the toys in it. She strokes it, grasps it, twines her fingers in it, etc.

2 months, 15 days.   October 4

TODAY Ruth was on her back. She raised her legs and her eyes fixed on them. She watched them intently for several minutes.

Her hands touched and grasped her feet (I'm sure she doesn't know they're hers). She opened her mouth and made sucking motions. [*Note 14: As with Ruth's first visual attention to her hands, her discovery of her feet is extraordinarily early. See Deborah, 4 months, page 15, and Benjamin, 5 months, 6 days, page 121.*]

The round rattle in her playpen interests her. She holds it for a while, sliding it back and forth through the loop of the ribbon from which it hangs.

Ruth "strums" the playpen netting. She spreads her fingers on the netting and watches intently.

Ruth spotted the colored balls hanging on the side of the playpen—either her hand or foot accidentally hit them and they made a noise like a rattle. She looked fearful and cried. They were within reach but she made no attempt to grasp them.

2 months, 17 days.   October 6

RUTH "sings" herself to sleep. She lies in her crib and when she's falling asleep (always the same position—left thumb in mouth, fingers of the left hand resting against her eyes, and right hand twisted in her hair on the back of her head) she chants in a sing-song voice, "Ahh-ahh-ahh."

2 months, 18 days.   October 7

RUTH smiles back immediately when she's smiled at. If I walk into the room in the morning (she's on her belly), she senses someone's presence, lifts her head and chest, and smiles.

Ruth is startled *very* easily. Anything frightens her. Her eyes widen, she stays suspended a minute, her lower lip protrudes, and then she cries—real excited. Her crying is not instantaneous. I gather that noises only frighten her when they are near but not necessarily loud. If the person holding or feeding Ruth speaks suddenly (even quietly), she jumps and cries. A movement nearby, a cough, a drawer closing, these noises startle her.

She seems to have excellent hand-eye coordination now. She grasps my hand with no trouble, holds bottle easily, and leads it to her mouth.

Ruth may be beginning to anticipate. When she is held in the feeding position, she looks around for her bottle. Even when she seems hungry, she cries if she is fed her solids first and will not eat—or else "gags"—but as soon as she is offered her bottle she stops crying immediately.

Ruth vocalizes constantly while awake. She lies in her crib and even if there is no one around she makes noises, chanting sounds. Last month her sounds could be described as unconnected, single utterances. Now she "talks" in what are connected sounds. If her previous vocalizations could be called "words," her new sounds are "sentences" or "paragraphs." A sing-song "ahh-ahh-ahh," a dove-like sound—sharp, trilled, with breath-intake, etc.

2 months, 25 days.   October 14

TODAY, Ruth noticed the chimes of the grandfather clock for the first time. When they sounded, she stopped drinking her milk. She looked around, the chimes ended, and she opened her mouth again for the bottle.

Ruth touches the flower design on a chair as she hangs over my shoulder while being burped. She spreads her fingers to feel things.

Ruth spends much time in her crib watching the colored designs on the sheet, touching and scratching them. She likes the feel or sound of scratching. She scratches with her nails against her sheet, crib bumper, toys, playpen netting, etc.

Ruth's small-muscle control and hand-eye coordination are improving markedly. Today she was on my lap, sitting near a table on which were colored plastic spoons. She managed to pick one up without much fumbling and held it for a few seconds.

Her vocalizations now include: "A eau-O eua," "Ugg-Uhg," "Eh-eh" (hard to describe—wish I could tape—many different sounds and pitches). "A-zeh, a-zeh"—sound she makes blowing out, using saliva to produce it.

3 months.   October 19

TONIGHT Ruth repeated certain motions like a game. She was in her crib on her back. I put my hand near her face—palm forward and fingers spread. I took her hand (she spread her fingers) and put her palm against mine. She curled her fingers and then mine. After this, I repeatedly put my palm before her and she put hers against mine, right where they were placed the first time. Did this six or seven times.

3 months, 1 day.   October 20

WHEN my palm was put up, she put hers against it again today.

Ruth doesn't cry when she is put in her crib if a teddy-bear toy is in the crib with her. She lifts her head and "talks" to it or smiles at it.

Ruth laughed for the first time. When someone goes "boo-boo-boo," bringing his face close to hers from afar, she gets very excited and smiles, and today she laughed.

Ruth visited the doctor for three-month check. She weighs 14 lb. and measures 23⅝ inches. She smiled at the doctor and made noises. Cried when he gave her injection but only for a few seconds. Then resumed smiling at him.

3 months, 2 days.   October 21

RUTH seems to prefer to have us make strange sound effects rather than use words. She smiles, seems to get excited at whistling, panting, gasping noises. [*Note 15: Ruth is probably reacting to the novel character of these sounds. See Benjamin, Note 9, page 117.*]

3 months, 5 days.   October 24

RUTH was put in her crib and she cried. As soon as a light was turned on and she could look around, she stopped crying and settled down to sleep. [*Note 16: There is an implied cognitive advance in the increase with age of babies' resistance to bedtime, and the role of illumination in enabling the baby to sleep. First, there is the baby's new awareness that life continues without him after he has gone to bed. Second, darkness does not carry the threat of dissolution to the very young baby that it does to the somewhat older one who has acquired a stable visual framework.*]

3 months, 8 days.   October 27

RUTH has been turning herself from tummy to back during the night. She cries in agitation because she usually can't sleep on her back and neither can she turn over again. She may turn over six to ten times a night. However, I have found her sleeping on her back in the morning and I presume that if it's light when she turns over, she can look around and presently is relaxed and tired and falls asleep on her back.

Ruth laughs now when you talk to her, sing to her, etc. She draws in her breath, her tongue is on the roof of her mouth and she actually sounds as if she is laughing.

Ruth never liked her bath until lately. [*Note 17: Compare entries on pages 173 and 174. It seems likely that Ruth went through a brief period of disliking her bath, obliterating her mother's recollection of earlier reactions. It is possible that bathing disturbed a newly acquired stability of spatial orientation.*] She seems more secure sitting directly in the water than lying on the rubber hammock. She used to cry when she was turned over and put on her tummy in the water. Then a few days ago she grabbed the side with her hands and held on fiercely. She must feel more secure, because now she grasps the edges and hangs on—never cries.

On October 21 (three months, two days) Ruth was given new foods. She couldn't swallow gelatin and cried (new texture). [*Note 18: Also at stake, no doubt, is the difficult neuromuscular task of keeping a slithery substance like gelatin in the mouth and swallowing it. See Benjamin, 6 months, 11 days, page 123.*] Liked green vegetable and egg yolk. Does not like mashed graham cracker or zwieback and chokes or cries when she's given meat. She seems to like vegetable soup and prefers fruit to custard. Her favorite is the bottle and she cries for it when given solid foods first. Midway in her milk, she will accept solids. She seems to prefer cow's milk to formula and drinks about three or four ounces more at each feeding than she used to.

Ruth is preoccupied with her hands. She often holds one or both hands in front of her eyes, moves them, stretches her fingers, and stares at them intently.

If Ruth is being fed in a room when the TV is on, she loses interest in the bottle and strains her head to see the TV. [*Note 19: It is doubtful that Ruth perceives meaningful patterns in the sights and sounds of television. It seems likely that young children watch television in the same way that adults watch the flames in a fireplace, or waves breaking on a beach. Indeed, the editor knows of one two-year-old who, when bored, would climb on the couch, put his thumb in his mouth, and sit staring at the blank and silent TV set.*]

Over this month, I would say Ruth's awareness of objects has become highly variegated. She spends hours in her crib just looking around. If she is on one's shoulder to burp, she turns her head looking around the room, her eyes fixing on her clothes tree, animals, pictures, people, etc. Her attention is more often directed to light fixtures and people than anything else. She still finds her mobile fascinating.

She now, at three months, is totally involved with her surroundings. She studies her environment visually, is beginning to explore by touch, is alert for noises, and communicates with smiles, laughter, and vocalizations. She is a "social" being. [*Compare Deborah, Note 18, age 3 months, page 13.*]

For the past week, Ruth has had a "bottle song." When she is drinking her bottle and begins to lose interest in it, she pushes it out of her mouth with her tongue and sings or chants—different from what she does at any other time of day. The vocalization is peculiar to this feeding time.

3 months, 11 days.   October 30

TODAY I held Ruth in her crib so that she was standing up. I supported most of her weight and she could only stand on tiptoes. I was surprised to find that she put one foot before the other as if she already knew how to walk, if only she could support her weight.

3 months, 15 days.   November 3

RUTH now clasps her hands, holds them together *constantly*, watches them intently. She overlaps her fingers or one hand holds a finger or two of her other hand. She brings them together to her mouth—even lies on her stomach supporting herself on her arms and watches her folded hands.

3 months, 16 days.   November 4

RUTH has discovered she need not stop sucking her thumb even when she drinks her bottle. She now holds up her hand, holds her thumb apart from the other fingers, watches it and puts it in her mouth while she drinks her milk. She thinks it is fine to have both thumb and nipple at once and cries if one removes her thumb.

3 months, 18 days.   November 6

RUTH has now started touching my face while I feed her. She watches me and puts her fingers or palm against my face.

Ruth no longer cries when she wakes up in the morning—she lies in her crib making noises and looking around. [*Note 20: This is an important transition that occurs regularly, at about this age. (To detect it, one asks the mother, "How do you know when he's awake in the morning?") It seems to imply an advance in self-awareness and autonomy.*]

For some reason, when Ruth is on her back in the tub she feels more secure if her feet are out of the water. She always rests her heels on the top of the tub side—out of the water—and if they fall in the water, she cries.

3 months, 20 days.   November 8

PERHAPS Ruth recognizes my *whole* face—or can't see well close to something. She rarely smiles at me when I'm holding her a few inches from my face, but when I hold her at arm's length, she smiles and talks to it. [*Note 21: At close range, Ruth probably becomes aware of individual features calling for earnest study. When she focuses on single features, she may lose the Gestalt of the face, or this Gestalt may be radically transformed. At arm's length, the adult's face resumes its normal identity.*]

Ruth has just noticed a small floral design on her crib headboard. She turns to watch it, lifts her head, etc.

3 months, 22 days.   November 10

TODAY Ruth's new nurse came to baby-sit with her—a 300-pound Negro woman. I was holding Ruth. Ruth looked at the nurse and did not smile. I gave her to the nurse and she seemed afraid. She cried and cried. The nurse tried to soothe her but Ruth screamed. She refused her food and kept crying. I took the baby from the nurse and she immediately stopped crying and she ate. The nurse wanted to finish feeding her. Ruth cried and would not eat. All day when Ruth looked at the nurse or the nurse spoke, she cried.

The next few days Ruth would smile at the nurse as long as

I was in the room, and would let the nurse feed her as long as I was in view.

3 months, 27 days. November 15

RUTH now gets along with the nurse. She smiles, eats, and plays when I am *not* around. If I come into the room now, Ruth cries—even when she's eating—as if to complain. As long as I am in the room, she cries when the nurse goes near her.

4 months. November 19

OVER the past week or so, Ruth has been changing rapidly. She laughs *out loud,* not only when one goes "boo-boo-BOO" with one's face drawing nearer and nearer to hers, but also if one playfully pinches her neck or stomach (ticklish?), or if one rubs Ruth's hand against his face, even when one talks to her.

Ruth now really enjoys her toys. She "talks" to them, reaches for them, holds them (for a second or two) in one or both hands, and tries to put them in her mouth.

Ruth opens her mouth when she sees anything suckable. She grabs the end of her sheets, blankets, sleeves, bibs, and holds them to her mouth so she can suck them.

She holds her bottle (does not support it herself) with one or both hands. She holds the fingers of the person feeding her and opens her mouth as the spoon approaches.

Ruth has begun to feel and rub the nipple of the bottle with her hands before it goes into her mouth.

Ruth refuses to eat plain baby's strained meat (since three months): she gags, closes her mouth, etc., but adores vegetables and meat mixed.

Ruth's attention remains on an object now for several minutes at a time. I wind up a little doll that turns around and around and Ruth watches it intently, singing and "talking" to it.

Ruth *seems* now to be understanding games, or perhaps anticipating. She laughs and smiles as I hold her teddy bear high, at a distance, bringing it closer to her and pushing it against her stomach. Now, as soon as she sees the bear at a distance coming closer, she gets real excited—arms and legs move at once and she laughs.

Another instance: when I am holding Ruth, jiggling her in my hands and chanting "ah-ah-ah" and then stop, she looks at me and says "ah-ah," as if it were a game. [*Note 22: If accurate, this is a case of extremely early imitation of a vocal pattern. Note, however, how Ruth's reproduction of the sound arises in a particular behavioral context—she might not have been able to perform the same act without the context.*]

Ruth seems aware of everything—watches the tiny pattern on her sheets, on my dresses, the small movement of a musical doll, the movement of trees outside. She listens to everything. Immediately looks to see where a voice is coming from, cried when I sneezed. Looking and touching are now two of Ruth's favorite pastimes. She also tries to put everything in her mouth. When she is held, she gets a tight grip on the person holding her and "bites" and sucks his face. She tries to grab one's fingers and put them in her mouth. It seems to me she may know her own fingers. When she takes my fingers to put in her mouth, I arrange them so that her own fingers go into her mouth. She stops sucking them, looks around, gets my fingers and tries again. [*Note 23: Ruth's mother has devised an interesting technique for studying the baby's self-awareness.*]

4 months, 5 days.   November 24

RUTH was with us at Thanksgiving dinner. She ignored candles burning on the table, but was totally engrossed in the chandelier and watched it for several minutes.

Today Ruth started to "feed" herself for the first time. As she would see the spoon approaching her mouth, she would open her mouth for the food, grab the handle of the spoon and put it in. She did this every time the spoon was refilled.

Ruth likes to be held in one's arms, but yesterday I noticed something else. She cries if she is held and is then put in her infant seat. If you take her out and hold her, she stops crying, and if you put her in the seat and hold the seat or carry it around, she's content. If you surreptitiously ease it onto a table or chair, she immediately notices the change and cries.

4 months, 6 days. November 25

TODAY was the first time Ruth did not ignore our reflections in the mirror. Today they fascinated her. She looked at herself and me in the mirror, looking from one to the other, smiling and making noises. Then she touched the mirror and intently watched the two pairs of hands in the mirror (hers and their reflection).

Trip to the doctor's for four-month checkup. Weight 16 lb. 4 oz., 24½ inches long. Ruth smiled and talked to the doctor. Enjoyed his attention.

4 months, 8 days. November 27

RUTH recognizes strange surroundings. We took her over to a friend's house. Although I held her, she screamed from the moment we were inside the house until the moment we left, and then she was fine. Either the strange house or two strange people frightened her.

Ruth is aware of all her small toys. She reaches for and grasps her rubber beads, colored balls, teething ring, and rattle (holds it correctly), and everything goes into her mouth.

Whenever I am feeding Ruth, she touches my face with her hand. If I rub her open palm against my cheek saying "nice," she always makes the same sounds: purring noises, using her saliva to make the sound.

4 months, 12 days. December 1

RUTH's fingers fascinate her. Her hands are familiar, but the fingers moving individually are new-found delights. I think she is aware that she controls them because she moves one finger at a time, watching it intently.

4 months, 15 days.   December 4

RUTH found her feet today. She was on her back and her legs were over her body near her head. She spotted them and grabbed at them but they got away. This happened a few times in succession. Then her hands caught them and she sucked on them, especially the big toe. [*See Note 14, page 176.*]

4 months, 16 days.   December 5

RUTH now feels secure in the bath. She does not mind getting her face wet; in fact for the first time today she splashed in the tub with her hands and feet.

Ruth has found that two thumbs fit in her mouth as well as one, so now she sucks them both at the same time.

Ruth prefers watching TV to playing with her toys, to people, or even to eating. She stares intently at the TV, and nothing distracts her. [*Note 24: It should be borne in mind that television is a source of sound as well as of light.*]

Ruth mirrors expressions that she sees. If one smiles at her, she smiles. If one frowns or pretends to cry, Ruth does the same.

4 months, 19 days.   December 8

RUTH became very excited today. She tried to pick up the colored pictures in her story book. She tried and tried. Then she tried to eat them and scratch them. She couldn't understand why she couldn't grasp them. [*Note 25: This observation supports the hypothesis that three-dimensional visual perception comes earlier in development than two-dimensional. We still must account for Ruth's not having grasped (as far as we know) some of the two-dimensional patterns to which she attended earlier. We might note that her first attention to patterns preceded her ability to grasp, and it may be that she now required novel two-dimensional patterns to gain her attention. It might be added that such behavior indicates what Piaget calls "picture realism."*]

Today was the first time Ruth showed real interest when she spat up. She squished the vomit around, tasted it (made a face), put her fingers in it, and tried to pick it up. [*Note 26: It is apparent that a part of self-awareness consists in coming to know about the substances that issue forth from the body.*]

4 months, 22 days.   December 11

TODAY a friend brought Ruth a furry bear, battery-powered, which lights up and shines shoes. It makes a noise also. Ruth saw the bear and was so afraid that she cried and cried until we turned it off. [*Note 27: Note that similar mechanical toys served as unconditioned fear stimuli for Harlow's monkeys. (Harlow, 1958).*]

There is a new game Ruth has learned. As mentioned earlier, she can turn from her stomach to her back, but cannot turn from her back to her stomach or sleep on her back. Tonight she turned over, couldn't sleep, and cried. When I went to turn her over, she laughed and smiled. As soon as I turned her over, before I was even out of the room, she flipped over and looked at me, then cried until I turned her over. This "game" went on for some time. [*Note 28: Ruth's mother does not describe the character of the crying. It would be most remarkable if Ruth, at this age, could produce a cry of sham distress, except in direct imitation, as in the entry for December 5, page 186.*]

4 months, 24 days.   December 13

RUTH notices the cut-outs and pictures in her room, smiling and vocalizing at them. She also "talks" to her dolls which are on the couch in her room. She adores jewelry and tries to eat the rings, pearls, etc., worn by people who pick her up.

4 months, 26 days.   December 15

TODAY we put the baby on an automatic swing. Although it was automatic, Ruth pumped herself with her legs. (No one had previously shown her how.) She loves the movement and chants loudly.

5 months, 1 day.   December 20

WHEN Ruth eats, she gets very excited and makes crowing vocalizations.

There is an 8 by 10 picture of Ruth's father in the den. Whenever she sees it, she "talks" to it and tries to touch it, and quite clearly thinks the picture is an actual person in the flesh. [*Note 29: Another example of picture realism, the lack of clear discrimination between a picture and the thing it represents. See Note 25.*]

5 months, 6 days.   December 25

RUTH says "da-da" loudly and clearly—but it is just part of her babbling and definitely does not mean her daddy. She says it all the time to anyone or anything around her. If someone then says "da-da" back to her, she laughs and repeats "da-da." [*Note 30: Once more it must be pointed out how precocious Ruth is in imitating sounds. We do not know whether it is easier for babies to imitate sounds they have already produced than other sounds.*]

Ruth also says "ga-ga," which does not refer to anything in particular either.

Ruth's favorite game is peek-a-boo. She crows and squeals and laughs out loud in delight.

Ruth now has discovered that one hand can control the other. She grasps one of her hands with the other, moves it through the air, opens the fingers, and feels her toys this way.

Ruth is most interested in and aware of textures now, and is fascinated by fabrics and paper. She strokes her fingers on anything she can reach—walls, sheets, cribs, covers, my slacks or dresses, books, toys, etc. She would rather have paper and cloth—to feel and put in her mouth—than her toys.

Ruth already shows some ability to control situations. If one is giving her a bottle, she grabs it with her two hands, puts it accurately into her mouth, and holds the bottle. She takes it out to rest.

She grasps objects and can let them go at will to pick up other objects.

5 months, 1 week.   December 26

RUTH has learned to attract attention. If one goes by her room without picking her up, she starts to squeal until you notice her.

She has also learned to make "gargling" sounds. She makes noises through her saliva—thinks this is funny.

Ruth reaches out with her arms [*to be picked up*] if she is on her back. If she is prone, pushing up with her hands, she lowers her weight onto her chest and starts flapping her arms and kicking with her feet, making crowing noises.

Ruth's main interest right now is textures—paper, cloth, wood—which she touches or bangs with her open hand.

She has been saying vowel sounds for some time. She says "da-da" all the time—refers to anything pleasurable. Also says "ga-ga" and "je-je."

5 months, 9 days.   December 28

RUTH enjoys chewing on her feet—preferably one toe at a time. She will suck her shoes or socks [*when they are on her feet*], but gets really excited when her feet are bare. Then she really grabs and sucks them. She also likes to watch the motions of her feet.

Ruth recognizes the nipple as the source of milk, I think, for no matter in which direction relative to her the bottle is held, she finds the nipple with her fingers and turns the bottle so that the nipple goes to her mouth.

If one takes away one of Ruth's toys, she looks at the place where it was and cries. She has no idea where it has gone. Nor does she look for it anywhere else. [*Note 31: Ruth's behavior provides another example of the young child's lack of conservation. Compare Deborah, Note 54, page 35.*] However, she seems to understand her own displacements in space. If I put her bottle on the table and then hold her with her back to the bottle, she turns around until she sees it again.

5 *months, 22 days.   January 10*

RUTH enjoys the piano. I had her in my lap while I played the piano. She seemed to look around, not knowing where the music was. [*Note 32: We cannot be sure from this wording whether Ruth was looking for the source of the sound or for the sound itself as some kind of material entity that could be seen if only it could be found. It seems clear from the behavior of some babies that they do attribute visible existence to some sounds.*] Then she started to bang on the piano.

Ruth remembers and anticipates. She had a cold and I had to clean out her nose with drops on a swab. She didn't like this and cried. Now, as soon as she sees the swab, even before I'm near her nose, she screams and turns her head away.

Ruth has plastic toys that squeak. Today she pinched one for the first time herself and kept looking around for the squeak. She didn't know where it came from. [*See Note 32.*]

Ruth cries when she wants to be picked up. Yesterday or the day before, when I went to pick her up, I stretched out my hands. Then I reached out and waited until she reached her arms out to me before I picked her up. Today, whenever I went by her crib, she cried and reached out her hands to me.

For some reason, Ruth's favorite position when one is holding her is with her head thrown all the way back until she sees everything upside down. She laughs and enjoys this position and/or sensation.

We put a higher crib bumper in Ruth's crib because she was banging her head. This one is too high to see over, as she could with her other one, so she pulls it down and rests her hands on it to see out.

5 months, 25 days.   January 13

RUTH again tried first with one hand, then with two, to grasp the figure print on her sheet.

If Ruth hears someone else cry, she cries.

6 months, 3 days.   January 22

I HAD Ruth on my lap in a chair. Her foot tapped against the arm of the chair rhythmically. Then she tapped with her hand. She then watched her foot as if waiting for it to tap again, as if she didn't know *she* controlled the foot's movement. Finally, her hand grasped the foot and tapped it against the chair. [*Note 33: This is a fascinating example of lack of internal integration of the body schema.*]

Ruth has always liked music on the radio—chanting with it, etc. But today was the first time, when I turned on the radio, that she looked around to see where the voice was coming from, and when she traced it to the radio she looked very puzzled and looked around behind the radio as though to *see* the source.

Ruth loves to play in front of the mirror. She smiles at herself and turns from her image to me, then looks at her image again, cooing all the while.

Ruth must realize that I am the only one to feed her. In the morning she plays until I come into her room. My husband or anyone else can go in and play with her, talk to her, and leave the room. If I even walk by quickly and she sees me, she cries until I pick her up. In the evening, she lets anyone else walk by her room, but when she sees me she waves her hands and legs and cries to be picked up. The strange part is that Ruth "senses" that I am near—perhaps she recognizes my footsteps or perfume or something. Even if I hold a newspaper blocking off her view of me, or close the door, she can tell I am going by and cries.

Although Ruth has only occasionally seen the TV set on (she was very interested in it), whenever she is in the room where the TV is she stares at the set, makes noises to attract our attention, looks back at the TV, straining her body toward it. If one turns it on, she stops crying, and if one does not, she cries. She must remember the TV even when it is off.

Another example of how Ruth can communicate her wishes. She has a battery-powered mechanical bear which one can start or stop. She watches its movements intently. If you stop the bear she looks at you, pokes you, looks back at the bear and says "ah-ah" until you turn it on. It is almost as if she knows that *you* make the bear go.

6 months, 11 days.   January 30

RUTH uses her feet instead of her hands to strike the bells hanging on her crib. She has good small-muscle control with her hands. She grabs the spoon with her fingers and feeds herself.

Ruth is very interested in novel materials. Someone brought her a musical teddy bear. She ignored the bear but crinkled the tissue paper, tore the wrapping paper, pounded on the box, and sucked the ribbon. She was fascinated with the sound of the tissue paper. [*Note 34: For several months after birth, the crackling of paper seems to be a decidedly aversive stimulus for many babies, whereas in later infancy it is a source of enjoyment.*]

She loves jewelry—stares at rings, earrings, and bracelets, and grabs at pearls to eat. I had my pearls inside my dress and I was very surprised when she pulled open my bodice looking for the pearls. This was taking a "detour," so to speak. [*Note 35: This behavior further implies orientation to something outside the perceptual field.*]

Ruth is ticklish and laughs out loud if one tickles her under the arms or on the abdomen. She goes into a storm of laughter if you butt your head against her belly.

If Ruth wants something which is not within her reach she can crawl to it or roll over to it.

7 *months, 1 day.* *February 20*

THESE things have happened in February.

Ruth has her first two teeth.

Ruth could always start her swing going by "pumping" with her legs, but today (accidentally?) she learned how to stop herself. She grabbed the stationary frame of the swing and hung on until the motion stopped. She did this several other times today also.

Ruth went for her seven-month checkup on February 13. (She missed her six-month checkup because of illness.) For the first time, she did not wait for the doctor or the injection to cry. The minute we went into the office she started to scream. She did not like the doctor's table and did not enjoy "socializing" with the doctor as in the past. She measures 26 inches long and weighs 18 lb. 12 oz.

Ruth puts everything in her mouth except a book she has with stiff cardboard pages. She just looks at the pictures, trying to grab them, and turns the pages. (We showed her how.)

Ruth's food tastes have not changed much. She still likes sweets the best. One thing I find interesting is that although the doctor says Ruth can have such soft foods as regular scrambled eggs, cottage cheese, etc., Ruth will not swallow the pieces, even if I have put them through a sieve. She spits the pieces out and makes a face. If I mix *my* food with her prepared strained food, she manages to swallow only the food from jars and spits out the rest.

Ruth was having a terrible time in her playpen today. The sun was shining into the room so that there were patches of sun in her playpen. She tried and tried to pick up the spots of sunshine—using first one hand and then both. One of her toys cast a shadow and she tried to grasp the shadow.

Ruth still cries when a stranger or half-stranger approaches her.

She crows with delight when she bangs either her toy piano or my piano. She bangs with both hands, listens, and bangs again. I feel sure she knows *she* is making the noise although she doesn't really seem to know where the music comes from and looks around as if to see the notes.

Ruth's favorite game is peek-a-boo. She enjoys the sudden "boo" or "hi" and laughs out loud. When I play it with her and she is in her crib, I notice when I hide behind the crib headboard, she puts her head down and hides it in the mattress for a second so that she plays the game, too. She never tires of playing it.

Ruth finds things fascinating which an adult wouldn't notice. For example, last night she was crawling on the rug and spent several minutes watching, feeling, and scratching a certain spot on the rug (trying to mouth it, also). The focus of all this attention was just an indentation in the carpeting left by a chair leg.

I believe that Ruth is imitating three actions. When someone kisses Ruth, she makes the kissing sound also. She waves at times when someone waves bye-bye. Then, too, she puckers up her mouth as if to whistle (and blows out air) when someone whistles. This happens only occasionally. There are also times when she makes these noises and movements with no stimulus at all.

Ruth is aware of the sounds she makes, likes the way they sound, and repeats them. This is true of squeals, which she knows we laugh at and imitate, and "da-da." Whenever Ruth wants to attract attention, she squeals in a very high-pitched voice until someone pays attention to her.

I put a "busy box" in Ruth's playpen. It is interesting to note that she did not have any idea that one knob controlled the movement of another mechanism. Instead of turning a knob which rotates a windmill, Ruth manipulated the windmill sails herself. She has no idea how to turn knobs, although she knows how to press them to make a noise. She was able to pull out the drawer, but did not even know how to begin to open a door (to see a mirror) or a sliding panel. [*Note 36: Observe how drawer pulls have a "demand quality" of graspability. It is likely*

that Ruth likewise grasped the knob of the door, but in general,
to judge by the babies I have tested, it is at about age one year
that babies can pull open a door held shut by a friction latch.]
She could turn a wheel by hitting it in a certain place. She is
really too young yet for such a toy, but I think the order of her
mastery of this toy should be interesting. [*See 9 months, 12*
days, page 206, and 14 months, 3 weeks, page 224.]

Ruth now enjoys feeding herself. She manages to hold and
eat a piece of zwieback herself, and is engrossed when she has
a banana to eat. She enjoys squashing and mushing it with her
fingers as well as the taste. Ruth refused to eat grapefruit at all.
She made a terrible face and spat it out. But she adores sherbet.
She licks her lips after each spoonful.

Ruth is more fascinated with the texture of hair on people or
her dolls than anything else. She loves to feel it, eat it, and pull
it. Whenever Ruth sees my father-in-law and she is near enough
to reach him, she goes immediately for his mustache and feels it
with her fingers, laughing, even without any provocation on
his part. Several weeks ago, he took her fingers and stroked his
mustache once or twice, and since then she has tried to stroke
it by herself.

Ruth's favorite companion is her image in the mirror. Whenever she is close enough to the mirror, she puts her face right
on the mirror image of her face and licks her mouth, looking
herself in the eye. She also puts her hand against its reflection
in the mirror and moves the "touching" hands around on the
mirror's surface, watching their movement intently.

She was playing in her playpen and fell, twisting her arm.
She cried and whimpered in a distinctive way indicating pain.
She could not be distracted by being rocked, held, or fed. This
was very different from her crying for attention, which stops
instantly when she is picked up.

7 months, 10 days.   *March 1*

RUTH has the best time with a mirror, talking to herself. Tonight
she looked in the mirror, smiled at me (I was holding her). Sud-

denly she pulled back and looked at me again, repeatedly. I think she is just beginning to wonder how it is that she can see me in two places.

Ruth crawls about on the floor a great deal. Her favorite objects are magazines from the magazine rack, crib sides or chairs (which already present action possibilities—she tries to pull herself up) and drawer pulls. She grabs the handles and tries to get real close and touch herself.

Ruth is a mimic! When a friend stuck his lower lip out at her and made a face, she did this, too. When someone banged the floor or table with his hand, she immediately did this. When one laughs, she laughs, and when her grandfather nodded his head, she also did this. Each time she squeals with laughter and looks up, waiting for the person to repeat the action. [*Note 37: I have incorporated these stimulus actions, and a variety of others, into a test of imitation. I have had only variable success in eliciting imitation, except in the case of table-slapping, which works with almost all babies in the 6–18-month range.*]

When Ruth is contented—most typically when drinking from her bottle—she usually taps one or both feet rhythmically.

New objects frighten Ruth until she becomes used to them. I bought her a "talking" (recording) doll. Ruth looked from the doll to me, as if she knew *I* made the doll talk, and then cried. Now she loves it—smiles and talks to it. [*Note 38: Contrast Ruth's reactions to novelty with Debbie's easy acceptance of new things and people, but observe the similarity in Ruth's and Benjamin's reactions to novelty.*]

Ruth eats strained foods as usual, but from the minute she cut her first two teeth, she literally makes chewing motions with her mouth. No one showed her how, and it is not made necessary by the consistency of the food.

Ruth is no longer content to sit still in her carriage. Instead, she climbs around, hanging out, making loud sounds to people passing by. She tries to grab the nearby bushes and trees, leaning out and opening and closing her fingers. She seems to lack any sense of distance, for these bushes are several feet away and she vainly tries to catch them.

7 months, 2 weeks.   March 5

THE playpen is interesting to Ruth only for its action possibilities. She is not content to look about, or hold or chew on her toys; she only wants to grab the netting, climb, hold on, etc.

When Ruth sees herself in the mirror, she laughs and laughs, tries to get real close and touch herself.

Makes distinct sounds of "ba-ba-ba."

Ruth hums if the radio is playing or someone is singing.

7 months, 15 days.   March 6

RUTH is now interested in chairs, tables, TV sets, beds, and any piece of furniture she can hold on to and pull herself up to a standing position. Ruth is discovering door stops (which she pulls, lets go, and watches vibrate), drawer pulls, wires, and electric outlets.

7 months, 16 days.   March 7

STOOD up in the playpen for the first time. Was so surprised that she screamed and cried. Was afraid to let herself fall and didn't know how to get down.

Ruth saw her father's picture upside-down. She cried until someone righted it, then smiled. Aware of direction, space orientation? [*Note 39: There is evidence (see Hunton, 1955) that young children are indifferent to the orientation of pictures. It may be that Ruth was reacting not so much to the inversion per se as to the consequent deformation of a familiar face. Compare Benjamin, Notes 9, page 117, and 13, page 121.*]

7 months, 20 days.   March 11

RUTH has good small-muscle control. She feeds herself bits of crackers, holding them between thumb and index finger. [*Note*

40: As mentioned previously, self-feeding entails, in addition to the necessary motor control, a knowledge of where one's mouth and hand are relative to each other.]

Said "ma-ma" for the first time. It was an accident. She tried to kiss and her lips were together and the sound came out. (It did not refer to Mother at all.)

Ruth does not know her feet as her own unless she *sees* them. She was sitting in her feeding table. All of a sudden she saw a blue leotard foot. She caught it with her hand and laughed. The foot slipped away and she looked around for it, but seemingly had no idea she controlled it.

7 months, 3 weeks.   March 12

RUTH uses people to hold on to, pulling herself up to a standing position.

Ruth noticed stairs for the first time, or at least showed the first signs of wanting to climb them. She crept over, knelt up, and tried to pull herself up.

7 months, 23 days.   March 14

RUTH has been "practicing" sitting down from a standing position. In her playpen, she holds on, lowers her seat slowly, stops mid-way, looks down at the floor, then lets go and falls. She tries this repeatedly, and each time she is more sure of herself.

Ruth loves magazines, to rustle them, tear them, eat them. She laughs when she sees a face, especially a child's.

7 months, 25 days.   March 16

RUTH took her first cruising steps, holding on around the coffee table.

Shiny, reflecting objects are favorites of Ruth's. She notices herself in chrome table legs and the rotisserie and howls with

laughter and tries to eat or hit her image. She crawls after shoes
and investigates their buttons, bows, or whatever.

She enjoys looking out the window. Hits the window when
cars go by, pulls the curtain aside herself, plays with the material, pulls it away and laughs—her own game of peek-a-boo.

Ruth is extremely interested in the shiny andirons and the
screen before the fireplace. She likes the noise the screen makes
when she pulls it along. She no longer likes regular toys or
quiet play. She only wants to be active.

7 months, 27 days. March 18

WHEN Ruth is put in her playpen, she cries, but she is content
to be set down on the floor.

Ruth crept up a flight of stairs today—BUT she has no fear.
She then turned around and wanted to come down head first.
[*See Deborah, Note 32, page 20, and Benjamin, 13 months,
2 days, page 141.*]

She has no fear of height or falling. On a bed, or chair, she
tries to throw herself to the floor, head first. She inclines *toward*
edges, not away from them. [*See Deborah, Note 32, page 20.*]

Ruth moves and rocks her body in time to the phonograph or
radio.

She now notices when people are eating something. She cries
and gestures toward their mouth with her hand.

Ruth now notices little pictures. She was being fed and her
eye caught the picture of the baby on the label of the baby-food
jar. She looked away and back to it and laughed several times.
It was a game of some sort to her. [*Note 41: It is conceivable
that the picture had the same stimulus-value for her as her own
reflection.*]

Ruth tries to grab the spoon from me to feed herself. She
manages to get it to her mouth but usually inverts it on the
way. She has no idea the food is falling out or why.

Doctor's visit—eight-month checkup. She was not relaxed or
happy, but she did not cry. She looked about skeptically and
uncertainly. She did not like the examining table and tried to

crawl off. She grabbed the stethoscope and tried to put it in her mouth.

8 months.   *March 19*

RUTH went up to her toy piano today and for the first time knelt before it and banged on it completely on her own initiative.

She loves music. She "dances" with her body and hums with the music. She recognizes certain songs all the time. When she hears "Never on Sunday," she crows with excitement and literally jumps rhythmically to the music. [*Compare Benjy at 11 months, 3 weeks, page 137.*]

There is something strange happening. Ruth has learned to pull herself up and stand holding on recently, and for the past few nights she stands up in her crib in the middle of the night and screams—as if she didn't want to stand up, but she *had* to. She is so tired that when I lay her down she's asleep in seconds. [*Note 42: This behavior sounds as though the accumulated tensions of the day are discharging themselves in sleep at a rate too intense to be handled by mere dreaming, and over-flow into motor activity that wakes her up.*]

Ruth is no longer afraid of strangers. Instead, she makes noises and grabs their clothing to make them notice her.

Ruth does not like ordinary toys. She prefers buttons, magazines, shoes, hair brushes, cords, bottle covers, cloth, paper, cups, glasses, tubes, door stops, hangers, powder cans—in short, the miscellany of everyday life. [*See Deborah, 10 months, 1 week, page 42.*]

All day long Ruth creeps around looking for crumbs to eat. She finds the smallest particle, picks it up, and either puts it in her mouth or hands it to someone near.

Ruth stops whatever she is doing when she hears the grandfather clock chime. If she is near it, she creeps over to it.

If Ruth is eating with us, she yells or tugs at our clothing until we put bits of food on her feeding table. She feeds herself meats, vegetables, scrambled eggs—does not get tired of this or lose interest. She picks up the pieces with her fingers. She ignores the spoon if we give her one, or sucks on it. She has no idea she can use it to scoop up food.

Ruth enjoys her bath. She creeps over when she hears the water filling the tub, stands up, dances, leans over the tub, and tries to put her hands into the water. One day she tried and tried to put her hands in the water. Finally the water rose up to where she could reach it. She splashed her hands, yelling with excitement, her body dancing. She tried to reach the faucets. When I put her in the tub, she stood up, knelt, got into a creeping position, and tried to lap up the water. She looked at me, as if to see if this was all right. She then sat down and splashed with her hands until her face was wet and her eyes were dripping. She rubbed her eyes and started to "complain" and fret. I wiped her face with a towel. She repeated this and now when she cried, I laughed. She opened her eyes and *she* laughed, then splashed, wetting her face, looked at me again, and laughed. It became a game and no longer did the water in her eyes bother her.

Ruth understands that "No" means do not touch—I think! She, of course, has not generalized and does not remember the "untouchables" from one time or minute to the next. But if she goes to touch a wire and I say "No," she creeps away. The first few times I did this the tone of my voice scared her and she cried. She turns to me, looks sheepish, and then goes away from it. Often, if she decides she'll touch it after all, she always turns to see what I'll do just before she touches it, with a big smile, as if she knows she's naughty. [*See Deborah, Note 37, page 23, and Benjamin, 11 months, 3 weeks, page 138.*]

I do not let her play on the stairs. Often she creeps toward them, but just before she reaches them, she stops, turns around to me, then smiles and creeps away.

Ruth can now move around by herself—climb stairs, creep, stand up, and walk holding on. She can also make herself understood. If she wants something in sight, she makes noises, looking at the object. She strains her body toward it, motions her hand for it, and finally strains out of one's arms (if she's being held) and creeps over to get it herself.

8 months, 12 days.   March 31

RUTH took her first plane ride. These are the things which fascinated her. She banged on the window, looked out, touched and pulled the light switch and other buttons, chewed on the safety belt, looked at magazine pictures, always smiling at one in color of a family, seeming to recognize it each time, and tried to tear the page, crumple it, and eat it. Ruth played with a paper cup, "drinking" from it, but these things were secondary to trying to attract the attention of the other passengers. If someone walked by, she would try to touch them or look at them or smile or make noises—"da-da, ma-ma, na-na"—or yell. She climbed and hung on the back of the seat, shouting at the people behind until they talked to her. Then she smiled and was happy.

8 months, 13 days.   April 1

RUTH has learned to play "pat-a-cake." This was the first time she opened her palms, instead of clapping with her fists. She does this all the time, getting very excited, whether or not one says "pat-a-cake." Ruth claps when one says the verse, and also imitates someone else's clapping.

If we pass a dog or a cat while riding in the car, she turns around, straining to watch it.

Ruth has had a carriage strap for many months, but for the first time today she learned that by pulling the elastic she can make the colored balls make rattling noises.

8 months, 19 days.   April 7

RUTH drank from a cup today, for the first time, without spilling the milk.

I was making sounds—"la-la-la-la"—by rolling my tongue on the roof of my mouth. Ruth, in a few minutes, was imitating my tongue movements and shortly after was able to imitate the sounds I was making, "la-la-la."

Ruth raises her hands above her head when one says, "How big is Ruthie? So big." I never showed her how; her grandmother must have shown her once or twice.

We have a game. I put my hand over my mouth and give an Indian call—"Wa-wa-wa"—and Ruth imitates the sound by putting her fist over her mouth. If I pat her mouth with my hand, she makes the sound.

Ruth likes all the prominent household noises, smiling and trying to get near them. She listens to the garbage disposal, crawls after the vacuum cleaner and climbs on it, adores records, telephone ringing, doorbells, clock chimes, floor waxer, etc. She gets very excited when she sees and hears a motorcycle. Loud noises do not frighten her at all. [*Compare Benjamin's reaction to loud noises throughout his biography.*]

Ruth loves her bath and laughs and hums when her hands are washed under the faucet. She splashes and laughs.

8 months, 22 days.   April 10

RUTH spends many minutes at the window, banging on it, watching cars and people go by.

Her toys are kept in a plastic laundry-basket on the floor. She has just learned to overturn it and take out the toys she wants to play with. She also turns over wastebaskets and tries to eat the contents.

Ruth loves dolls; she holds them, mouths them, pulls their hair, etc.

If Ruth is holding something and wants something else, she puts down the first object and reaches for the second. [*Note 43: This behavior, commonly observed in babies late in the first year, represents a crude ability to organize temporal sequences.*]

Ruth touches all the objects on the table now, throwing them or eating them. She pulls out drawers and explores their contents and opens cabinets, pulling everything out.

When Ruth sees herself in the mirror, she recognizes herself,

laughs, crawls up to the mirror and kisses herself. Last week she
learned to wave bye-bye, at least some of the time, when someone says bye-bye and waves at her. The last few days I have
found her standing and waving at her dolls several times; or
she waves to her image in the mirror.

If my back is toward Ruth and I am standing before a mirror,
she watches my reflection and when she catches my eye, she
laughs and laughs.

Ruth chews on straps—bath strap, bathinet strap, etc., especially the metal buckle. Her favorite pastime is pulling out
her shoe laces and chewing on them. She also tears ribbons off
her stuffed animals and eats them.

9 months, 11 days.   April 30

NOTES from the last two weeks:

Ruth noticed the lock on the car door for the first time and
now spends her time in the car trying to work the knob.

She gave her most elaborate vocal imitation so far when she
said, "Hi, Da-da" today after my husband had said it. [*Note 44:
Such an imitation does not qualify as a spontaneous combination
of words into a sentence since the baby probably hears the
original phrase as a single unit.*]

More examples of imitation. If one whistles, Ruth puckers up
her lips and tries to whistle. If one breathes hard, she makes
panting sounds.

Ruth says "Hi" and waves to pictures of people all the time.

She looks for objects now that go out of sight. She was playing
with a ball—rolling it, creeping after it, etc.—and it went under
her playpen. She saw this, crept to her playpen, lay down, and
looked under the pen to find her ball. If one hides a cookie with
his hand while Ruth is looking, she grabs the hand and pulls it
away from the cookie.

I put a colored object in Ruth's clear plastic glass. Ruth tried
to reach through the side of the glass for the object, knocking
it over. She did this several times, not understanding why she
couldn't get the object that way. (Does not understand trans-

parency.) [*Note 45: See Deborah, Note 84, page 65, and Benjamin, Note 24, page 138. Observe that the baby does not profit from his considerable experience in drinking from transparent containers or from pouring or spilling liquids out of them.*]

Ruth was wary of the doctor's office during her nine-month checkup. She cried and looked frightened when she was put on the table, although she relaxed and did her "tricks" for the nurse. Weighed 20 lb. 6 oz., measured 29½ inches. Did not cry at all when she was vaccinated.

Ruth discovered that blowing into a hollow tube made a funny noise. She does this often, laughing with delight.

She is fascinated by shoes, which she chews on or fills with small toys, and by all types of buttons—buttons on clothing, TV knobs, car knobs, etc. She pushes them in and out and chews on them, too.

Ruth enjoys listening to voices on the telephone and even picks up the receiver to listen to the dial tone.

She saw a little girl a year and a half old. Perhaps Ruth thought she was a doll, because she cried when the child walked and talked.

Ruth is completely unaware (and therefore unafraid) of thunder and lightning. There was a terrible storm the other night, but Ruth went to sleep as usual, completely disregarding the storm.

She is not afraid of animals. She saw a dog and only wanted to touch it.

Ruth invented her *own* game of hide-and-go-seek. She was standing in her playpen. I was feeling tired and rested my head on my arms on the playpen railing, so that my face was hidden from her. Suddenly Ruth knelt down, putting her face against mine, and laughed and laughed. Then she stood up so she couldn't see my face, then knelt again until she could see me and laughed again. She repeated this sequence many, many times.

Ruth discovered her navel today when she was in the bathtub. She was splashing with her hands and her finger touched something. She looked down, stuck her finger in her navel, and laughed. She felt it several times and laughed. [*Note 46: Here we have another example of how the baby comes to know his own body.*]

Ruth is mischievous. If she is creeping and you call her, she looks over her shoulder, gets excited, and creeps very quickly in the other direction. [*Note 47: Again note both the self-awareness and the awareness of others implicit in playful negativism.*] When Ruth goes out of the room I am in, she turns around to make sure I'm still there.

She gets excited and laughs and yells when she sees baby faces on jars and boxes of baby food. She likes to put her face right against the pictures.

9 *months, 12 days.   May 1*

THE TV was on and there was a shot of the audience applauding. Ruth thought they were playing pat-a-cake, I suppose, and she sat there happily clapping her hands.

When someone smokes, Ruth sniffs and sniffs the smoke.

When Ruth is outside and feels the wind, she blows, as if she recognizes the sensation of the wind is like the one she can produce by blowing on her own skin.

Ruth remembers objects, even if they are out of sight. Whenever she sees a scrap of paper on the floor and I cover it with a book or my foot, she takes away the book or my foot and grabs the scrap. If I hide a toy behind a pillow, Ruth moves the pillow away. And she will not be distracted from her search. [*Note 48: Here is one more instance of object conservation.*]

Ruth enjoys games and we play hide-and-seek. I hide behind chairs, tables, etc., making sure some part of me can be seen, and Ruth creeps around until she can see me, yanks at my clothing, and laughs until I turn around.

Ruth knows how to open doors. She pulls on the door stop until the door opens, then pushes the door shut. She can be occupied doing this for several minutes.

She is learning to do things with her "busy box." She can

pull out the drawer, pull open a door (which has a mirror behind it) and push a sliding door (which has a picture behind it). [*Compare age 7 months, 1 day, page 195.*]

I was curious about your described phenomenon of a baby picking up pieces of food with his hand from a tray to eat, but lowering his mouth to it when the food was in a bowl. [*Church, 1961, page 47.*] I tried this several times: If the bowl was large enough, Ruth would hold it steady with one hand and pick up pieces with the other. When the bowl was too small, she just picked it up and turned it upside down and ate the crumbs from the table. For some time, the baby has been picking up bits of solid food and feeding herself, but she does this from a bowl as well as from the table top and she does *not* lower her mouth to the bowl.

Last week Ruth reached for the candy dish on the coffee table. I moved the candy out of her reach. First she tried to climb the table, boosting herself up, to crawl across the table to the candy. When this failed, she finally got down and crept around the table to the other side to get the candy. [*Compare Benjamin, Note 25, page 139.*]

I showed Ruth her father's picture upside down. She looked puzzled and then turned her head as far as she could—about a 45° angle—and then smiled when I righted the picture and she recognized her father. [*Note 49: In this case, Ruth's head-tilting implies a response to inversion of the picture. See Note 39, page 197.*]

9 months, 26 days.   May 15

RUTH *may* be using words. Whenever she sees the picture of dolls in one of her books, she says "dayee," which I think is an imitation of "dolly" which I always say when I show her that book.

Whenever I read the book to Ruth and we come to the picture of flowers, I put my nose against the flowers and sniff, "hmm." Now, whenever Ruth "reads" by herself and comes to the page with the flowers, she bends down, puts her nose and face flat against the book, and sniffs and sniffs and sighs in imitation of what I did (there's actually no aroma at all).

Yesterday, Ruth picked up her cloth doll, took its two hands, and clapped them together, making the doll go pat-a-cake. I was surprised that Ruth knew her hands could easily control the doll's hands. [*Note 50: It is interesting, too, that Ruth recognizes the analogy between her hands and the doll's.*]

Whenever Ruth is eating crumbs, she offers some to whoever is nearby. Now, when Ruth eats, if she's near her book, she turns to the picture of three dolls (she loves turning pages) and puts crumbs on each of the doll's mouths. [*Note 51: Ruth seems to be at the very beginning of dramatic play. She must have a conception that crumbs go in everyone's mouth, not only her own, and she must also recognize the pictured mouths as mouths.*]

Yesterday a dog came over to the playpen and tried to lick Ruth. She screamed with fear (first time she's seemed afraid). [*Note 52: It is probably the dog's movement in approaching Ruth that frightened her, rather than the dog itself. See Shiff, Caviness, and Gibson, 1962.*]

Ruth played in the grass for the first time. She enjoyed pulling out the grass with both hands. First she tried to taste it, but when I wouldn't let her, she was perfectly content to let it drop from her hands and watch it as it fluttered down.

Ruth has only now learned that dropping objects is a game. She leans out of her playpen, holds a toy at arm's length, opens her fingers, and laughs as the toy drops to the floor.

Buzzing noises now seem to bother Ruth, whereas before she never paid them any notice. She screamed when my husband used the electric razor in the same room, and she cried when she heard the buzzer for the door release.

10 months, 1 day.   May 20

RUTH's development during the past two weeks has been in the vocal sphere. She listens to sounds and then repeats them, imitating the first syllable sound. She has also shown an understanding of the words she says.

Cock-a-doodle-doo. When Ruth sees a picture of a rooster in her book or if someone says "cock-a-doodle-doo," Ruth says "Ca-ca."

Cookie. Ruth says "ca-ca" or "ca-ghee" if she wants a cookie. If you ask her if she wants a cookie, she gets very excited and smiles, then looks for the cookie box, and, when she has located it, says "ca-ca."

When Ruth sees a car go by she points to it and says "ca-ca." [*Note 53: Observe that the child can use identical sounds to designate different things. That is, his semantic range is not limited by his phonetic range, any more than his ability to construct sentences, later on, is limited by his knowledge of grammar and syntax. It is not usually until the school years that the child notices the existence of homonyms. One child, for instance, used the vocable "ahmah" to designate both airplanes and his grandmother.*]

Ruth imitates the "c" sound. Although her word for car, cock-a-doodle-doo, and cookie sounds the same for all three, she understands these as different words when someone says them to her. I'm sure she can only imitate the first sound and that's why all of these are "ca-ca."

Mama is "ma-ma," and so is milk. Daddy is "da-da." Down is "da." Dolly is "da-yee" or "da" (for doll).

Ruth understands words very well. She creeps over to the grandfather clock or sees someone's watch and immediately says "dick-dock." If she hears the clock chime, she says "dick-dock." Ruth listens to a watch tick and concentrates intensely.

If you ask Ruth, "Where are the buttons?" she touches the buttons on your or her clothes.

If you ask her, "Where are your teeth?" "Any new teeth?" etc., as soon as she hears the key word she puts her finger in her mouth. [*See Deborah, Note 63, page 42, and Benjamin, 10 months, 9 days, page 136.*]

Ruth, at ten months, has learned the power of "No." She

cannot say no, but she shakes her head in refusal. I don't know where she learned this, but when she has had enough food, or doesn't want to be changed, she just shakes her head, no, and stands pat.

Ruth is eating regular food now, in small pieces, and feeds herself well. She adores meat, fresh banana, and, especially, sponge cake. She can be very full and refuse to take another bite, but if she sees sponge cake, she says "ca-kee," and gets very excited, and stuffs it into her mouth.

Ruth imitates many actions. The other day I blew on a piece of her food to cool it. When I gave it to her, *she* blew on it and then ate it. One day, when Ruth was eating, I pushed the pieces of food from one side of her tray to another, which I thought would make it easier for her to eat. The next minute, Ruth was pushing the food back and forth on the tray.

Ruth is getting her own language. When she wants a drink of water, she makes the sipping or drinking sound with her lips, puckering them up and drawing her breath in. Each time she does this, it is because she wants a drink and when she sees the glass she gets very excited.

Ruth understands quite a few words now. If you ask her, "Where are your socks?" or mention socks, she points to her socks. When Ruth is hungry, she either says "ca-ca" or "mum-mum-mum," which means she wants to eat.

Something most unusual happened. I took Ruth to a friend's apartment and as soon as we got into the elevator, Ruth started to scream. This was the only elevator she has been in except at the doctor's, and I really feel she connected the elevator with the doctor and thought that was where she was going. At her last checkup, Ruth started to cry as soon as she got to the doctor's office, before she even saw the doctor. [*Note 54: Ruth's mother seems to be referring to the ten-month visit to the doctor, which she did not chronicle. See age 11 months, 1 day.*]

Obviously Ruth notices things I don't even realize. Yesterday, she stood up, picked up the telephone, put it to her ear the right way, and said "Hi." She did this several times though no one had ever shown her how. She just watched and imitated. [*Note 55: This is a particularly good example of the kind of learning that occurs without overt practice and without reinforcement.*]

Ruth has just learned to stand up by herself, without holding on to anything. What amazes me is that she has no fear of falling or any idea of her capabilities. She has no idea how to walk, but she tries to run and naturally falls on her face.

New words. Banana is "na-na." This is "dis." Thank you is "ta." Hat is "ha-dd." Ruth imitates the phrase "good girl" and it comes out sounding something like "ga-gee."

I just realized that getting ready for bed is ritual behavior for Ruth. The last three nights have been very hot, so I just put Ruth into her pajamas, leaving off her wear-a-blanket sleeping bag. She couldn't fall asleep and just fussed for hours. In desperation, on the third night I went in and put on her sleeping bag and at that minute, she lay down and went to sleep immediately. I suppose this was part of bedtime, necessary for sleeping.

Ruth's great-grandmother always has cake tidbits in her pocket for Ruth. Now, whenever Ruth sees her, she searches Gram's pocket for the cake.

10 months, 27 days. June 15

RUTH likes to wave and talk to strangers if I am holding her, but if I let anyone else hold her, she cries and reaches out her hands for me.

Her behavior at feeding time may be ritualistic. Ruth grabs her *right* foot when she is eating and rests it on the table top. When I am holding her in my arms giving her the bottle, she holds her right foot in the air—either by grabbing the foot with her right hand or pinching the right leg to grip it and hold it in the air. (She has little black and blue marks from this.)

Perhaps it is too early to tell, but consistently for about a month, Ruth has been using her left hand—I really think this means she'll stay left-handed. If you give her something in her right hand she switches it to her left before she'll play with it or eat it, and if you put food near her right hand she'll go into contortions until her left hand can pick it up. Before this she used either hand.

Ruth's favorite part of the bath is sucking water from the washcloth.

She listens to birds singing and then looks for them. When she spots them she gets very excited.

11 months, 1 day.   June 20

RUTH is suddenly turning pictures of peoples around as though to see the other side of the people. She did not do this before and was satisfied with the front surface of the picture. [*Note 56: We must bear in mind Ruth's earlier attempts to pick up pictured objects (see Note 25, page 186, and 7 months, 1 day, page 193). Most people have to be reminded that a picture is both a two-dimensional representation of something else and a three-dimensional object in its own right. Ruth may indeed be looking for the far side of the people, or she may only be inspecting the back of the picture.*]

Ruth shakes her head to mean "No" or "No more"— consistently! Once she has shaken her head, she refuses to eat another mouthful, to hold still to be dressed or have her face washed, etc.

Ruth's behavior almost imitates a puppy's. (We have none.) She is content to put something in her mouth and creep around. She uses her mouth as a third hand, and carries her toys around by biting them, leaving her hands free to creep.

At Ruth's eleven-month checkup, she started to cry when we went into the elevator and did not stop crying until we left the doctor's office. Height, 29 inches, weight, 22 lb. 4 oz. [*See age 10 months, 1 day, Note 54, page 210.*]

I am realizing that I "see" a different world from that of the young child. For instance, I put sun glasses on one of Ruth's stuffed animals and she screamed with fear. One of the funniest things Ruth ever saw was a plastic bag of candies being "walked" along a table by a visitor. She laughed and laughed. When *I* try to make her laugh, she doesn't think I'm very funny. I never would have thought pushing along a candy bag would be so hilarious.

Ruth must have seen me shake her fruit juice cans at some time because now whenever she sees juice cans or baby-food jars she holds them up and shakes them.

Ruth understands the word "kiss." If I say "Kiss the baby" (in the mirror), she puts her face against the image to kiss it and does the same with pictures if someone says "kiss."

Ruth recognizes and generalizes from pictures to real things. We taught her to smell the flowers in her book—she inhales and then gives a big sigh. Now, whenever she sees flowers—in a book or outside—she smells them.

Ruth's senses are confused—or, at least, *fused*. She loves to hear a watch tick and listens very intently when one holds a watch against her ear. When she wants to hear the ticking she takes the watch and puts it against her *eyes* and listens, concentrating deeply.

I see signs of "learning set" or transfer in Ruth's behavior. She was playing with the dials on the TV. She turns it on and off, softer and louder. When she turns up the volume too high and it blasts, she gets scared and creeps away. [*Note 57: It seems likely that Ruth knew how to regulate the volume but found the noise so frightening that she did not dare approach it and apply her knowledge. Babies at this age "know" that radios and TV sets may take a while to warm up. What they find hard to master is leaving the volume low during the warm-up period, instead of turning it high and having the sound suddenly blast out at full intensity.*]

Her hand hit the side of a little door on the TV which covered more dials. The door had no handle, but after the door opened accidentally she knew she could open it by pressing on the side, prying up the opposite side with her fingers. Since then she pries up the covers on cigarette boxes, silent butlers, etc., with no trouble, even though they have no handles. She has generalized or transferred her learning so now she pries up many box covers by inserting her fingers and pulling up.

11 months, 15 days.   July 4

TODAY Ruth saw a picture in a magazine of a little boy with his back to the reader. I was surprised for she smiled and recognized it as a boy without the facial features being visible. She turned her head to the side as if trying to look at the picture from the side to see the boy's profile. I imagine she still does not react to cues for two-dimensionality. She thinks the boy must be in three dimensions. [*Note 58: Even at later ages this form of picture realism may recur. One two-and-a-half-year-old boy, looking at a profile picture of an unfamiliar make of car, asked, "What does the front look like?" and tried to peer around to see.*] She also rights a magazine if it is given to her upside down—if there are pictures—so I guess her space orientation has become fixed. [*Note 59: But note that "up" in a picture means away from the center of the viewer, as when we look at a picture placed flat on a table top, and not necessarily upright in three-dimensional space. In fact, the child usually looks at pictures laid flat on the floor.*]

This month we started to put Ruth on the potty-chair to train her when we saw signs that she was ready. To give her the idea I made appropriate grunts and thought she would understand. Since that day, every time she creeps into the bathroom or is put on the toilet she makes straining noises—thinks it's a game—but does not connect it at all to having a bowel movement.

Last week I put Ruth into a rocking chair. As soon as she rocked once (accidentally), she got the idea and started rocking back and forth—she *knew* she was controlling the movements of the chair. Since that day she thinks all chairs rock. She sits on her potty-chair or on her car seat holding on to the armrests and rocking her body back and forth.

Ruths says "pa-pa" whenever she sees her grandpa.

She can brush her hair with her brush.

Today Ruth saw a round thermometer outside the window and

said "tick-tock"—she thought it was a clock. [*Note 60: This is a frequent sort of generalization which may extend to quite unclocklike dials, signs, etc.*]

11 months, 3 weeks. July 10

RUTH's vocabulary has increased in the last few weeks. I have found that she *repeats* a word or sound that she has heard and can duplicate them. While at first she said words only in immediate echo of those said to her, now Ruth can say the words she knows in response to an object, spontaneously, not as an imitative response.

Ruth says "kie-kie" when she wants milk. This misnomer is entirely my fault, I realize, as I several times referred to milk as "milkie." It is interesting, I think, how she took only the *last* syllable to refer to milk.

"Owdt" for "out." Ruth says this when I open the door.

"O-pen" for "open." Ruth says this when she wants someone to open a closed door, box, cupboard, etc.

Ruth says "shoos" (shoes), "tsox" (socks), and "cas" (cars)—she does not pronounce her *r*'s.

While Ruth mostly talks in monosyllables, when my husband taught her to say "hubba, hubba," she was able to put these nonsense syllables together the first time she heard the expression.

Within the past few days Ruth repeats "sed done" (sit down) when I tell her to, and "don toch" (don't touch).

Ruth seems to understand a great many things. When I say something about a bath, she repeats "bath" and walks into the bathroom to the tub.

Ruth has been walking since the beginning of August. [*The entries under this date span an entire month.*]

Ruth seems to be pretty well oriented in space. She climbs onto tables and chairs, etc. Turns around and sits down and can turn herself around, hold on, and slip down from the chair, holding on until her feet touch the floor. This is new. Until now, Ruth would have tried to get down head first.

Ruth walks pushing a doll carriage, stops, pats her doll and goes "Ah, ah, baby." (She says this well.) Either she is doing what she sees other children do, or is imitating me.

If Ruth is barefoot and she sees her shoes and socks, she picks up one foot and tries to put on her sock and shoe.

Ruth imitates my gestures. She often takes a diaper and dusts the furniture, floors, etc. [*See Deborah, 9 months, 13 days, page 37.*]

I wonder if Ruth is insensitive to cold. I was at the seashore three weeks ago and took the baby in for the first time. The water was icy, yet Ruth wasn't afraid, and walked right in as though it was the temperature of her bath. [*Note 61: Young children indeed do not seem to mind immersion in water as cool as 50° F. and seem impervious to their own chilling, even after they have begun to turn blue. Nevertheless, they are certainly aware of the iciness of ice and the heat of hot pavements or sand.*] The waves didn't frighten her either. They just made her squeal with delight. It was the same in a big pool.

Ruth is no longer afraid of buzzers. The only thing she cries at now is being alone in a room with the door closed.

When Ruth sees ducks on a lake near our house, she doesn't say "duck," but "quack, quack, quack." If you say to Ruth "duck," she says "quack, quack."

When Ruth sees a dog she says "wow-wow," imitates the dog's panting, and says an excited "ah-ah-ah." She stands back a bit, loves to watch but is hesitant about touching it.

About two weeks ago when I was dressing Ruth, I said "Say 'baby.'" Ruth watched me intently, put her fingers on my lips, then put her fingers on her lips, as if to feel the sound, and said "baby." It was almost what a deaf person would do.

I drew a face on my thumb, wrapped a diaper around it as a hood and Ruth was hysterical with laughter. She touched it and was very excited and thought it hilarious. I doubt that she knew it was my thumb. She saw me draw on it, but when I took off the diaper, she kept looking inside it and shaking it out, saying "ba-bee."

Ruth saw a pigeon the other day and said "quack-quack."

Ruth notices more and more things: she can spot an airplane, stops and listens to the singing of the birds, notices the drops of water on the side of the bathtub, sniffs loudly when she sees flowers and goes over to smell them.

Whenever Ruth wants something and she can't say its name, she points to it and says "dis" (this). She now says "egk" (egg), "tzeeze" (cheese), and "bed" (bread). She says "Mimmi" (Minnie) and "Bob-ba" (Barbara). Ruth loves to feel the wind and when she's riding in the car I find her sticking her hand outside the window.

She has discovered that she can get out of her playpen and crib.

Ruth found a new trick for herself which beats walking. She puts her two hands on a record envelope (is in a creeping position), pushes with her feet and glides along the carpet.

Whenever Ruth sees an infant or a child in a carriage, or even a toddler, she says "Hi, babee."

If one says "Good girl," Ruth tries to repeat it and says "goo ga."

Ruth really has an idea of negation, as I have noted before. If you say "don't" do something or "no," she shakes her head "no," and speaks gibberish in a scolding tone of voice. Which reminds me that, along with all these recognizable words, Ruth has started using expressive jargon.

If I scold Ruth and slap her hand for doing something she shouldn't, she either hits her own hand or mine and says in a scolding tone, "Da-da-da," which means "bad," I think, in addition to "Daddy" and some other things. But while "Da-da" means several things, "Ma-ma" now means only Mother.

When someone brings Ruth home, if she has been visiting, and I'm not at home she walks around the house looking into the rooms and sobs, "Ma-ma." If I'm home, she's all excited. Whenever anyone she doesn't know well lifts her up, she looks at me and cries "Ma-ma."

Ruth doesn't seem puzzled by the telephone any more. She just accepts the voices. In fact, she seems to recognize her grandmother's voice and "replies" to her, repeating words Gram says. For example:

Gram: Ruth, are you going bye-bye?
Ruth: Bye-bye.
Gram: In your car?
Ruth: Ca.
Gram: With Mommy?
Ruth: Ma-ma.
Gram: To get a cookie?
Ruth: Coo-kie.
And so forth, repeating key words.

Ruth walks up and down stairs if someone holds her hands, but she puts only *one* foot on each stair.

If someone is holding Ruth and she hears music, she picks up the person's hand and holds it out in the dance position. She loves to dance.

Ruth always looks for—and finds—her navel when she is being dressed. One day she was playing with a clown that squeaked. The squeak hole must have seemed a navel to Ruth, for she picked up her shirt, and touched hers, touched the clown's, and laughed. [*Note 62: This is a very advanced understanding of the similarities between one's own body and those of others, including effigies.*]

When Ruth's milk spills on her feeding table, she tries to lap it up with her tongue, as a dog would do. She never did this before. She is weaned to the glass.

Ruth understands many things. If you say, "Bring me the lion" (or book or ball or picture, etc.), Ruth brings it to you. If you say, "Let's eat," she says "eat" and walks to her high-chair.

Ruth loves her wading pool with or without water. She likes to walk to it, climb in, sit down and say "Hi" to everyone passing by.

She imitates the sound of the word "pretty" as "peppy." (She does not know what it means.)

If you say "Sh" (be still) to Ruth, she puts her finger over her mouth and goes "Sh" also.

As for food preferences, Ruth much prefers water to milk, green vegetables to meats, especially asparagus and fresh fruit (bananas) and fruit salad (canned). Ruth spits out rice and potatoes (sticky consistency).

At age one year, Ruth weighed 22 lb. 10 oz., and was 29½ inches tall. She didn't cry at the doctor's, but showed mild distrust and didn't enjoy the visit.

1 year, 22 days.   August 10

RUTH laughs whenever she sees anyone putting on lipstick. If you give Ruth the lipstick, she puts it on her lips, imitating the adult's gestures.

She now imitates shaking the index finger in the gesture of "no-no-no." She also says "Don toch" (for "don't touch") in a scolding voice. "Poc pa" is pocketbook. "She-a" is Sheila, the babysitter. "Sa-shin" is sunshine.

Ruth noticed my bare skin in a halter dress and thought it was the funniest thing—as if she was surprised to find skin instead of cloth. She pinched it and touched it so as to be sure. [*Note 63: It is possible that Ruth's surprise came from the unprecedented interruption in the continuity of her mother's costume.*]

Ruth has no fear of height, unfortunately, because she has no idea and is unaware of the height, I think. She continually tries to turn around and slide down backward from her bathinet as she does from a chair. She holds on with her hands and expects her feet to touch the ground, two and a half feet away. [*Note 64: At stake here is not the perception of downward depth but the ability to gauge such depth against her own body.*]

13 months, 1 day.   August 20

RUTH today showed her awareness of glass. She saw a glass-topped table and put one hand on top of it and one under it. She then went and got her doll, put the doll on the table, bent down and looked up through the glass at her doll and laughed. Then she held her doll under the glass, stood up, and looked down through the glass at her doll.

If you say "Smile," Ruth practically shuts her eyes, and gives a wide grin, with her lower teeth sticking out—as if she is imitating smiles she has seen.

Ruth says "op-u" (open) and I am surprised she understands the meaning in different instances—she says this of a door, window, pocketbook, box, lipstick—she repeats her shouts of "open" until she gets you to open whatever it is. Or she does it herself.

Today I was reading Ruth nursery rhymes and she said "Ba-Ba" when I came to the picture of "Ba-Ba, black sheep." I hadn't realized she was ever aware of the picture before.

She points to eyes, nose, hair, and knee on someone else, when asked, but seems to have trouble doing this on herself. In this regard, Ruth still has trouble finding her ear when she tries to listen to a watch. She pokes her cheeks and neck first.

When Ruth wants to chase a ball she brings you the ball to throw.

Ruth does not obey "No" any more. She used to, perhaps because she used to be afraid. She still shakes her head "no," or shakes her index finger "no," or says in a scolding tone "don toch" (don't touch), but she still touches. She is unafraid of a scolding voice or a slapped hand, although she shuts her eyes and grimaces when she thinks I am about to smack her.

Ruth has been able to comply with purely verbal commands for several weeks: "Get me a shoe," etc. She understands words I never made a point of using before.

Ruth does not respond to her name all the time, though she sometimes comes when you call her by name. When shown a picture of herself, she says "ba-bee."

I believe I mentioned "dis?" (this?), one of Ruth's first words. She pointed to things and seemed satisfied when we supplied a name for it.

At thirteen months, Ruth's utterances seem to embody all the operations described on page 4 [*of the editor's instruction sheet*]: naming, verification, imperative, pleasure, contrition, assent, refusal, greeting. She has not yet used self-assertion as she does not yet refer to "me."

Ruth combines a few words. She says "car key" and "mama car." But she does not combine most of her words yet. They are single, unconnected verbalizations. She understands the words "in," "up," "down," "under."

If one hides a toy, Ruth knows it still exists and knows just where it has been hidden. She also engages in detour behavior, goes around obstacles, etc.

Ruth plays "Ring around the rosy" with me. We both fall down. She says "don." Then she stands up and says to me "up." If I don't get up, she takes my arms and tries to pull me.

She sniffs flowers and loves to come over when I am putting on perfume. She sniffs, then tugs at me until I let her smell the bottle.

[*A gap appears in the records between August 20 and October 10 because Ruth's parents were abroad. During this time Ruth stayed with her maternal grandparents in a city on the Eastern seaboard.*]

14 months, 3 weeks.   October 10

RUTH says and understands the following words:

Mamma	neck or necky	appu (apple)
Daddy	hap (happy)	nana (banana)
Nanny (Grandma)	cake	coat
Papa (Grandpa)	puc (cup)	outs (outside)
Elsa (Elsie)	bock (block)	bace (bracelet)
Andy	hi-cha (high-chair)	nice
She-a (Sheila)	buggy	med (meat)
baby	hot	pad (pat-a-cake)
duck	cold	aopane (airplane)
quack-quack	baa-baa (black	puppy
horsie	sheep)	tow (towel)
book	ah-ah-baby (sleep	woof-woof (dog)
ball	or crib)	meow (cat)
bas (bath)	pay (play)	red
shos (shoes)	head	pease (please)

socks
pish (fish)
rip
down
opu (open)
mush (mushroom)
gape (grape)
knee
toe

pocke (pocket and
　pocketbook)
su-shi (sunshine)
Pafp (Philip)
bod (bottle)
don (down)
pin
keys
head (heart)

wol (roll)
petty (pretty)
bed (belt)
shsh (water sound)
hamme (hammer)
again (aspirin)
dis (this)

These are words I remember Ruth saying. I must make clear, though, that she now talks expressive jargon. [*See age 11 months, 3 weeks, page 217.*] She loves the sound of her own voice and she squeals. She perhaps says many other things that are unintelligible to me. Ruth says these words without necessarily seeing the object. She can recognize pictures of objects and talk about them, ask for something, demand something, etc. Ruth speaks in words, not yet in phrases or sentences. If you ask Ruth to get something in another room, she brings it without delay.

Ruth likes to play with pots and pans. She puts them on her head and says "hat" and laughs. One day she found a wooden spoon. She stirred the pots, then "tasted" the spoon, then stirred, tasted, etc. She loves to pretend!

It surprises me that Ruth plays make-believe. If you offer her an imaginary grape, apple, or strawberry, she takes it daintily in her fingers, puts it in her mouth, and licks her lips. She thinks this is funny. (I showed her this only once and she immediately copied my actions.) She also "eats" food from pictures, pottery, etc. She says "gape" (grape) and offers me an imaginary fruit.

Ruth loves to imitate animal sounds—in fact, she calls animals by their cries rather than their names. "Quack-quack" is a duck. Ruth loves this sound and walks around all day saying "quack-quack-quack." When you mention a lion, Ruth growls. If you ask her to talk like a fish, she opens her mouth wide and then closes it like a fish making bubbles.

Ruth loves to play with dolls. She carries them on her shoulders, pats them and says "Ah-baby," lays them down, feeds them with a little bottle, etc. Her favorite pastime is looking through books. She constantly says "book" and brings a book to me to read to her. She turns pages and names all the objects she knows. She first says "Open" and then "hat," "horsie," "box," etc. I am amazed that she understands such words as "open" or "up." If a door, pocketbook, breadbox, book, box, bag, etc. is closed, she will say "open." When she wants to be picked up or when she wants something which is too high for her to reach or when the car goes up a hill or when she climbs on a chair, she says "up, up."

At Ruth's first birthday party we sang "Happy Birthday" many, many times. Finally Ruth joined in with "hap" and mimicked blowing out the candles. Since then, whenever she sees a cake, or a picture of one, she sings "Hap. . . ." Last night, when I lighted the Sabbath candles Ruth started to sing "Hap. . . ." So I imagine "Hap" means (birthday) cake and candles or either one alone also.

Ruth generalizes a great deal. Apple is "appu" but so are a lemon, pear, peach, etc. [*Note 65: It would be interesting to know if Ruth generalized* apple *outside the domain of fruit to include, for instance, light bulbs or rolls of red crepe-paper or rocks, or other things having something in common with apples.*]

Ruth knows how to refer to a purse as "pocke" (pocketbook). She also plays "grown-up." She suspends the purse from her forearm the way I carry mine, and does not grasp the handle. She also carries around her musical top and says "pocke," as it looks somewhat like a purse. Whenever Ruth finds shoes or hats around—anyone's—she tries to put them on. She loves to find our shirts or shorts, etc., and try to wrap them around herself.

Ruth can now say "head," "eyes," "nose," "mouth," "neck," "toes," and she can point to her own body parts (or anyone else's, or in a picture) when these are named. She can also point to her teeth, arm, hand, foot, belly button, and nails, although she can't say these words yet.

Ruth has a sense of humor, I think. She says "hat" and knows what a hat is. Sometimes she puts a pillow on her head, laughs, goes to the mirror, and says "hat."

Ruth does not dance any more, even to her favorite records. It's as if she has forgotten how to dance. Nevertheless, she walks around humming all the time, imitating animals in a sing-song voice, etc.

Ruth's grandmother taught her, if she hurt herself on an object, to hit the object and say "da-da." Now, I often find Ruth crying or rubbing some part of her body and hitting something and saying "da-da-da" in a scolding voice.

Ruth makes a fist and knocks on doors that are closed and says "knock, knock."

During the six weeks that she spent with my parents, Ruth did not see a "busy-box." Yet the minute she saw hers again she was able to do all the tasks that she had been unable to do six weeks before. It was, I think, "readiness," certainly not specific experience. [*Note 66: Readiness does not have to be a choice between maturation and highly specific learning. Ruth's intervening general experience could have taught her to perform the new busy-box tasks.*]

Ruth's tastes in foods surprise me. She adores sharp cheddar cheese, sucking a lemon, etc.

She walks around with a cloth "dusting" the furniture and "drying" pots and pans.

When Ruth finds a handkerchief, she makes believe she is blowing her nose (she actually blew her nose once and was very surprised; she couldn't do it again).

Ruth pushes her doll carriage. Yesterday it tipped over on its side, so she turned a wheel, watching it spin around. Then she gripped the wheel with both hands and used it as a steering wheel.

Ruth has a large wicker toy box with a hinged cover. She tried to open the top two or three times and each time it fell shut and hurt her. Finally she lifted the top with two hands and moved it past the halfway point and it stayed open. Now she can open it without trouble.

She always says "hot" before she tastes something or goes near the stove or into the bathtub, but I think "hot" also means cold—ice cream is "hot," too. [*Note 67: Confusion of opposites is very common in the speech of toddlers, and is not unheard of in adult speech, especially when the speaker is distracted or tired or under pressure.*]

Ruth says "b'ush" which means either comb or brush, and she brushes her own and her dolls' hair.

The other day Ruth wanted a doll which was on the quilt of my bed—way out of her reach. She said, "Doll," asking me to give it to her (I didn't). Then she tried to climb on the bed (she couldn't), so she pulled the quilt toward her until she could reach the doll. [*Note 68: It is likely that Ruth discovered the relationship between movement of the quilt and movement of the doll through her efforts to climb onto the bed. This kind of operation was first recorded by Piaget and has been incorporated by Uzgiris and Hunt (1964) into their baby scale.*]

Ruth cannot yet eat with a spoon. The best she can do is pick up pieces of food with her fingers, put these on a spoon, and sometimes manage to get the spoon (and food) into her mouth.

I brought Ruth a doll from Spain, which has a large skirt and a head at both ends. It took about fifteen minutes before Ruth saw both heads and she could turn it upside down, back and forth.

She likes to play "catch." She retrieves the ball if you throw it to her. She can now let it go from her grasp, too, and throw it with some force.

Ruth loves clocks and watches (both "tick-tocks") and carries them around. This week she put a watch on her wrist and said "bace" (bracelet). [*Note 69: This observation seems to imply that the name of the object changes (in this case from "tick-tock" to "bace") according to its function.*]

Ruth adores babies (even ones that are older than she) and she screams, "Ba-bee!"

Now Ruth understands and follows fairly complicated directions: for example, just now she was walking around with a covered dish. She followed these instructions: 1) Put the dish on the table. 2) Get the cover. 3) Put the cover on the dish. She understood everything. I didn't even gesture.

Ruth now knows her own feet. She sat in her highchair and saw her feet over the tray. She knows she can control her feet: she raises them up past the tray edge and says "toes" (even though they look strange from that angle).

Ruth makes associations to the names of people she knows. She goes to the closet to Pa's coat and says "Coat, Pa-Pa." When you say "Barbara," Ruth repeats "Bob-ra" and says "Me" (Mel—Barbara's husband). If you say "Steven," Ruth puts her finger over her lips and says "Shh" (because when Ruth was staying with my parents, whenever she cried, she was told, "Shh, Steven is sleeping"). If you say "Nanny" (Gram), Ruth says "cake," because Gram gives her cake every time she sees her. If you say "cheese," Ruth says "Pa," because Pa always is eating cheese.

Throwing kisses and waving "Bye" are favorite pastimes.

The other day I found Ruth trying to put a hairpin in her hair.

For some reason Ruth cries in elevators. I thought this was because she knew she was going to the doctor's [*as noted at age 10 months, 1 day, page 210*]. However, she cries when we leave the doctor's in the elevator, too. She screams "Ope" (open) as if she is afraid of being closed in—claustrophobia in some form? She also cries "Ope" if one closes the door of a room she is in, whether or not she has company in the room.

Ruth enjoys pulling people's glasses off ("gasse") and putting them on herself. Then she walks to the mirror to see how she looks.

The mirror intrigues her. Whenever you dress her, put a bow in her hair, put a hat on her, etc., she walks over to the mirror to see herself. There's no doubt she knows who it is in the mirror. She smiles and turns from side to side (she must have seen someone do this) in front of the mirror to see herself from all angles.

On the last visit to the doctor (fourteen months) Ruth cried the minute she entered the examining room. A few days ago,

the doctor made a house call to check her, and she screamed
the second she saw him, even though he was in a regular business suit in her own home. Ruth must have recognized his face
or voice.

My mother must have told Ruth to say "Ach" when she was
having a bowel movement. For a few days when Ruth had a
bowel movement in her diaper, she'd say "Ach." One day she
said "Ach" but she was clean so I put her on the toidy. She had
a bowel movement there, pointed to it, and said "Ach." Since
then she tells me "Ach," I put her on, and nothing happens. It
has become a game, and Ruth knows how to get my attention.

Trying to discipline Ruth often turns into a joke. I just want
to give her an idea of what "No" means. First I tried hitting
her hand and saying "No" if she did something she was not
allowed to do. She'd then slap her own hand and say "Pad"
(pat-a-cake). Even when the slap was hard enough to hurt, she
felt that this was a game. So I tried scolding her and putting
her in the corner for a minute. However, after she was in the
corner once, she took her toys there to play. Now this is also a
game. She purposely does something that isn't permitted—
making sure I see her—then marches off to the corner, looks
over at me, sees my disapproval, comes over and puts her head
in my lap or tries to hug me. This, too, is like a ritual game by
now. Ruth, I think, likes the attention of a reprimand. She always comes over to show me that she has torn up magazines or
chewed the paper because I scold her when she does this. If
I pretend not to notice, she nudges me. One afternoon she did
this and I took the paper away. She then took a piece of imaginary paper and made believe she was eating it. She already enjoys the sport of teasing. [*Note 70: Already, barely out of
infancy, Ruth can turn the manipulation of emotions into a
game.*]

When we returned from our trip, Ruth greeted us with
"Mamma" and "Daddy" immediately, with no reserve or hesitation. She ran to us and hugged us (fourteen and a half months
old). But then she wouldn't let us leave the room. Now she
cries if we leave the house and in general cries much more easily

than before when frustrated, and screams if she can't have her way. I find her much more easily upset than before our trip and more clinging and affectionate. She is constantly hugging our legs or asking us to pick her up. The first night we were home, she kept saying "Mamma, Daddy, Mamma, Daddy, etc." in her sleep. I really think the separation affected her greatly.

The day we came back from Europe was Ruth's first time home in six weeks. For an hour she just walked around taking inventory, as it were. She went from room to room checking to see if everything was the same and if everything was in its proper place. She didn't touch anything but her eyes took in every piece of furniture, every picture, every knickknack—she would bend down to see what was on the shelf of the end tables, look on the fireplace mantel for the candlesticks, etc.

14 months, 26 days to 16 months, 16 days.
October 15–December 5

RUTH loves to "read" books. She has several stories memorized. If you read to her and skip a page, she fills in the missing words and turns back to the skipped page. She supplies the motions for the story (she points if the boy in the story points, etc.).

Ruth names animals and makes animal sounds. She recognizes a dog (any kind) in any book and says "doggie" (it is surprising to me that she can see an entirely new dog picture and label it properly). Examples of animals, animal sounds, and associated terms: "Horsie—gallop—neigh-neigh." "Pig-oink." "Goat—billy—beard." "Cat—meow." "Puppy—doggie—woof-woof." "Bunny—carrot." "Frog—hop—Dick." (Dick gave Ruth a stuffed frog.) "Deer." "Duck—quack-quack." "Chickie—peck-peck—egg." "Birdie—tweet" (or hums). She flaps her arms and hands in imitation of wings.

Ruth has a book about a boy who can't name objects but knows their sounds. When I read *Johnny says*, Ruth gives Johnny's lines: *Airplane*—"Z-z-z" (Ruth pretends she is holding a toy airplane and flies it as Johnny does). *Hammer*—"Bang, bang" (Ruth pretends she is hammering with her fist as Johnny does). *Cow*—"Moo-moo." *Train*—"Toot-toot."

Ruth seems to have a kind of word readiness now. If you read or say a new word once or twice, she mimics the word (or action) and remembers it—it becomes part of her vocabulary or her repertory of behavior.

Ruth participates empathically in many actions. She saw us learning the twist and in a few seconds she was twisting too.

Ruth knows how to imitate songs. She says "Papa" if she wants me to sing *Papa, Won't You Dance with Me,* "Baby" for *Baby Face,* "Tootie" for *Toot, Toot, Tootsie, Goodbye,* and "Sunshine" for *Oh, Let the Sunshine In.*

Ruth knows parts of songs and poems. She brings her nursery rhyme book to me and says "London" and then turns to the page with the poem and picture of *London Bridge.* When I come to the next stanza she says "Keys" for *Take the keys and lock her up.* When I sing one popular song of the Twenties, Ruth joins in with key words.

Ruth likes to dress herself. She puts on her own hat and can get one arm into her coat sleeve. One day when I was putting on Ruth's slippers, I said, "push, push" and she repeated "push, push." Now every time I put on her slippers, shoes, or mittens, she yells, "Push!"

I have found myself jumping to conclusions and assuming Ruth perceives things the way I do. Two examples:

(1) Ruth pinched her finger in a door and I told her to come to Mommy and I would kiss it to make it feel better. She held out her finger to be kissed. The next time she hurt her finger she immediately ran to me and held out her finger to be kissed— I thought she remembered and understood. The next day she got a bump on the head and came running to me—with her *finger* held out for me to kiss. It was just a ritual.

(2) Ruth usually says "please" when she wants something. When she doesn't say it, I ask her, "What do you say?" and she replies "please." One day someone asked Ruth how she was. Ruth usually replies "Fine," but this time she didn't answer, so

I said, "What do you say, Ruth?" and she replied "Please." This shows that "please" has no meaning for Ruth as yet, that this is just a ritual, a conditioned response as it were. I was simply reinforcing "please" and the signal for "please" became "what do you say?"

When Ruth has the hiccups she announces "hiccups," and when she coughs she says "coughing."

When Ruth had a cold I gave her medicine just before her meals. I must have asked her if she was hungry, for now whenever she sees medicine she announces "hungry." This shows how you form a child's reality and how easily they can misunderstand you. Hungry to Ruth now refers to medicine, rather than the desire to eat. [*Note 71: The remarkable thing is how rare such deviant associations are.*]

Ruth says "paper" and "pencil" and "pen." If she finds a pencil she asks for "paper," and if she finds paper she asks for "pen" and says "write."

Ruth can say a great many things now, but her pronunciation is terrible, although consistent. She pronounces *l* as *y* ("yike" for "like"), *r* as *b* ("bite" for "write"), *th* as *s* ("bas" for "bath"), *f* as *p* ("pish" for "fish").

Ruth has added the following words to her vocabulary and uses them appropriately:

meat	coat	picture	wipe
hamburger	hat	hug	bottle
napkin	mittens	kiss	bad
wash	pot	boy	sweep
beef	spoon	girl	towel
toys	raisin	tear	bath
beads	robe	hanger	yes
pin	leaf	book	knife
bracelet	hair	belt	cook
ring	nails	nice	book
picture	ah-ah-baby	broom	up
pumpkin	monkey	sweep	down
peas	bear	push	candy

bow	bone	toidy	out
shoes	mirror	closet	dress
socks	bobby (pin)	bicycle	cold
stockings	brush	grape	no
pants	powder	diaper	tie
overalls	money	house	fan
peek	mimic	bagel	birdie
blouse	good girl	fuzzy	door
sweater	big lady	sour	beans
broke	like it	light	sip
good	scissors	zipper	pretty
highchair	orange	piano	suitcase
lunch	dish	heart	fingers
eat	water	flower	nails
glass	milk	breakfast	
glasses	messy	clock	
egg	cheese	dust	

Peep (for Little Bo-Peep)
Panaca (Chanukah—any resemblance is purely coincidental)

Ruth labels round objects as either "ball" or "apple." She called a [*mercury?*] thermometer a "tick-tock," perhaps because of the numerals. [*See Note 60, page 215.*]

Ruth takes a pot and spoon and stirs and tastes and says "cooking." She pretends there is food in the pot, or puts cookies or raisins in if she finds them.

When Ruth finishes her glass or dish of food she says "All gone."

Ruth likes to dress up. She holds out her skirt and says "mirror." She stands and pirouettes before the mirror.

When she sees either a cup or a percolator or a can of coffee she says, "Coffee, Daddy." When you mention a story, Ruth immediately goes and fetches the correct book.

Ruth says "hot" when she sees cigarettes or matches (or pictures of them). She says "eight" if one asks her how many teeth she has and "ten" if one asks her how many toes or fingers she has. (We taught her these answers. She doesn't really understand. If you asked her how many hands she has, she could say "eight" just as easily as "two.")

One day I said "one" for some reason and Ruth replied "two, three" out of nowhere. I don't remember ever counting to her. Someone asked Ruthie how old she was and I jokingly whispered to her, "Say one." Ruth replied, "Two." I repeated, "No, say one" and Ruth reiterated "Two." She must have memorized these words as a sequence, so that my saying "one" provoked her to follow with "two."

When Ruth sees a picture of a cuckoo clock she chimes, "Coo-coo."

As in your notes [*Ruth's mother is referring to the editor's instructions*], when Ruth tries to look through a cardboard tube she holds it between her eyes—the "Cyclops effect." [*Note 72: Between the ages of one and two, the baby's awareness of his own body has evolved to the point where looking through a tube is a possible form of action, but he experiences his visual field as a unitary whole centered somewhere around the bridge of his nose. Even though the baby may be able to tell you that he has two eyes, functionally they are a Cyclopian unit. See Church (1961, pages 47ff).*]

Ruth uses such exclamations as "Oh boy" or "Wow." She walks her dolls in the buggy, saying "Ah-ah-baby." She also pretends to feed her dolls, hugs and kisses them, puts them to bed.

Ruth now says "happy" (for happy birthday) whenever she sees a cake, candles, candlesticks, or a lighted match.

Ruth's Grandpa gives her a horsie-back ride now and then, getting down on all fours. Whenever I kneel, looking for something, Ruth climbs on my back and yells "horsie." Sometimes *she* gets on all fours and yells "horsie."

This brings another incident to mind. Ruth was playing with two small cans of fruit. She called them "cans" and tried to put one on top of the other; then she shouted "blocks, blocks" (because of their function, I assume); then she became very excited and repeated "horsie, horsie." Perhaps it seemed to her the same as people getting on top of one another for a horsie-back ride.

Whenever Ruth's shoe comes untied she goes to an adult and says, "Tie, please."

It is amazing how a child as young as Ruth (now sixteen months) tries to control situations. When it is her bedtime and I get her ready for bed she gets very affectionate. When I carry her over to the crib she hugs and kisses me (naturally, I hug her and hold her longer). Ruth then stops hugging until I start to put her in the crib. Suddenly she starts hugging again. I guess she realizes that if she is affectionate she will be held for a few minutes longer and have bedtime postponed by that much. Ruth also uses the excuse of "water" before she goes to sleep if she wants attention. The other day, when I put on my coat to go out, Ruth went up to the *new* baby-sitter and hugged and hugged her. She wouldn't even look at me when I talked to her. It's as though she wanted to make me jealous and punish me for leaving her.

Ruth enjoys trying to get out of sight and yelling "Hide." She wants to be discovered and squeals until she is found. [*Note 73: Ruth's squealing can be attributed to the tension associated with waiting eagerly to be found, and also to the fact that not much before age four does the child realize that hiding requires that one be inaudible as well as invisible.*]

Ruth must observe actions, even when she seems oblivious. One day she pulled a hanky out of a guest's pocket and blew her nose, then put it back in the pocket.

She cries when she is scolded for doing something she is not permitted to do. However, she laughs and laughs if she is scolded jokingly or if I give her a glance of mock despair.

Ruth has tried tantrums to get her way. She lies on the floor and cries. If I ignore her and leave the room she stops crying, comes to the room I am in, lies on the floor and screams. I go into another room and she follows. When she discovers she cannot get any attention this way, she comes over to me, puts her head in my lap and puts her arms around my legs and says "hug."

Ruth is afraid of: pumpkins [*jack-o'-lanterns?*], fur, doodles of faces, masks.

Ruth has learned that people think it is cute for her to kiss them, and now she spends a great deal of time throwing kisses at pictures, people passing by, etc.

When someone comes with a pocketbook Ruth says "pocke" and puts the handle over her arm. She brings it to me and says, "Open, please." Then she finds the wallet and brings it to me and says, "Money, open." She plays with the contents, then says, "Close." Then she puts the purse on her arm and walks around. If you ask Ruth where she is going she answers "Out" or "Bye-bye."

Ruthie has her own private jokes which she can repeat over and over. I say to her every morning, "What would you like for breakfast?" and she says "Apples." She thinks this is the funniest thing when I say that apples aren't for breakfast but for lunch or dinner.

Ruth is ticklish and if anyone tickles her she shouts "tickle, tickle."

She has three dolls—each with its own name which she never mixes up. If I ask her to get Cathy, she brings Cathy, not the other two; and if Ruth asks for Nancy at bedtime she gets very annoyed if you bring her the wrong doll.

It is interesting that Ruth can play the emotional roles of others. A child of two named June visited us last week and spent the day crying. Now, Ruth, either spontaneously or on request, starts to sham-cry—eyes closed, sobbing, etc. Then she looks very pleased with herself and shouts, "June, June." She thinks this is great fun. If you tell Ruth to laugh, she goes, "Ha-ha-ha-ha" (learned from a story). If you ask her to smile, she grins sheepishly. A related episode: a few days ago, she fell off a chair and banged her head, and I comforted her. She went to the chair and pretended to fall off, rolling on the floor, and ran to me to be comforted again. [*Note 74: See an account of a similar bit of behavior in Church (1961), page 60.*]

Ruth seems to distinguish people clearly in terms of age and sex—much to my surprise. Whenever she sees pictures in a book or sees people on the street she identifies them as boy, man (or daddy), girl, lady (or mommy). She never makes a mistake. [*Note 75: But I have known slightly older children to ask, for instance, about women with a somewhat masculine style, "Why is that man wearing a dress?"*]

RITUALS: Ruth must have a drink of water while she is in her crib before she will go to sleep. She will not sit on the toidy unless she has a book. She must wear her robe when she gets up in the morning. I guess you could call it a ritual that whenever she sits on a chair in the living room she says, "Big lady."

When Ruth wants you to turn the page of her book she says "up" instead of "turn" (which is understandable).

EVIDENCE OF LEARNING AND MEMORY: When Ruth sees any of our friends who have babies, she says, "Baby, baby," whether or not the baby is present. Ruth recognizes policemen. There is one in her book and she can say "policeman." Whenever we get to Ruth's grandmother's street, she screams "Nana house." Whenever Ruth sees a lemon she says "sour" (she tasted one once). If a picture is upside down, she rights it immediately.

Ruth both names and points to these parts of her body:

head	hair	neck	forehead (doesn't
eyes	nose	mouth	say this yet)
knees	feet	toes	nails
arms	hand	fingers	belly button

tuchis (Yiddish word for buttocks, pronounced "tooshy" in baby talk)

Last night when she was taking a bath and playing with the washcloth, I told her to wash her face, knee, other knee, etc., and she really scrubbed herself.

When Ruth finishes eating she shoves her food from the tray to the floor. I have scolded her a few times, calling her messy. So now whenever she throws food on the floor she says, "No, no, messy."

Ruth says "beads" whenever she sees pearls and I thought it

was a synonym for necklace. Today she brought me her moccasin, which has bead trimming, and Ruth said "beads."

Ruth sometimes calls her father and me "honey," I suppose because she hears us call each other "honey." We call her "honey." If we ask her what Mommy or Daddy calls her, Ruth says "honey" or "precious."

Ruth's new skills seem to be all-encompassing. For example, she learned to tear paper. Now she goes around tearing everything she can get her hands on—her favorite books, photographs, etc.—and proudly shouts, "tear, tear."

Ruth understands the concept of *more*. Whenever she drinks a glass of water and finishes it—or I take it away—she says "more." Also, when she finishes a glass or dish of food she says, "No more."

Ruth now tries to control her eyelids. She walks around saying, "Open, close" and tries to open and shut her eyes at will.

Today she was chewing on a bone and I gave her another one. Out of the blue she held them up and said "two." Later this afternoon, she was playing with two balls and again announced "two." She seems to have gotten the concept of two somehow, although there is no evidence that she even understands the concept of one yet.

Ruth says her own name and realizes, I think, that this name refers to herself. She stands before a mirror and says "Ruthie," and if someone asks "Who wants to go bye-bye?" or "What is your name?" or something similar, she points to herself and says "Ruthie."

Ruth seems to be internalizing some restrictions, almost as if she were getting a conscience. I do not have to reprimand her or tell her repeatedly what she can't touch. She walks around saying "No-no" or "Not" (Do not touch) and shaking her finger at *all* the objects she may not touch. She enjoys this game—perhaps because of my approval, perhaps because she is proud of herself for remembering. She says "No" in a scolding voice (like mine?) and she does this when I am near. This does not mean that she is consistent or has learned the things she is not permitted. If she finds a dish of candy she says "No," but at the same time she is grabbing a candy to eat. Saying "No" seems to be a way of showing off.

I have another example of Ruth's internalizing. One day she did something she was not supposed to do and I told her to stand in the corner. A few days later she did the same thing and I scolded her. I was busy and let the matter drop. Ruth pulled at my skirt and became very upset and yelled "cor-cor" (corner) and tried to pull me near the corner. She wanted me to put her in the corner.

Ruth seems to have toilet-trained herself. When she was staying with my parents (thirteen to fourteen and a half months), my mother gave Ruth a label for bowel movement ("Ach"). Now, whenever Ruth has to have a bowel movement she announces "Ach" and goes to the bathroom door and waits for me. When she's had her bowel movement she says "Good girl" and then "Off." Lately she has announced "Sis" when she has to urinate. When she wakes up with a bowel movement in her diaper she looks amused and says "Ach—toidy."

Ruth seems to be entering a "copy cat" or imitative stage. She saw a little girl sucking her fingers, glued her eyes on the little girl, and sucked the same two fingers. When the little girl cried, Ruth cried. When the little girl squealed, Ruthie squealed, and when the little girl screamed "Mama," Ruth screamed "Mama" too. Empathy?

Signs of time orientation: Ruth understands that she must wait for certain things—for example, if she wants a cookie, I say she may have it *after* she drinks her milk, and she drinks her milk quickly to get the cookie. I often tell Ruth she must nap before going outside. As soon as she wakes up she says, "Out, out."

Ruth learned by herself how to open a zipper. One day this week I found she had unzipped her sleeping bag and had gotten out of it.

Ruth doesn't really understand how some things work. She turns on her mechanical monkey, or the TV at full volume, and then runs in fear to get me to stop it. [*See Note 57, page 213.*]

She is aware that certain features come in twos—knees, ears, eyes, etc. She points to one when asked where her knee is, and points to her other knee when asked where the other knee is, etc.

Ruth enjoys imitating animal sounds and actions—growls like a lion, gets down on all fours like a horse, etc.—role playing.

Playful negativism: Ruth has just begun to run away when I call her to dress her or put her to bed. Occasionally when I ask if she wants more food, she answers "No" with an emphatic shake of her head—she may or may not eat more.

Ruth recognizes people's pictures in our wedding album— Mommy, Daddy, relatives and friends. She can point to them when you ask her where they are. She seems to recognize them inverted, but immediately rights them. She also recognizes her own picture, in any orientation, and says "Ruthie."

Ruth seems to perceive the action as well as the objects in magazine pictures. For example, she said to me, "Boys—peek out door" to describe boys looking out a door at Christmas decorations. She also says "Ah-ah-baby" when she sees pictures of babies sleeping, or "Splash—bath—water" when she sees a picture of anyone in a bathtub or swimming.

Ruth tries to put large blocks in small blocks—no sign of size relationship yet.

Contrary to the observation guide, Ruth could not [*yet*] put my coffee pot together correctly. [*Note 76: In a sample of eleven babies between the ages of 1 year, 3 days and 2 years, only three (ages 1:0:13, 1:7:3, and 1:10:29) did not completely disassemble and reassemble a double-boiler-like lunch pail.*]

Ruth does seem to remember things past and to anticipate things in the future. For example, she found a broken giraffe which I had put away about two months ago, and she said "neck," meaning long neck, I think. Asks a friend for her "baby," or says the friend's name when she sees a carriage, etc. Also, Ruth goes to the window late in the afternoon and says "Daddy," or asks me for a bath.

Ruth is on a definite schedule and my baby-sitters say that she adheres to it faithfully. She gets up in the morning and says "breakfast"; at around 10 A.M. she puts her doll and dog in the crib and says "Ah-ah-baby" or climbs on her toy box (at the edge of the crib). At lunchtime she announces "eat," and later in the afternoon she announces "Ah-ah-baby" again. Often in the afternoon she goes to the door or brings her coat to me and says "Out" or "Car." She says "Up—highchair" when she sees me getting her supper ready, and around 7 P.M. she lays her head on our lap, a chair, etc., to show she is ready for bed. [*Note 77: Observe that not all these behaviors have to be regulated by an internal clock, but may also be in response to environmental cues.*]

16 months, 16 days.   December 5

WHEN Ruth stopped doing something she was not allowed to do, I used to tell her she was a good girl. Now she has the wrong idea. She starts doing forbidden things, then stops herself and proudly says "Good girl." She thinks she's being great as long as she stops herself. Doing these forbidden things has, to her, become a way of getting praise.

Before Ruth will go to sleep at night she must say "Nighty-night. Sleep tight" and throw a kiss. It has become part of the bedtime routine for her.

Ruth looked at one of my bridge books and pointed to a picture of a man. I said, "That's Goren." Now, whenever she sees a picture of Goren—on pamphlets, etc.—she announces, "Goren."

Function seems more important than form for Ruth—function determines what an object is. For example, she put her hand in my pocket and said "Mitten." She put a milk cover on her head and said "Hat." When she washes her hands she calls a towel a "towel," but when she pretends to wipe or blow her nose on the same towel, it's a "hanky." A scarf around her neck is called a "necklace." [*Note 78: These observations point to the important principle that semantic generalization can proceed along dimensions which the adult would not ordinarily antici-pate. Not only may an object change verbal identity as it*

*changes functions, but an old name may be applied to a new
object, as when Ruth called a thermometer a "tick-tock."*]

Ruth imitates many strange words, usually said singly—
"diarrhea," "macaroni"—but everyday conversation must just be
absorbed into her reality without outward signs. One day she
was playing with a drawer. Suddenly, she yelled "Caught"
(proper tense), and her arm was indeed caught. I never even
remember using such a word and she had never said it before,
but when the opportunity arose, she had the correct word
stored away. Another day she pulled my skirt and said "Broke."
In her hand was a piece of glass from a soda bottle she had just
broken.

Ruth makes believe all the time. She gives her horse imaginary
sugar, she feeds her dolls imaginary food, she brushes her teeth
with an imaginary toothbrush, etc. If you ask her to carry an
imaginary doll, she takes the doll tenderly.

Ruth played with children three or four times in the space
of a few weeks and the difference from one time to the next was
amazing. One day Missy, age two, came over to our house. My
in-laws were here and thought Ruth's possessiveness was cute—
I think Ruth sensed this and was encouraged by it. She wouldn't
let Missy touch any of her toys. She would scream or have a
tantrum and yell, "No, Ruthie's!" Ruth's toys were only de-
sirable to her when Missy wanted to play with them. Ruth kept
running to her family to seek "justice" and have her toys
returned. A few days later there was no commotion when Missy
came to play with Ruth. They were left alone and, since there
was no one for Ruth to run to for support, they played nicely
(though not together). They did talk to each other: "House, man,
car," etc. (Missy is a shy, timid child.) Another day Jeff, age
two, came over. Jeff was not so timid. He chose a book and a
piano to play with. When Ruth approached to get her toys,
he shielded them and screamed and hollered. Ruth was afraid
of him—she mimicked his screaming from a distance, but got
herself another toy to play with. One day I took Ruth over to
Laurie's (age thirteen months) house. Ruth didn't take her toys
and was happy wandering about until Laurie took Ruth's snow-

suit. Ruth ran over to me screaming and grabbed it away—"No, Ruthie's!" To keep peace, someone gave Ruth Laurie's snowsuit to play with. Ruth took it over to Laurie and tried to grab her own snowsuit. She seems to know what is hers and is very possessive, but she isn't so aggressive with someone else's toys. Another example of Ruth's ideas of ownership was shown when my sister was a house guest. Whenever Ruth saw my sister wearing my robe, slippers, coat, or scarf, she would yell, "No, Mama's!" and try to pull it away.

Ruth's self-image is becoming more elaborate. If one says, "Where is Ruthie?" or "What's your name?" etc., Ruth points to herself and says, "Me Ruthie Stern." She always recognizes photographs of herself.

Ruth tries to connect names to colors. Whenever she sees a traffic light, she says, "Light—color—red" or "Color—green," although she's only right some of the time. These are just lucky guesses. She does correctly identify and name the color pink. Ruth counts, although she has her own system—"1-2-3-6-9-10."

Ruth does seem to know how some things work. One day she discovered a string to make her "talking" doll work. She pulled it and said, "Mama, Mama." That's what she thought the doll said, for some reason, although the doll doesn't say Mama. When the doll says, "Please carry me," Ruth carries her around, and when it says, "I hurt myself," Ruth bangs her head on a wall or chair and pretends to cry. Somewhere she must have learned the meaning of "hurt."

One morning, Ruth noticed some drops of orange juice on her feeding tray. She seemed upset and said, "Orange fell down."

One night Ruth said "Kiss." (Until now, she mostly threw kisses.) She put her arms around my head and wanted to kiss me on the lips. I tried to turn my head, but she said "lips" and tried to hold my face still to kiss me on the lips. I suppose that is how she thinks one should kiss—she must watch my husband kiss me and is trying to imitate.

Ruth says "toys," "children," "people." She seems to like to lump objects together under one name. "Food" and "clothes" are other examples.

It's amazing how a child can remember certain things. I named Ruth's three dolls Cathy, Nancy, and Daisy. One day she called one Peggy instead of Nancy and I couldn't understand this. A few days later I heard the baby-sitter refer to Ruth's dolls by three other names. For several weeks Ruth has been referring to her dolls by the names I gave them when I am present, and by the names the sitter gave them when the sitter is present. Each doll has two or perhaps three names, which Ruth simply accepts.

17–18 months.   January

WHEN Ruth's father was on a business trip for five days, she seemed to be lonesome. She kept repeating "Miss. Miss Daddy." She would go to the window at the time of his usual arrival and wait at the door. At bedtime, she called for her Daddy over and over and cried because she didn't want to go to sleep without Daddy. When he got home, she only wanted Daddy to hold her, put her to sleep, etc. It was the first time he has been away that she really seemed to notice his absence.

Ruth seems to be getting a conscience—*partly*. She is not allowed to eat candy. Somehow, she got two candies from the dish (I was in another room). She could have eaten the candy there and I wouldn't have known but instead she came into the kitchen with the candy and said, "No-no." She then quickly put the candy in her mouth. It was interesting that while she ate the forbidden candy, she didn't do it behind my back, so to speak.

A combination of words that appeared a week or two ago was "Ruthie do." One day I was feeding her. She hit my hand, grabbed away the spoon and said, "No-no, Mommy. Ruthie do."

Another example of function overruling form: Ruthie puts a pencil or a stick in her mouth and says "cigar" or "pipe."

Ruth puts her books and toys in her toy chest and says "Neat. Lydia" (the woman who cleans).

Space must look different and exciting to Ruth when she is

upside down. She loves it when she stands with her head on the floor between her legs or when her father holds her upside down: "More, more."

Whenever Ruth sees me undressed she points to my breasts and says "hands," and thinks this is very funny. I wonder why she thinks of them as hands.

When you ask Ruth where her ear is she points to one of them and then says, "Other." Her hand travels across her face until she finds the other ear. (The same with her eyes.) She knows which finger is her thumb and can say "thumb."

Ruth found an emery board. She stuck out her tongue, opened her mouth, put the emery in her mouth and said, "Ah, Docka Yehma." (Dr. Lehman—she still has trouble with *l*.) She apparently saw it as a tongue depressor.

Ruth was playing with a muffin tin. She said "Light—green, red." The arrangement of cup holes must have reminded her of traffic lights. When she turned the tin upside down, she said "pucs" (cups).

Ruth has added phrases, as well as single words, to her vocabulary: "glass of water," "not in mouth" (which she says to scold herself when she has put something in her mouth she knows she shouldn't), "money to store—to buy apples," "bake a cake."

She likes to hear herself talk. Even in the middle of the night we hear her repeating names of people she knows out loud over and over: [*people's names*], "go bye-bye," etc. [*Note 79: See Weir (1962) for a detailed account of bedtime verbalization. Miller, in a foreword to Weir's volume, expresses surprise at the existence of such a phenomenon, but its reality seems beyond dispute.*]

Ruth uses the past tense of verbs correctly in her speech, such as "Nana baked," "did," "made," "ate," "said," "saw," etc. [*Note 80: Compare Church (1961, page 64). It is only at a considerably later age, when the child is adapting his speech to the regularities of adult conventions, that he produces such hybrid forms as "I branged" or "I wented."*]

It isn't confusing yet to Ruth that I am "Mother," "Ellen," and

"Mommy" or that my husband is "Karl," "Daddy," or "Father."
She laughs when she calls us by our first names or as Mother
and Father. Lately she calls me "Mommy Ellen."

Ruth plays with cards. She refers to the kings as "Old King
Cole" (or as "Jack," by mistake) and the jack as "Papa" (her
grandfather's name is Jack), and she recognizes the joker.

I have heard Ruth play what may be called word games by
herself. One day she was playing with a saucepan, saying
"Pot." All of a sudden she started to say "potty" and laughed
and laughed. She then tried to sit on the pot. Her own potty is
actually a small toilet seat, but we refer to it as a potty. Another
day Ruth was having lunch and she said, "Fruit salad—cherry."
Then she laughed and said, "Cherry" (picking up the cherry),
and then "Sherry—Sherry Jones" (her friend).

Whenever Ruth asks for something—"Eat," "Go car," etc.—
I ask her who wants to do this and she replies, "Ruthie do—
Ruthie Stern."

Ruth can pronounce "water" correctly, yet whenever she
says water, she prefaces it with *wa*—"wa-water." This is the only
word she does this with—it has become routine.

Ruth's pronunciation still has a few peculiarities. Usually she
pronounces initial *l* as *y* ("yike" for "like"); *l* is silent in the
middle of a word ("bock" for "block"); she says "ky" for "sky";
she says *d* for *n* ("macarodi" for "macaroni" and "Rondie" for
"Ronnie"); she says *b* for *r* ("bite" for "write"); *g* for *d* ("Ging-
gong" for "Ding-dong").

Interesting mistakes: Ruth pronounces cup as "puc." [*Note
81: Such reversals of consonants are by no means rare, e.g.,
"oosh" for "shoe." Note, too, such common deformations as
"pisghetti" and "aminal" and "hangerberg."*] I told her to say
"cat," and she did; "cap," and she did; and "cup," and she said
"puc." Also she refers to milk as "nilk," yet she says "milkman"
correctly, and "mail." Whenever she sees her vitamins she says
"vitamins" or "medicine." But even though she knows what they
are, as soon as she sees the dropper she says "nosedrops."

Ruth is an actress and she is also able to adapt her actions
to different situations. For example, at Nana's house whenever

Ruth (sham) coughs, Grandma gives her honey and Ruth says "medicine." There she is constantly "coughing." At home she does not cough because she knows I will not give her honey. She tried that trick in vain a few times, then stopped.

Ruth is expert at mimicking intonations as well as words. One day she threw down all the towels from the closet. In desperation I howled "Oh, Ruthie!" in a high, sing-song voice. Immediately I heard her say "Oh, Ruthie!" in the same manner I had said it, and she laughed and laughed. Since then, whenever she spills milk, messes up, etc., she says, "Oh, Ruthie!" and thinks this is very funny.

To get attention, Ruth opens a drawer and puts her finger in or tries to catch her foot between her car pedals; then she yells with mock urgency, "Hurt–hurt" or "Caught."

I find Ruth's cries at moments of "crisis" very interesting and revealing. When she is put into bed and she doesn't want to go to sleep, she starts calling: "Mama? . . . Mama? . . . Daddy? Wa-water. Ach! Ach!" [*i.e.*, *B.M.*]. In a crying voice, she calls "Nana, Nana!" (Ruth cries for Nana whenever she wants something I will not give her.)

Ruth has started to assert herself and command others. She pulls my hand and says, "Come me" (come with me) or tugs at my skirt and says, "Up–Pick up."

Another routine. Before Ruth will go into her crib—at nap or bedtime—she says, "Hupa-hupa." This means she wants to snuggle into your shoulder and be carried around and patted. Also soothes herself this way—if she hurts herself or is afraid she says, "Hupa."

Doctor's visit: Eighteen-month checkup. Height 32 inches, weight 24 lb. 11 oz. Ruth was not afraid today, even when she went into the office. She showed the doctor her tricks and was very friendly until he gave her an injection, when she cried. Later, when I was putting on her coat in the waiting room, the doctor came in and Ruthie immediately covered her (correct) arm and pointed to the place of the injection, looked at the doctor, and cried again.

If you ask her what she does with money, or if she sees

some money, she says, "To store—buy apples" or "To bank."
[*Note 82: In the affluent portions of our affluent society, children learn early a pragmatic command of money; but it is
important to remember that any conception of where money
comes from or how it functions escapes the child's realization
for many years.*]

Ruth makes jokes. She sometimes refers to her milk as "beer,"
"wine," or "ginger ale," then laughs and laughs.

She can't tolerate dirty hands. When she is eating she says,
"Sticky hands—wash!"

One day when Ruth was playing with her doll, the arm came
off. Ruthie cried out in fear, ran over to me and hid her face in
my lap. She kept looking at the doll from the corner of her eye,
but would not look at it directly. Ever since then she has
avoided the doll completely. [*Note 83: Such fear (as opposed to
simple distress) over broken or incomplete playthings, peculiar
to toddlerhood and the early preschool years, seems to represent an empathic identification with the broken object, as
though the child's own newfound and still precarious integrity
were threatened. See Note 88.*]

Ruth seems to understand and use the word "No" all the
time, but she never says "Yes." In fact, whenever I ask a
question the answer is always "No" so, instead, I just make a
statement. Her "No" is sometimes serious, sometimes means
"Yes," sometimes is a show of independence, and sometimes is
whimsical. [*See Deborah, Note 66, page 44.*]

The only Negro Ruth knows is a man named Fred. [*We can
assume that Ruth has no recollection of the Negro nurse she
had in infancy.*] Two illustrations: One day I gave Ruth a
brownie. She looked at it closely and said, "Fred." The color
brown must have reminded her of Fred's skin. Whenever she
sees a picture of a Negro man, she says "Fred."

Ruth seems to know the difference between big and little.
She has two toothbrushes, pencils, etc., and if you ask her for
the little one or the big one, she hands you the correct one.
[*Note 84: Here one needs to test the generality of the distinction
with unfamiliar pairs of objects as well.*]

When we drive to Ruth's grandmother's and get in front of the house, Ruth says "Nana's house."

Ability to anticipate: I gave Ruth a little piece of cake and even before she finished her first bite, she asked me for "more." Another example of anticipation: One day Ruth asked for raisins. I told her she could have them as soon as her milk was all gone. Immediately she turned her glass over and spilled out all her milk, then she repeated, "Raisins."

Ruth seems to remember who calls her what endearing names. If you ask her who calls her:

Chickabiddy — "Mommy say."
Honeybunch — "Daddy say."
Princess — "Papa Jack."
Icky-Pu — "Nana Thea."
Yungatz — "Nana Rosen."

Ruth has a private form of humor. She mumbles things to herself and laughs heartily; yet she is the only one who knows what is funny. She doesn't care if no one else laughs.

Ruth is learning to walk downstairs. She does very well when I hold her hand, but when I take away my hand, she is afraid and turns around to go down backward. Just holding my hand gives her the security to go downstairs frontward, one foot at a time.

I'm always playing "Hide" with Ruth. One day I pretended not to see her and I said "Where's Ruthie?" She excitedly pointed to herself and said "Here I am. Me." [*Note 85: Since this use of the first-person singular is remarkably early, it seems likely that Ruth has learned "Here I am" as a unit.*]

Ruth demands all my attention—whenever I am on the telephone she runs to get a book and says, "Read, read."

She calls the stove, cigarettes, and matches "hot." She likes to go outside, and several times a day she dresses herself in a hat, mittens, and overalls, and says, "Outside. Nana's house. Car." Ruth refers to everything as "this" and "other." She puts on one shoe and then says "other one," etc.

Ruth has a new "game." She goes into a room and shuts the

door. Then she cries and tries to open the door. Finally she calls "Mama" and cries if I don't come immediately.

Often Ruth says "Ach" (B.M.) and then when I put her on the toidy she says "Tease" or "Kidding."

Ruth points to her fingernails and says "fingu nails." She also knows her "toes." I asked Ruth what her toenails were and she replied "fingu nails" (not toenails).

One day I asked Ruth to bring me a clean sheet. She brought it and said, "New sheet." I then told her to put the old sheet in the hamper and she did. She understands fairly complicated verbal requests now.

I think I reported before that whenever Ruth sees two objects she says "two," but she does not have the concept of *one* or *three* yet.

18–19 months.   February

RUTH's imitative responses are becoming very frequent. One evening my husband was dressing and Ruth imitated these gestures: putting on shaving lotion, putting deodorant under the arms, massaging scalp.

Ruth often runs away when I call her, but she returns a few seconds later (whimsical negativism).

She understands these spatial-relational words: up, down, on, under, in, out.

We noticed something interesting. Often when I sing a song, Ruth mouths the words as if she were singing. Could this mean that she thinks *she* is singing?

Ruthie says "zippu" and can work her own zippers. She also says "tie" and "untie" when she plays with her own shoelaces.

One day Ruth brought me the cap, which had been missing, for her tube of medicine and said "ointment." I don't know how she recognized it without the tube. She must see things as separate parts—not as a whole?

Whenever Ruth goes by a light switch she says "Off—on. Ruthie do light."

One night at dinner, Ruth's grandma brought a package of lady fingers to the table and asked Ruthie if she wanted a lady finger. Ruth repeated fearfully, "Lady fingu. No! No! Nana's fingu." She cried until we took them out of the room. Explaining that it was cake and showing Ruth how to eat it did no good. She kept saying "fingu" and hiding her face. [*Note 86: Here we have a striking case of nominal realism, in which the word takes precedence over the fact. Unlike the cases in which the child unquestioningly accepts an old label as designating something new (see Note 53), the pastries have enough perceptual resemblance to actual fingers for the name to seem to designate them as the same thing.*]

Ruth has a remarkable memory. She found a toy car at Grandma's and said the full name of the child who had left it there three or fourth months before. She had not seen it since.

She knows the difference between "hot" things and "cold" things.

Ruth does not seem to be confused by (or maybe is not aware of) the phonetic identity and semantic differences of *two* and *too*. She calls two objects "Two." Before drinking her milk, she says "Too hot." When I give my husband soda, she says "Ruthie too."

It is easy to misunderstand a child's reality. One day I took Ruth outside and said something about it being cold and windy. After that, whenever Ruth went out, even on better days, she would say "Windy" (I had thought she understood the wind). Later, I gave her some sherbet and she said "Windy, Mommy." For Ruth "windy" was synonymous with cold.

Ruth loves to role-play. My husband once showed her how Frankenstein's monster walked. Since then she walks around the house like a monster and says, "Frankenstein. Monster."

Ruth is not permitted to touch wires. Yesterday she called to me, very upset. She brought me her pocketbook and said, pointing to the chain handle, "Wires—no touch."

Ruth put a knitted coaster on her doll's head, said "shower cap," and laughed.

She knows how to open a ball-point pen. She turns it upside

down and pushes the release down against the floor or table until the point comes out (no one showed her this). She likes to scribble on paper and says, "Write. Pictures." Then she says, "Other side" and turns the paper over.

Ruth wanted to roll in the snow and eat it.

She adores raisins. When she is given several, she eats them quickly, using both hands to feed herself. (When she particularly enjoys her food, she hums while she is eating.) When she is given a single raisin, she holds it in her fingers and takes tiny bites of it. She will not swallow it whole—it is too precious.

The subject of raisins reminds me of how Ruthie has people pegged. One night Papa told Ruth she could not have any more raisins. She didn't say anything but walked quietly to Nana Rose, took her hand, brought her over to the raisins, and said, "Please."

Jerry, two and a half years, was having supper with Ruth. She grabbed his milk and spilled it on him. Jerry screamed and cried, and in a minute Ruth was screaming and crying. She wasn't superficially imitating him; she watched him and participated empathically.

Ruth has learned several verbal stimulus-response sequences. She answers "Good" to the question "How are you?" But I've discovered that if you ask how she is going to do something, her response is also "Good." "How" is the stimulus for the response "Good." Another example: "Where was Daddy?" "Chicago." But if you ask her where she put her dog, again she may answer "Chicago"—"where" elicits "Chicago." It is easy to be misled and, by omission, think that a child understands more than he really does.

Ruth loves the sensation of being dizzy.

One day I mentioned to my husband that the day seemed like a Thursday. Ruthie piped up "Sunday, Monday, Tuesday" —learning by osmosis again. At some time she must have heard the days of the week recited.

When I go out, Ruth's behavior depends on the behavior of the sitter. If the sitter (Gram) says that Mommy will be back soon, Ruthie is fine. If she says "Mama has gone away," Ruth cries.

One must repeat the words Ruth says—to reaffirm her reality, perhaps. If you don't repeat the words, Ruthie gets upset and says them over and over.

Ruth will not eat things she finds on the floor. She brings them to me and says, "Pah."

Ruth pointed to the TV screen and said "Window."

Ruth connects words incorrectly. She must hear them this way:

> "How-ya"—How are you?
> "See-ya"—See you.
> "Come-gain"—Come again.
> "Wakeup"—Wake up.
> "S'long"—So long.
> "Not-ē-mouth"—Not in mouth.
> "Biggy-strong"—Big and strong.

Although, as I mentioned, Ruth calls all pictures of Negro men "Fred," she had no trouble recognizing Fred himself in a group of Negro men.

Whenever Ruthie finds clothes on the floor, she puts them in her laundry hamper or brings them to me and says, "Cleaners."

Ruthie has rigid rules. The door to the den is usually shut. One day it was open and she took me by the hand and showed me how *she* "shut de door."

Ruth has a game. She took a stocking and put it around her neck and said "scarf" (laughed), "tie" (laughed); put it on her head, "hat" (laughed); finally put it on her leg and said "stocking."

She likes to stand on her head, to cross her fingers, to pinch herself and other people.

Ruth looked at some drinking glasses with a repeated chevron-like design and said "birdies."

Whenever one tells Ruth not to touch something, she says, "Looking."

Ruthie answers questions very well. For example: if one says, "Who washes clothes?" she says, "Maggie washes clothes," repeating question catechism-fashion.

Before Ruth eats anything, she says "Hot? Too hot," and if I say "No, it isn't!" she says "Just right."

Ruthie omits most prepositions: "Sit lap," "Build blocks," "Come me," etc.

One day, Ruth tried to put on a bracelet—not slipping it over her hand, but from the side, as though there were an opening for her wrist to go through.

One day, a little girl came to play with Ruthie; she was wearing patent-leather Mary Jane shoes. Ruthie pointed to her shoes and cried, "Ruthie shoes too—Ruthie Janes!" and tried to pull them off the little girl.

Today (February 10) I bought Ruth nesting blocks. She had no trouble putting the very little blocks into the very large ones, but with blocks close in size she was stymied and whined in frustration. She had no idea why the big one wouldn't fit into the little one. When I told her to remove the small boxes so another (medium) block would fit in the largest one, she did this immediately and replaced the small ones correctly, but had no idea how to do this on her own. [*Note 87: Such observations support the idea that the perception of relative size depends on learning and is not given innately. There seem to be two independent functions here. The child's ability to place small things in much larger ones implies that he perceives a relationship of container to thing contained before he can judge things purely on the basis of size. When the two objects are nearly the same size, they seem to exist ambiguously, each as a potential container of the other.*]

Ruth was eating a graham cracker. Accidentally, she broke it in two and got upset and yelled, "Broken! Fix! Fix!" Naturally I couldn't put it together, and Ruth was very distressed that her mother couldn't fix it. She threw the two pieces on the floor and wouldn't eat them. [*Note 88: To continue Note 83, the particular case of distress over a broken cracker (a developmental universal in cracker-eating societies) seems to express an almost esthetic disturbance at the interruption of a stable temporal sequence according to which the baby consumes the cracker. We note incidentally that the baby learns only with some difficulty what kinds of brokenness can and cannot be repaired.*]

Ruth imitates almost everything now. The TV was on and showed two men wrestling. Suddenly Ruth rolled on the floor, yelling "Oh—Ah," kicking her feet, etc. Another day, a little girl on TV was playing the piano. Ruth ran to the other room, brought her piano in front of the TV, and played it. The little girl's father (on TV) hugged her, and Ruth threw her arms around the TV screen ("window") and hugged the father, too. Empathy? [*Note 89: While empathy may indeed be at work here, it is likely, too, that Ruth sees the images on the TV screen as flesh-and-blood, huggable people.*]

Ruth walks around with her hands in the air above her head whenever one says "Caroline," because Ruth saw a picture of Caroline Kennedy looking gleefully at her Christmas tree with her hands raised. The first time she raised her arms this way, I didn't know what she was doing. Then when I saw the picture in the newspaper that evening, I told her it was Caroline who did that.

One day I was standing on a chair hanging curtains, and when I looked around, Ruth was also standing on a chair.

A little boy in a department store didn't want to leave the store, sat down on the floor, rocked back and forth, shook his head, and cried "No!" Ruth immediately mimicked his action exactly. She could hardly be dragged away. She occasionally repeats the action and says, "Boy—store."

Last night Ruth was trying to open and close a cupboard in the kitchen. She couldn't close it because a large flour-sifter was on the floor in the way of the door, and she was getting frustrated and angry. She kept slamming the door harder and harder. It didn't occur to Ruth to remove the sifter. Finally we told her to remove it, she did, and the door closed; but I don't think she realized the connection.

FEARS: Ruth is not afraid of the dark or of strangers. However, lately she has had unexplainable fears. One night, she noticed the box that covers the doorbell (it was silent). She yelled, "Box!" and ran out of the room crying. For a few days she would go into the room only holding onto me and whimpering. She was afraid of my husband in his Army fatigue hat and yelled, "Hat—off!" She started crying one day when I was dressing her on the bathinet, and yelled, "Fall! Fall!" and grabbed me. (She's never fallen from it.) The thing which scared her most, however, was when I drew a face on my thumb, wrapped a hankie around it, and sang "Thumbelina." She screamed in *terror* and cried for almost an hour and hugged me in fear for several hours—she wouldn't let me put her down. [*Compare Ruth's reaction to thumb-doll at age 11 months, 3 weeks, page 216. In general, fears increase through childhood as the individual's greater awareness of self brings with it a greater awareness of his own vulnerability.*] Whenever she hears even the *tune* of "Thumbelina," or the word "Thumbelina" she literally trembles with fear and says, "No, no Thumbelina."

18–19 month word inventory.

New words: Scarf, nail, ribbon, curler, garters, cradle-cap, diarrhea, honey, medicine, vitamins, nosedrops, cough, hiccough, pail, basement, garage, eye-glasses, stove, television, radio, paper boy, mailman, diaperman, cornflakes, raisins, apricots, veal, tomato, applesauce, string, tea kettle, tea party, coffee, soup, can, ginger ale, window, knife, blouse, jacket, muff, breakfast, lunch, sardine, walk, Nana's house, farfel [*barley*], cover, dry, change, check, money, twist, honeybunch, sweetheart, chickabiddy, hit, spank, dirty, messy, corner, drawer, Mommy's toy, wire, fireplace, key, lock, blueberries, leotards, closet, floor, wall, fingernails, haircut, knit sweater, fur, off, on, down, up, like, fix, hurt, carry, good, naughty, pretty, big, little, wash, lap, lips, sit, seat, house, home, cellar, stairs, chair, broom, shovel, mouse, pocketbook, Mickey Mouse, love, dear, soap, tea, sugar, clothes, boots, slip, toidy, fork, juice, caught, broke, Mr. Sunshine, lipstick, perfume, gloves, uncle, aunt, do, run, jump, eat, drink, see, go, fall, look, touch, covers, blanket, mirror, kids,

busy, dizzy, queen, clock, later, yourself, me, Huckleberry
Hound, Yogi Bear, package, presents, slippers, stockings, pick,
peek, Mama Goose, tie, sit up, catch, box, toothbrush, drive,
blue, yellow, llama, clown, whippoorwill, hummingbird, dots,
fuzzy, sort, other, any, toys, bobbypin, bathtub, push, pull,
gorgeous, records, table, I love you, upsy daisy, not, wallet, of
course, bedroom, sure, dining room, Shalom (Hebrew for
"hello"), living room, Frankenstein, wrestle, exercises, stars, hers,
yours, mine.

Uses, but inaccurately: draw, count, show, boyfriend, pal,
cousin, Cuba, iron, bell, ding-dong, stamp, horn, back (i.e.,
come back), lucky, poor, candle, bank, butterfly, monster,
record, newspaper, soaking wet, undress, up a tree, toilet seat,
nail polish, hold, tight, bow (verb), sleep tight, nitey-night,
windshield, cleaner, hamper, broken (past tense), downstairs, all
right, American, cheese, whoops, new, good girl, toast, butter,
refrigerator, peek-a-boo, snowing, all gone, hide, playroom,
build (blocks), morning, cards, fat, kitchen, operator, throw
away, sherbet, either, somersault, sour, lemon, dishwasher.

SONGS AND NURSERY RHYMES: Ruth knows these songs and
nursery rhymes, and puts in the italicized words when I say
(or sing) them:

Teensy, weensie, spider went *up* the garden *wall. Down*
came the *rain* and *wash*ed the *spider out. Up* came the *sun* and
dried away the *rain.* And the *Teensy, weensie,* spider went up
the *spout again.* (All the finger motions, too.)

When I sing "Little Sir *Echo,*" Ruthie is the echo with
"Hello," "Play," and "Away," right on cue. Also, *Happy talk,
Happy talk,* etc., "Golly Baby, Lucky Guy" (finger motions),
"Pop Goes the Weasel," "Papa, Dance with Me," and "Six Little
Ducks."

Ruth also puts in the right word if you say one of the following rhymes. She doesn't recite the rhyme herself, but continues
if you stop.

Little *Miss Muffet* sat on a *tuffet, eating* her *curds* and *whey.*
Along came a *spider* and sat down *beside her* and frightened
Miss Muffet away.

Pussy-cat, Pussy-cat, where have you *been?* I've been to London to visit the *Queen.* Pussy-cat, Pussy-cat, what did you *do* (it should be "there")? I frightened a little *mouse* under the *chair.*

She says these words in these rhymes: Little Boy Blue . . . horn . . . sheep . . . meadow . . . cow . . . corn . . . boy . . . sheep . . . haystack . . . asleep.

Three little kittens . . . lost . . . mittens . . . cry . . . Mother dear look . . . here . . . mittens . . . lost . . . naughty . . . pie.

Jack Horner . . . corner . . . pie . . . thumb . . . plum . . . good boy . . . I.

This little piggy . . . market . . . home . . . roast beef . . . none . . . wee-wee-wee . . . home.

Rock-a-bye baby . . . tree . . . wind blows . . . rock . . . breaks . . . fall . . . down . . . cradle . . . all.

Tom Tucker . . . supper . . . eat . . . butter . . . knife . . . wife.

Mary . . . lamb . . . snow . . . sure to go.

Old King Cole . . . soul . . . he . . . pipe . . . bowl . . . fiddlers three.

Simple Simon . . . pieman . . . fair . . . *cakes* (should be "wares").

(Ruth does the finger motions of "Johnny, Johnny, whoops.")

Nineteen-month doctor's visit: Ruthie enjoyed this visit to the doctor. She said poems for him, counted, and generally showed off. She cried for a second when she had her injections, but immediately was the doctor's friend again and hugged him goodbye.

18 months, 29 days.   February 17

RUTHIE opens ball-point pen by herself, holds paper with one hand, and scribbles on it with the pen. One day her pen wouldn't write; she threw it down, and said, "No write." Her grandfather said it had no ink, and Ruthie replied, "No ink. Papa get ink tomorrow morning."

Ruthie says *a, b, c, d, e.* She recites 1-2-3-4-5-6-7-8-9-10, and

Sunday, Monday, Tuesday, Wednesay. She says "your(s)," meaning "mine" (or hers), as she repeats what I say. Example: "Wipe *your* hands" for "Wipe *my* hands." Ruthie goes to the mirror and says, "See *me*." (In this case, the correct pronoun.) Ruth uses "cover" as both verb and noun: "Here's the cover." "Cover the cake."

Ruth has a silver cup with a red, yellow, and green traffic-light design on it. She says, "Red light—stop," and when she sees a policeman, she holds up her hand and says, "Stop" (as the policeman does). Ruthie must take in everything. One day, out of the blue, she said, "Up a lazy river" (song).

A great deal of Ruth's verbalization involves commands: "Bring it in—chair"; "Take off glove, Mommy, Ruthie put on."

Another mistaken pronoun: Often when I'm changing Ruth, she says, "Fall down and hurt de self (yourself), Ruthie" (instead of myself).

Ruth looked at the grandfather clock's insides and said, "Dark —sleep." She comes to me and says, "Ruthie wet her diaper. Soaking wet. Change her diaper. Clean diaper." Ruthie unzips her sleeping bag at night and greets me every morning with, "Oh, Ruthie zip de self."

When I light the Sabbath candles, Ruth orders, "Put on scarf, Mommy. Good Shabos (Sabbath)."

Ruth's sitter is German, and Ruth counts from one to five in German; she also says "Du bist eine schöne Mädchen," and then translates, "Girlie"; she says "Wiedersehn" (for "auf wiedersehen"), and then translates, "See you." She says "Shalom," and then translates, "Hello."

19 months, 6 days. *February 25*

ROLE PLAYING: Ruthie says, "Lenses," and imitates how I put on my contact lenses. She says, "Daddy's razor shave," and imitates the sound of the razor and the motion of shaving. When her father leaves in the morning, Ruth says, "Daddy go bye-bye, sell furniture." Ruthie found a key and said, "Yale lock."

Ruth and her father have a joke which he taught her. When he asks her what college she wants to go to, she says, "Sing-Sing," and laughs.

Ruth has been taught, in case she is lost: What is your name? "Ruthie Stern." How old are you? "One 'n' a half." Where do you live? [*City and state*.] What street? "Elmhurst." Mother's name? "Ellen Stern." Father's name? "Daddy dear."

Whenever Ruth sees bags or boxes, she gets excited and shouts, "Presents—Ruthie!"

When Ruth is ready for bed, she must first kiss Mom and Dad and say, "Good night. Ruthie go in crib. Sweet dreams. Sleep tight." (It has become a ritual.) Ruth loves to nap, and finds her crib very secure. Whenever she gets scolded or spanked, she says, "Ruthie tired—in crib, please" (to get away from it all).

I gave Ruth the doll whose arm fell off (it had been fixed). [*See age 17–18 months, page 246*.] She still wanted no part of it. She remembered the incident and said, "Dolly lost arm. Poor dolly. Mommy fix it."

Whenever Ruth sees me polishing my nails, she says, "Get scissor. Ruthie manicure—cut nails." Whenever Ruth sees a squeeze-tube, she says, "Zinc ointment," or "Vaseline."

19 months, 17 days.   March 8

WHENEVER Ruth hears the bell, she says, "Doorbell ring, Mommy" and when she hears the phone, she says, "Answer telephone—ringing."

Sometimes Ruth holds the phone while I dial her grandmother, and if it's busy she announces, "Nobody answers—busy."

After Ruth has been scolded, she comes over and puts her head into my lap and says, "Love, Mommy."

If anyone says, "Where's Ruthie?" she says, "Here she is" rather than "Here I am." She says "yours" meaning "mine," and "her" meaning "me."

Everyone's name that she doesn't know is Stern.

19 months, 3 weeks.   *March 12*

RUTHIE connects couples. Whenever she hears someone's name, she adds the name of the spouse and baby. Example: "Herb— Elaine and baby Janet." (She knows twelve or fifteen couples by name.)

Ruth saw a baby crying—the next minute *she* was crying. She recovered herself, and said, "Oh, poor baby. Don't cry."

Whenever Ruthie sees something on a table, she says, "Just looking—no touch." She dials her play phone and says, "Hello, Operator—Ellen Stern." Ruth differentiates correctly between "car" and "truck." Ruth touched the dishwasher, which was hot. She said "Dishwasher hot. Burn de self. Blow." (She blew.) "Colder."

Whenever anyone says, "It's a shame," she says, "shame, shame," and motions with her fingers. (Baby-sitter taught her.) When Ruth sees me dusting, she says, "Mommy's cleaning the house."

Ruth is so literal. Whenever she picks up something from a table and I say, "Don't touch. Put it down," she *always* puts it on the floor, *not* on the table (as far down as possible).

Ruth turns up the sound of the television and says, "Loud." She plays word games. Her baby-sitter's name is June Gumb. One day Ruth said, "June Gumb—chewing gum," and laughed. She kept repeating this.

Today I tried to wash Ruth's face, and she said, "Keep away."

Ruth not only plays on the white and black keys on her piano; somehow she discovered (no one showed her) the metal strings which produce the sound and she plucks them through an opening in the back to make different notes.

Ruth was drinking her milk. Suddenly she dropped two (im- aginary) things in it very carefully and stirred it with her finger. She must have seen my puzzled look, for she explained, "Mommy's sugar pills."

I tried a bathing suit on Ruth. She got hysterical with laughter and yelled, "Fat lady!"

Ruth has just learned how to walk up and down the stairs standing up. Now she says, "Ruthie big girl, hold on banister. Careful—no talk." When she feels unsure, she announces, "Backwards," and turns around and creeps down, saying, "All the way."

Whenever Ruth hears a noise or sees something overturned or messed up, she asks, "Happened?"

20 months, 2 days.   March 21

RUTH is mostly both bowel- and bladder-trained. When she has to go she comes to me and says, "Ruthie on potty, Ach, bathroom," and after she has gone she says triumphantly, "What a angel."

Ruth saw a dish of candy and said, "Candy." I said, "No." She replied, "Candy please, please, Mommy dear." I said "No" again. Then she asked, "Just a tiny bit?" I said "No" again. A few minutes later Ruth brought her doll to me and said, "Please, candy for Peter, Peter cry."

Ruth scolds herself in my tone of voice. When she spills milk, she says, "Be careful, naughty girl, mustn't spill milk." She tests and teases. She playfully pinches and tries to bite me (forbidden). Then she says, "No pinch, no bite, kiss."

Ruth's counting is interrupted now: "1-2, button my shoe, 3-4, shut de door." She has been experimenting with rhymes. She says "ducksie-wucksie" (duck), "fingy-ingy" (finger), "Daddy-fatty," "toesy-woesy" (toes), "clocky-wocky" (clock). Associations confuse Ruthie's songs and rhymes, e.g., "Rock-a-bye your baby to a Dixie Melody D'amour," "Ding-Dong Bell, Pussy-cat Pussy-cat where have you been?"

20 months, 1 week.   March 26

WHENEVER Ruth cries she tries to see how she looks in the mirror. She tearfully wails, "Don't cry, Ruthie." [*Note 90: Observe the complexity of self-awareness required to be in dis-*

tress and still be curious about what one's distress looks like.]

Ruth's ear and speech seem well trained and coordinated. She can repeat anything she hears once or twice if she's asked to. For example, "Mrs. Mergenthaler," "Hippoponamus" (*sic*). Ruth says her *l*'s clearly now, e.g., "listen," "block," "please," etc. She also says "cup" (not "puc"). She now says "dog" (not "gog"), but she says "carf" (for scarf), "pank" (for spank). The impure *s* is silent.

Occasionally, for no obvious reason, Ruth will imitate a person in every movement. She watched a woman sitting in a delicatessen and mimicked her, crossed her arms, scratched her arm, crossed her legs, pulled down her dress, etc. Whenever Ruth sees a child, she wants to touch him and talk to him.

Ruth must remember everything. One morning she surprised us. She pulled me and said, "O.K. Mommy, lazy-bone, get up, Ruthie breakfast." Her behavior is very ritualistic. When it is warm outside and I tell her she doesn't need her winter things, she cries and carries on. "Ruthie need boots, Ruthie's mittens." She calls her father "Daddy-pie," and laughs. She frequently gives orders. A piece of sheet music fell off the piano and she said, "Mommy pick up, give Ruthie."

20 months, 9 days.   March 28

IF YOU ask Ruth who something is for, she answers, "Ruthie for," instead of "for Ruthie." I burned myself. Ruthie assumed the burn came from the stove, although it didn't. Every time she goes by the stove now, she says, "Burn, hurt Mommy."

When someone calls her, Ruth now answers, "Here I am."

Ruth says, "Don't tickle" or "Mustn't tease," etc. She was naughty and I slapped her hand. She said, "Hurt hand," and gave me her other hand to hit, too.

I told Ruth to sit on the bottom stair when I had to run upstairs for something. I kept yelling, "Are you waiting?" When I came back down, she said, "Ruthie just waiting and waiting."

Her father asked Ruth whom she wanted to marry. She looked delighted and answered, "Marry-Mary-Janes" (shoes).

Whenever she wants me and I tell her to wait a minute, she replies, "Mommy little busy now." She puts on and takes off her own shoes. She says "malicious" instead of "delicious." She also experiments with sounds. She repeats "Malicious Margaret" (baby-sitter's name).

Ruth sometimes attributes human feelings to inanimate objects, even though she knows her dolls can't talk (she looks to see who's talking), and don't eat (she pretends to feed her dolls but eats the food herself). But she dropped a bone on the floor and cried, "Fall down—poor bone." Sometimes she hugs a table or rocker and says, "Love you."

One night she asked for water. Her father gave her milk. Ruth wouldn't drink it and said, "No, water." He said it was water and she replied, "Other water."

20 months, 13 days.   April 1

THE first time Ruth saw a bandage on someone's finger she became very upset, cried, and ran out of the room.

For Ruth everything is "time to." She defines her day as "time to go out," "time to eat," "time to go ah-baby."

When Ruth hears the phone, she says, "Telephone ring, answer." When she is wet, she says, "Accident, change your diaper" (instead of "my diaper").

20 months, 15 days.   April 3

RUTH really counted for the very first time (coincidence?). She took cards from one pile and made another pile, counting 1-2-3-4-5-6, for every card moved.

Ruthie is beginning to use "I" correctly, sometimes. Today she said, "I dropped it, milk." When she does something wrong, she says, "Oh Ruth, Mommy mad."

Her body sensations are becoming better defined. When she has hurt herself, she's able to say where it hurts—nose, head, fingernail, etc.

One day Ruth's baby-sitter put her in to nap. Ruth's Gram

went into her bedroom and played with her. When the sitter, Frieda, looked in, Ruth said in a teasing voice, challenging, "No ah-baby, Frieda Simons."

Whenever Ruth hears the word "exercise," she says, "Exercise your charge-a-plate at [*name of department store*]" (a radio commercial).

Ruth saw a family picture. She pointed and said, "Papa, Daddy, Nana Rose," etc. When she came to herself, she said, "Ellen Stern's baby" (instead of "me" or "Ruthie"). She says "Sharp" when she sees or touches a sharp instrument.

When someone comes to visit, Ruth takes his hand and says, "See house, come with me, this way."

The song *Thumbelina*—even just the tune—still terrifies Ruth. [*See entry on page 254.*]

20 months, 19 days.   April 7

SHE says and understands far-near, up-down, in-out. She has used "Yes" correctly for the first time. Before this everything was "No."

Other sounds she plays with—"Jimmy (her doll), Mommy."

She has books about seals and talks about seals. One day we took her to the zoo and showed her the seals. She showed little interest and said, "Dog."

Ruth saw her father kiss me goodbye and said, "Daddy Mommy's father." (To Ruth he is not only her father but her mother's father, too.)

Ruth is very independent. When she is put on the potty she will not let me take her off until she is finished. She says, "No, more ach," and when she's done, she says, "No more—finished—off."

Grandpa asked Ruth a question which she couldn't answer. Kiddingly he said, "She's not smart, she'll have to go to school," and Ruth immediately retorted, "A-B-C-D-E-F-G-H-I-J-K-L-M-N-O-P—Cuba—T-X-Y-Z."

When Ruth sees a pen she says, "Write a letter to my mother."

Her latest trick is watching herself spit on her stainless steel highchair tray.

Two imitative actions seemed to come out of the blue. One morning at breakfast, Ruth said, "Potty, please." As she left the room she said, "Excuse me, Daddy, right back." Also whenever anyone sneezes, Ruth says, "Od (God) bless you."

One day in a restaurant, Ruth looked around and said, "Younger kids sit in highchairs."

"Yes" is now an important word in Ruth's vocabulary. She consistently uses it correctly. At breakfast today Ruth used the correct pronoun (she usually doesn't): "I do it for myself" (referring to feeding herself). Whenever I scold her she says, "Mommy mad, spank Ruthie." One day on the potty, she recited, "Tinkle-tinkle" (another name for "wee-wee") "little star."

20 months, 4 weeks.   April 16

WHENEVER Ruth sees anyone cry she gets a cloth and says, "Hanky wipe a tear."

When I took her to the doctor, she said, "Dr. Lehman, doctor, lawyer, merchant, chief, rich man, poor man, beggar man, thief." She recites this when she counts buttons, chandelier crystals, beads, etc. The word "doctor" triggered her.

Whenever she steps on a book or a brief case, she reaches up her arms and says, "Fix a light." (She must have seen someone changing a bulb on a ladder.)

Ruth says, "I am hungry" or "I am tired" before meals and bedtime.

She carries on conversations by herself, taking on both roles. For example: "Ruthie, dear." "Yes, Mommy."

Word play—"Mind the music and the Band-Aid and the mother."

She can't stand to be messy. She says, "Sticky hands, wash off."

Ruth is a back seat driver. She cautions, "Stop, go careful, too fast, slowly."

She does something strange. Whenever one asks her how old

she is, she usually says, "One 'n' a half, Larry Hyman." When someone says, "Sweet dreams," Ruth says, "Janet." When someone says, "Pretty," Ruth says, "Thank you, John." These people told her or asked her these things first, and although she's only met these people once she associates them with those words.

Ruth has memorized entire lines of her records. She goes around saying, "Every time I pick it up it makes me feel like singing" in response to nothing in particular. She seems to like the sound of the words.

Ruth asks questions constantly. "Where is . . . ?" "What is that noise?" "Which one?" [*Note 91: Note the multiple motivations to ask questions: a craving to know, a desire to maintain contact with the adult, reassurance, and a striving to master one's own experience, to make it coherent and one's own, by putting it into words. Observe how Ruth learns both catchphrases or formulas, some with only ritual meaning, and also ways of giving her experience an original formulation.*]

She met a boy named Bobby and she said, "Bobby—bobby pin."

New words—April—almost 21 months.

salty	listen	younger kids
sturgeon	dinner	myself
cream cheese	with	I
out to dinner	lunch	yes
goodies	visit	warm
sharp	busy	blow up [*balloon?*]
cramp	poached egg	pick up
wind (the clock)	record	colors
feed (the fish)	come again	match (verb)
need	see you	exercise
want	itchy nose	charge-a-plate
dress (*de* self)	Hurry up!	Yamalka (Hebrew
wipe (your hands)	shampoo	skull-cap)
crumbs	rushing	Leave it alone
tomorrow morning	hit	maybe
draw (a mouse)	message	army

golf lesson

rush

help

hurry

ink

silver

rash

accident

absolutely

push

carry

I'm sorry

Excuse me!

God bless you

tomorrow

flashlight

nursery rhymes

Yankee Doodle

shut

rub your eye

glass of water

back door

front door

breakfast

spaghetti

whiskey

model

healthy

white

Oh boy!

have

music

zip

funny

What time?

four o'clock

pedicure

present

march

teapot

mustn't

mad

angry

tired

sad

don't

adorable

slowly

fast

brush (verb)

shave

deodorant

food

box

imitate

excellent

playmate

flu

cellar

spider

squirrel

friends

wine

spill

happy

yawn

draw

poor

button (verb)

gorgeous

What else?

fresh

manicure

Be careful!

notebook

little while

zoo

close

caught

ride

scream

you're welcome

lovable

comb (verb)

first

count

up-sa-daisy

love

like

web

dry

clean

dress (noun)

undress

company

pills

fashion show

strong

turn

piece of paper

take

abacus

daisies

smart

beautiful

school

package

tiny

just

little

smoke

visit

wet

toilet seat

clean (verb)

many

office

Band-Aid

busy

hippoponamus
   (*sic*)

impossible

paint

milkman

mazuzah [*a scroll
   of part of the
   Torah*]

mine

friend

slide

everybody

alphabet

rubber pants

under

in behind

covers

bit

sip

lot

operator

sexy

buy

sell

fix

mailman

bubbles

I'm

cousin

swing

nobody

minds

drive

blow

smells

pinch

bite

burn

daffodils

tulips

sew

sandwich

hurt

torn (clothing)

gate

answer

delicious

malicious
   (confuses)

horn

nude

basement

climb

tomboy

mind

put on

take off

change pants

rug

laundry chute

all right

a

frighten

[*Note 92: The reader should bear in mind that these lists
represent an accretion of less than a year. The particular words
tell us a good deal about Ruth's home environment, and also
about her conceptual scope. The list is probably a conservative
statement of Ruth's vocabulary resources. Such a list does not,
of course, tell us anything about a baby's command of syntax
or his ability to perform logical operations.*]

21 months.   April 19

IF I scold Ruth and her father is home, she goes over to him,
hugs his legs, and says, "Just love you, Daddy." If he is not

home, she tries to hug me and says, "Love Mommy."

I bought her two turtles. She had no fear and also no idea that she could hurt them. She carried them around, wheeled them in her carriage, rocked them in her rocking chair, and tried to make them play her piano, etc.

Whenever she overhears a conversation she says, "What about a ride," etc. When she is full, she announces, "Had enough." I asked Ruthie where her socks were, and she said, "*I took them off.*"

She spends many moments in role playing. She adores putting on my shoes and clothes and walking around saying, "Little Red Riding Hood." She plays mother to her dolls, feeds, soothes, puts them to sleep, walks, carries them, etc.

I took Ruth out of her bath and she shouted, "Stay in tub, Ruthie not ready out yet." [*Note 93: Throughout the above section, observe how easily Ruth masters such seemingly difficult "concepts" as* just (= *exclusively*), enough, stay, yet, *and* ready.]

Ruth mimics me, "Call you sweetie." Whenever she spills her milk or does something she shouldn't she says, "Accident, poor Ruthie." One day I was changing her, and out of the blue she said, "Thank you, Mommy." I asked what for, and Ruthie answered, "For giving me clean diaper." One night when her father came home Ruth asked, "What's new? Selling furniture?" Ruth touched the hair on her father's arm and said, "Daddy have mustache." [*Note 94: It seems that for many children "hair" refers only to hair growing from the scalp. Two children I have known designated arm, leg, and body hair as "threads." Beards and mustaches often seem to exist for the young child as unitary masses rather than as constellations of hair.*]

Ruth gets very frustrated playing with other children. They take her toys and she just cries. She doesn't know how to hang on to her toys or hit another child.

Ruth is learning something about taking turns. She was trying to get on her swing with her doll. Thinking aloud, she said,

"First Lee-Lee, next Ruthie on swing," and put her doll on the swing and then climbed on herself.

Ruth knows and recites about fifteen nursery rhymes perfectly. Says "Yankee Doodle" in its entirety, sings "Do-Re-Me" (a few stanzas). Example:

> Do—a deer, a female deer
> Re—drop of golden sun
> Me—name call myself
> Fa—long long ago
> So—Needle putting thread (etc.)

Also sings or says: Come on, baby, do the twist; Playmate, come out and play with me; Bring dollies three, climb up apple tree; Up a lazy river; Melody d'amour; Oh-Oh, little girl; and many others.

21 months, 11 days.   April 30

RUTH must have a good ear even for meaningless sounds. She recites after me a prayer (about twenty-five words) in Hebrew and although it makes no sense to her, her pronunciation is excellent. [*Note 95: Ruth has the advantage of being without preconceptions about what sounds a language should consist of. By contrast, an adult, in listening to an unfamiliar language, tries to find phonetic equivalents in his own tongue, even though no equivalences exist. Even the International Phonetic Alphabet gives only crude approximations for the sounds of non-European languages.*]

Ruth is now afraid of Negroes. One day at a friend's she saw the Negro cleaning woman, ran to me and said, "Mommy hug Ruthie." She hung on to me. At one point she forgot about the cleaning woman, started into the kitchen, and stopped dead in her tracks when she saw her and ran out of the room. She peeked around the door and said, "Goodbye, lady, go home." [*Note 96: It seems likely that Ruth's fear is not specifically of Negroes (or of this particular Negro) but of an object that simul-*

taneously conforms to and departs from a familiar pattern. Ruth is behaving according to the same principle as Hebb and Riesen's (1943) chimpanzees.]

Ruthie now pronounces initial impure *s* but makes a separate syllable of it: "sc-arf," "es-pank."

I noted in earlier records that Ruthie correctly identified by label boy, girl, man, and lady. Lately, however, she says, "Hi, little boy" to little girls and vice versa.

New words—May 5 to July 22—21 to 24 months.

sometimes	male ⎫ (mixes these)
closer	female ⎭
afraid	station wagon
accident	gasoline
excellent	gas station
congratulations	anyway
"Ma-nish-ta-na-ha-lay-la-ha-	Heaven's sake
zeh" (prayer in Hebrew	find
for Passover)	go
come	went
graduation	push
needle	away
thread	ocean
sew	beach
airplanes	tubes
long-mower (lawn mower)	old
belong	new
automobile	scale
powder	favorite
calomine lotion	measure
zinc oxide ointment	can't
sweetie	not
just	don't
also	doesn't
every	welcome
some	fix

please—thank you very much   resting
help   sorry
picnic   swimming pool

[*Note 97: This list illustrates how nearly impossible it is to keep track of the child's growing vocabulary. It omits words, such as numbers, which we know Ruth uses. See the entries immediately following.*]

21 months, 16 days.   May 5

RUTH announced today, "The sun is too hot. Ruthie stay in the shade." Ruth nevertheless uses, "I'm." For example, "I'm tired. I wanna rest."

I stopped to talk to someone and Ruth asked, "What's this name?" (Instead of "What's her name?")

She is full of questions now—"which one?" "who?" "whose?" "what?" "when?" and "where?"; she has not yet asked "why?" as consistently as the others.

Most of Ruth's routine activities are prefaced by her singing: "This is the way we (wash our face, eat our breakfast, go to sleep, take a ride, etc.) so early in the morning."

Most times Ruthie can count from one to twelve. [*Note 98: This entry does not tell us whether Ruth can count as many as 12 things, or whether, having done so, she then realizes that the number assigned to the last thing counted is also the sum of things counted—counting, counting things, and summing seem to be three developmentally distinct operations.*]

Most soft noises bother Ruth—at least mechanical noises do, such as lawn mowers, fans, and air conditioners.

Ruth astonished us by demanding "What else?" when we told her our plans for the day.

When Ruth hurts some part of her body, she says, "It's broken." And when something is torn, she says, "Torn—buy a new one—bib." Ruth's constructions are odd. She often says, "Ruthie wants one. Raisin," etc. [*Note 99: Here we see the use of what Braine (1963) calls sentence frames, standard forms into which are fitted differential terms like "bib" and "raisin."*]

21 months, 22 days.　May 11

OWNERSHIP and possession seem important to Ruth. She identifies almost every object by "Belong to Ruthie" or "Belong to you, Mommy." [*Note 100: The assignment of ownership seems to be a classificatory device by which the child makes his world orderly and manageable.*]

Ruth's memory is fantastic. I was talking to a friend, Sally Rieger, on the phone, and Ruth said, "Sally Rieg-rieg, feel better, Sally—soon. . . ." I had told this to Ruth several months before when Sally had been in the hospital.

We have been telling Ruth she is going to be two, and isn't "one 'n' a half" any more. One day someone asked how old she was, and Ruth replied, "Two in July."

Ruth was on the potty, and I tried to take her off. She yelled, "No—one more drop—ach," and she did then finish her bowel movement. Then she looked in and yelled, "Raisin."

Ruth usually says, "Mommy, help you," but now occasionally she says correctly, "help me."

Whenever Ruth sees her pajamas or sees me turning down her bed, she yells, "No nappie" (no nap), but her resistance is not real. Most of the time she seems glad to rest. As soon as she thinks it's bedtime, she asks, "Just play for de little while in the playroom."

Ruth's best treat is "In Mommy's bed—under covers—watch TV one drop."

21 months, 25 days.　May 14

RUTH found a silver pin in the shape of a duck and said, "Mamie gave Ruthie this—from Mexico" (two months ago).

Ruthie pleaded for some soda one night. When we refused her, she asked sweetly, "Just a tiny sip?" (I might mention that

Ruth has a special soft, sweet voice which she uses when she wants something.)

Ruth knows that I don't like her to have candy, and therefore she never asks for it—*exactly*. Instead, she says, "Ruthie not eat candy, Mommy," and waits, sadly eyeing the candy dish.

Ruth still explores everything by tasting. However, when she puts something in her mouth now, she comes to show me.

It's great fun walking around in Mom's and Dad's shoes. But Ruth *does* put on her own shoes, sweater, and hats correctly.

Ruth's latest announcement to most activities is "Ruthie do—Mommy help."

Ruth shows signs of jealousy. Whenever I kiss her father, she runs to him and says, "My daddy." [*See Deborah Note 92, page 84.*]

Ruth was waiting in line for a frozen custard. She saw a strange little boy and ran up to him and tried to hug him. She kept saying, "Play with you," and when he ran away she cried.

Ruth is afraid when she hears a fire engine, or when someone says "lion" or "Thumbelina." One day I spelled "T-h-u-m-b-" and she started to scream, yelling "Thumbelina." On the other hand, Ruth is not afraid of the dark, new places, etc.

Ruth adores brushing her teeth, which consists in biting on the toothbrush.

Often Ruthie asks, "What time?" and answers herself, "Tem o'clock."

Ruth understands and uses these words: before, after, first, closer, far, behind, in front, in, out.

Ruthie is beginning to carry a tune—at least her notes vary in pitch, and there is a hint of timing in her songs. She no longer sings in a monotone.

One morning I asked Ruthie why she was looking out the window, and she answered, "Just waiting for the mailman."

Ruthie now wants to pick her own costume. "Not wear this one, wear this yellow one."

She carries out roles. One day she was dusting, and said, "Clean up—be neat—Fanny" (the cleaning woman).

22 months, 1 day.   May 20

RUTH loves to climb on the scale and say, "Weigh on scale."

She has begun to try to scratch and pinch people. Her new game is testing the limits. She is allowed to pinch *things,* but not people, and she seems to understand the distinction. "Pinch the table? Okay?" "Pinch the sofa?" "Pinch the shoe?" "Pinch the dress?" "Pinch Mommy just a little pinch? A big pinch? No?" (She gets a mischievous grin on her face.)

She looks out the window and announces, "Rain, rain, go away" (if it's gloomy) or "Sunny day."

Ruth is getting more sensitive to temperature and often announces, "It's cool in here" or "It's hot in here."

A friend used to have a motto for her son, and she told it to me. Now whenever I ask Ruth what Margie tells Seth, she replies, "No whining, no crying, no screaming, and no acting like a baby."

Ruth can cry, scream, whine, sob, or whimper at will. She sobs and gestures. "He loves me not."

Ruth is afraid of the shower, and every bath time she pleads, "No shower—just a bath." She washes herself well with the washcloth and knows how to wash two hands—one washing the other.

Yesterday I was leaving the house, and Ruth said, "Please come back, Mommy."

Whenever anyone mentions a haircut, Ruth says, "At the Ladies' Beauty Shop."

I must have been thinking aloud, and I said, "I wonder where my purse is?" Suddenly Ruth answered, "Well, I don't know *either.*"

Ruth surprised me. I offered her more sweets, and she replied, "No, thanks. I don't want any more. I'm full. I have enough."

Ruth is a tease. Whenever I ask what she'd like for dessert, she says, "I want my Mommy for dessert."

Ruth is very observant. She announced one night, "Daddy drives Mommy's car now." Often she sees another station wagon and says, "Looks like my Daddy's car, but it isn't. It's somebody else's." [*Note 101: Note how Ruth is becoming able to manipulate relationships linguistically. Here she specifies resemblance without identity, draws a contrast, and uses the indefinite form "somebody else's."*]

Ruth must have some sense of direction. When I've told her we're going to Grandma's, and I turn out of the driveway in the opposite direction, she cries and screams, "No—other way—to Grandma's house." [*Note 102: It is likely that Ruth knows the route as a sequence of discrete operations rather than the direction. Many adults, too, know how to get from one place to another without any idea of where the two points lie relative to each other within a larger frame.*]

When I moved Ruth into a big bed, I put the bed in the guest room and she didn't want to sleep in it. She protested, "No—not Ruthie's—Aunt Betty's bed." (Betty had slept in the bed for a few nights last January, five months ago, when Ruth was seventeen months old.)

Ruth must pick up different intonations. She immediately repeated "Oh heck" and "Damn it," and seemed to wait for our reaction. From the first time she repeated the words, she would say, "My Mommy says, 'Oh heck.' "

Ruth saw a picket fence the top of which slanted to the ground, and said, "Slide." The directional line must have reminded her of her slide.

Whenever Ruth sees new children, she approaches them, tries to touch them, smiles at them, and keeps repeating, "Ruthie Stern, Ruthie Stern," almost as if she were introducing herself.

She put two chairs front-to-front and said, "See—a playpen for my doll."

Ruthie found a bra, put it on correctly, and walked around saying, "My bra—Ruthie needs a bra."

Ruth finally learned to throw a ball (i.e., to let go with her fingers), and says, "Here comes."

Ruthie has known Frances, our housekeeper, for almost two

years, but for the first time noticed that one of Frances' fingers is missing. She asked, "Where's your finger? Frances' finger is broken." A few days later, Ruth bent her finger and said, "Ruthie's finger is broke too. Lose a finger like Frances."

22 months, 2 weeks. *June 2*

I WAS drying Ruth one day, and she handed me a towel and said, "I don't need it any more—towel—I'm finished."

I asked Ruth to play a game with me (she was playing with her toys), and she replied, "Why? Don't you like my game?"

I asked Ruth if she was ready to go for a ride, and she answered, "Any time you're ready."

Ruth has started to play with words. She said, "*Eat* your *milk. Drink* your *cookie,*" and then laughed and laughed. Another example: She heard the song, "Oh, my darling Clementine," and she said, "Clementine—like *lemon.*"

After Ruth had hurt her finger, and I asked her how it was, she said, "I think it's getting better." For the first time, Ruth referred to yesterday. "Yesterday I went for a walk with Daddy." When you ask Ruth something, she often responds, "I suppose."

Ruth heard me say that she was so *rational,* and she said, "Ruth has a rash, too," and pointed to her diaper area.

My mother, Grandma Thea, asked Ruth if she loved her. Ruthie answered, "I love Grandma Nana." Then she hugged Grandma Thea and said, "I love *both* Grandmas."

When my husband was out of town, we couldn't mention his name, or Ruth would cry, "My Daddy. Where's my Daddy?"

When Ruth was away with us on a trip, she talked about her grandparents all the time. However, when she was reunited with them, she ignored them.

Ruth was playing with some little toys, placing them on a table one by one and counting, "One, two, three, four," etc.

Ruth was in the den with her uncles, and they said to her that she should call her Mommy on the telephone. She said no, and when they asked why not, she replied, "Cause Mommy's already here—in the kitchen." [*Note 103: Two sorts of knowledge are implied here: the whereabouts of her invisible mother, and that telephones are used to communicate only with distant points.*]

I asked Ruth if she wanted to hear a story or not, and she answered, "Not."

Ruth likes swimming pools, ocean, etc., but doesn't like to get her face wet.

Babies fascinate her.

Ruth now tries to get me to stay with her at bedtime. "Watch me from the door" or "Stay on the bed with me."

22 months, 25 days. June 13

WHEN we took Ruth to the beach, she kept pointing to all the people in bathing suits, laughing and shouting, "Nude."

Ruth pretends to read. She sits with an open book and recites the pages from memory.

Someone asked Ruth how her Grandma Thea was, and she replied, "I have two Grandma Theas. One is Grandma Stern and one is Grandma Rosen." (No one had ever told her she had two Grandma Theas.)

Ruth still cannot arrange her nest of blocks correctly one inside the other. It's hit or miss.

Ruth has a doll she named Jimmy. One day I put a dress on Jimmy instead of his suit. This didn't bother Ruth; Jimmy was still a boy.

She knows how to tease. She knows her uncles perfectly well, but she calls Fred and Paul by the other one's name and laughs.

Ruthie has a talent for copying personal traits. She walks around with her hands behind her back saying, "I'm Grandma Nana." (We had never noticed, but this is Gram's particular gait.)

My mother in the East has a pair of shoes just like a pair Ruth's Grandma here has. Ruth was visiting my parents and saw Mother's shoes. She screamed, "Take off the shoes— Grandma Nana's." She could not understand that both her grandmothers could have the same shoes.

Similarly, Ruth saw a little boy sleeping with a rubber Mickey
Mouse toy just like hers. She screamed, "Mine!" and could not
understand that he could have one just like hers until we
showed her her own toy. Then she was perfectly happy to let
the boy play with his Mickey Mouse.

Ruth sleeps through thunderstorms. Yet, before she will sleep
in a room, one must remove unfamiliar pictures and all clocks
and radios.

Ruth's sentence structure often goes like this: "Where are you
Mommy went?" [*Note 104: Another child, a year older than
Ruth, formed questions by prefixing a declarative sentence with
a verb, e.g., "Can I can have some?" or "Is it's all right?"*]

Ruth usually uses "my" and "your" correctly. She has just
started referring (correctly) to "tomorrow"—e.g., "Tomorrow I
go to see Joey."

Ruth remembers promises. I told her that after her nap we
would go for a ride. She woke up and said immediately, "I had
my nap—now go for a ride."

Whenever Ruth is pretending, she announces, "I'm making
believe" (I'm sprinkling the flowers, having a party, etc.).

Ruth saw an anklet on a woman and laughed, "Lady has a
bracelet on her foot." She then immediately stretched out her
wrist to the lady and said, "See Ruthie's bracelet."

One morning Ruth came over to me and said, "Ruth made
wee-wee with the mouth in her big bed." I couldn't understand
her at all, but later, when I made her bed, I found she had
vomited all over it. [*Note 105: This is an excellent illustration
of the way children extend limited linguistic means to apply to
new situations.*]

One day we had driven past Betty's house, and Ruth asked,
"Which one of these is Betty's house?" I said, "None of these.
We passed it." Ruth replied, "Well, what does it mean, passed?"

I've discovered that Ruth sneaks out of bed to read, and
when she hears me coming she scurries back to bed and pretends to be asleep.

Ruth makes the distinction perfectly clear: "Don't tell a story;
read Ruthie a story *from the book.*" She repeats to herself all of

the stories I read to her. When I read about a little girl and her activities, Ruth interrupts very excitedly with "*I* go swimming, too," "*I* have a sweater, too," "*I* see dogs, too."

I wonder how Ruth knows what swimming is. She must have seen people swimming somewhere, because the first time she was in the kiddie pool she lay on her belly, kicked her feet, moved her arms, and yelled, "I'm swimming and swimming." She tries to drink the pool water.

I've told Ruth that a new baby is coming, but she doesn't understand what I'm talking about. The same for the house we're going to move to. Ruth keeps asking, "What kind?" "What kind of sister?" "What kind of house?"

Ruth seems to have imaginary friends. She always talks about "Oddie" and "Polly Guserai." [*Note 106: Since this is not a work of fiction, I must spoil the suspense and say that a more prosaic explanation of these terms will emerge shortly.*]

Ruth says, "I'm jumping," and bobs up and down—but her feet never leave the ground.

When Ruth arrives at someone's house, she says, "I came over to visit you."

23 months, 5 days.   June 24

SUDDENLY Ruth is aware of money. Whenever I pay for something, she cries, "No! Mommy's money—give it back. Mommy's change!" She also says, "I need some *money* in my pocketbook," and she pretends, "Here is a dollar—a penny—a nickel."

Ruth turns herself around and around, and then yells, "I'm *busy!*" (for dizzy). She asks everyone, "What can you do?" Ruth often makes requests such as, "I like a spoon," or "I need some milk."

Ruth took her dolls to the table, took a wooden milk bottle, used her beads for food, and said, "I'm having a tea party."

We just discovered where "Oddie" (imaginary friend) comes from: "Mel-*ody* d'amour," a song she knows.

Ruth plays telephone. She dials, picks up the phone, and says, "I'm calling my uncles in [*name of city*]. Operator, this is Ellen

Stern. Oh, the line is busy. Nobody answers. Hold on a minute."

Ruth now announces, "I have to go to the john."

I asked if Ruth was ready for a spanking. "No, I don't think so. No, thank you, Mommy."

Things are very real to Ruth, even when they don't exist. My mother was telling her that she would buy her a swing for her new yard, and a slide and a see-saw, and all the little children would play on her swing and slide and see-saw. Suddenly Ruth started to cry uncontrollably. Mother got upset and asked Ruth what hurt her, what the matter was. Through her tears Ruth sobbed, "My see-saw—Ruthie's see-saw."

One morning Ruth caught her finger in the dresser drawer, which she is not permitted to open. She came crying to me and said, "I hurt my finger. Kiss it, make it better." I kissed her finger, and Ruth said, "That's why my Mommy Ellen told me, 'Ruthie, don't play with the dresser drawers.'"

Ruthie was playing with a balloon and it broke. Ruth looked around in amazement and cried, "Where did it go?"

At the kiddie pool a little boy took Ruth's tube. She screamed, "*My* tube." The boy paid no attention to her. Watching him from the corner of her eye, she began to collect her other five or six toys from the pool, and said, "Ruthie's toys" (just in case he should decide to play with them). It was as if her tube was a lost cause and she would salvage what she could.

Ruth used the comparative today. At the dinner table she announced, "The iced tea glass is bigger than the milk glass." [*Note 107: This is an important observation because it indicates both perception of relative size and visual perception without motoric mediation. Note also the occurrence of the comparative form "better" three paragraphs below.*]

I had forgotten: Several weeks ago Ruth kicked me and I scolded her, telling her that the new baby was in my tummy. The incident passed. Today Ruth pounded her tummy and told my husband, "The baby is right here." She thinks *she* has a baby inside her tummy, too.

Last night Ruth went over to her father and said, "Daddy, would you like some candy?" He said yes. Ruth came over to me and said, "My daddy needs candy." I held out the candy dish and she took *two* pieces. She gave her father the two pieces and then said, "Daddy has two pieces—one for Ruthie, please."

I was praising Ruth and said, "You're my big girl." She replied, "Better be baby than big girl."

Ruth has started asking me, "What shall I do?" She'd rather be amused than have to amuse herself.

23 months, 12 days.   July 1

RUTH's uncles asked if she had ever been on a merry-go-round. Ruth, remembering her ride of two or three months ago, replied. "Yes. Daddy took me. Mommy wait at the gate. Ruthie wave to Mommy. It was fun."

Ruthie is very excited about escalators: "Stairs going up."

Ruth notices all smells—perfume, flowers, bathroom odors, food aromas, etc. Once she passed her cousin's carriage and said, "What smells?" Her aunt replied, "Dinner." Ruthie answered, "No—something smells in the carriage." The baby had vomited.

My husband, Ruth, and I were having dinner in the dining room, and I went into the kitchen for something. I returned and Ruth said resentfully, "Mommy go in the kitchen. Ruthie and her husband are eating. Mommy don't sit with us." [*See Deborah, Note 92, page 84.*]

Ruth pointed into her potty and asked, "What's this?" I answered, "Wee-wee." Ruth asked, "Where does it come from?" [*Note 108: It seems clear that babies do not at first connect the act of eliminating with the products eliminated. This state of affairs continues longer for little girls than for little boys, the latter having the advantage that they can see urine issuing forth. It is considerably later that children comprehend the connection between food and drink and elimination, although the continuity of water and urine is fairly easy to establish.*]

Ruth recognizes red, yellow, blue, and pink—not green. She also recognizes white and black.

Ruth is engrossed in role playing. She gets on all fours,

meows, crawls near one's legs, and says, "Pet me—I'm a kitten." Another example: She said to me, "You're Elizabeth." I was puzzled until she said, "I'm Gregory"—a mother and baby we had seen in the East several weeks before. Another time: "I'm Amos—I'm gonna take away the plates. Are you finished, Miss Ruthie?" (Amos is the man who serves dinner at Gram's.) "I'm Sidney Braun. I cry and cry." (Another baby we know.)

Ruthie's finger got caught in the car's electric window. We took her to the hospital and she screamed. A little later in the car, she said, "I'm sad. I cried a little."

We sold most of our furniture preparatory to moving and as people carried pieces away, Ruthie sobbed, "It's my rug. Where is the lady taking my rug?"

Ruthie came to me with wet pants and announced, "I'm the baby sister." Evidently she is more aware of the coming baby than I imagined.

Ruth knows right from left—hand, foot, eye, etc. If asked which is her right nose, she points to her right nostril. [*Note 109: While it is perfectly possible to teach a two-year-old left and right, left-right discrimination seems not to stabilize much before age five.*]

Ruth went to the potty at Gram's house. When she finished, out of the blue she announced proudly, "And I have a *flush* in my new house too."

One night Ruthie was going to sleep and the sitter was sitting in the room. Ruthie pleaded, "Would you please go downstairs and send my mother up?"

The skin on Ruth's thumb is cracked from sucking. She showed me her thumb and I told her it would get better if she didn't suck it. She replied, "But I have *another* thumb. I suck the other thumb."

23 months, 20 days.   July 9

As AN illustration of the verbal distinctions Ruth can draw, she saw a truck and suddenly said, "That's not a firetruck—it's just a truck."

Ruth's cousin was showing Ruth her toys. She brought out a large dog, which Ruth asked for thus: "Amy, let's *share* your toys." (Sharing someone else's toys is fine with Ruth.)

Ruth sat in her car seat at Grandma's house. She said, "My very own car seat—two car seats. One is in Mommy's car and one is in Grandma's car."

Ruth always teases. She hugs her father and says, "My husband."

I was collecting the dirty laundry and Ruth pulled away one of the towels and said, "I'm saving this towel for Daddy."

Ruth constantly role plays: "I'm a monkey eating a banana," "I'm a duck in the water," etc.

She absorbs more than I give her credit for. She was playing with a little friend who took away Ruth's toy. Ruth went to her toy box, and I heard her mutter, "Get yourself another toy." (It was like hearing myself speak.)

Uncle Paul asked Ruthie if he could visit her in her new house. She answered, "No, you stay in your own house."

Ruth's grandma had a plastic tablecloth on the table. Ruth touched the cloth and asked, "What's this?" We replied that it was a tablecloth. "Well, what *kind* of a tablecloth is it?" She picked up the corner of the cloth and felt it with her fingers like an old woman.

Ruthie likes to play with words. When dessert came, she yelled, "Honeydew—just like Ruthie do." Another time she laughed, "Hamburger—Molly Berger" (baby-sitter).

Most amazing to me: Ruth recognizes and identifies [*a particular make of car*]. Whenever she sees one, no matter what color, she cries excitedly, "A car just like Nana's!" This happens all the time, and she is always right. (It is the styling, not the color, which she notices.)

23 months, 27 days. July 16

AT A restaurant, Ruth looked around at the Negro waiters and cried, "A few Amoses." (Amos is the Negro houseman at Grandma's.)

Ruth asked me, "Where did you went, Mommy?" and I replied that I had gone to change my shoes and put on more comfortable ones. "Well, where are the other shoes?" she wanted to know.

Ruth's worst punishment is for me to ignore her. After I scold her and walk away angry, she fears I won't talk to her. She follows me, pleading, "Hi, Mommy, hi, Mommy. Talk to me."

I was telling a friend that Ruth had done the funniest thing. My story was interrupted by a phone call. Afterward, Ruth prodded me (I hadn't even realized she'd been listening), "What about the story of Ruthie?"

One day Ruth went over to the cleaning woman and said, "Take the hangers out of the crib for Michele." I had put hangers in the crib. (Michele is the proposed name for the October baby.) [*Note 110: Apparently not only Ruth but her parents as well were prepared for a second girl.*]

Ruth got a scolding and started to cry. In the midst of her crying, she asked, "Pick me up, please. I want to cry in the mirror."

When you hum a song, Ruth immediately recognizes the melody and sings the words.

Ruthie saw a train of three streetcars and shouted, "Look, three Rapid Transit." Until now, Ruth only seemed to understand "one" and "two" (i.e., more than one).

Ruth referred to the basement as "the other downstairs."

I was telling Ruth how proud of her I was for going on the potty. She said, "Sometimes I wet my diaper and sometimes you are not proud of me. Now you are proud of me." She thought for a minute and added, "And I am proud of myself, too." [*Note 111: This is an extraordinarily early age at which to verbalize such aspects of self-awareness as pride.*]

Ruth was given a red lollypop and she became excited. "Everything is red—the lollypop and the steering wheel on the car."

I was brushing crumbs from Ruth with my hand and she said, "Oh, you're sweeping my skin."

Grandma called Ruth a "Yungatz" (imp), and Ruthie said, "Ruth Stern, yungatz."

Ruth loves to throw a ball now that she has learned how. She yells, "Here, Mommy—catch."

Word play: "succotash—mustache."

When someone asked Ruth if she wanted a baby sister or a baby brother, she answered, "A baby mother." [*Note 112: Here the editor is ineluctably reminded of the three-year-old who answered the same question with, "A boygirl. You know, a girl with a penis."*]

Ruth rebuked her father, "Don't call me buddy—I'm Ruthie."

Ruth returned from a trip of one week, greeted her grandmother, and said, "Where did *you* went, Grandma?" She had forgotten it had been *she* who had been away.

After lunch (about 1 P.M.) Gram gave Ruth a doll from Papa Jack. When Papa Jack came home after work at 6:30 P.M., Ruth —without anyone's mentioning the temporarily neglected doll —said, "Thank you for my doll, Papa Jack."

When her father was at reserve camp, Ruth told everyone, "Daddy's in the army—selling furniture."

Ruth told her father, "Turn off the air conditioner—it makes it cold inside."

After a rainstorm I took Ruthie for a ride, and she said, "It was raining and *now* it's not raining."

Ruth recognizes "bridges."

Ruth remarked one day, "Let me fix your hair, Mommy. I'll stand behind your *own* chair. You got another little bit of cradle cap."

Ruth's behavior is very inconsistent. Someone brought her a bottle for her doll. Ruth thought it was for her, and said in an insulted tone, "No. Ruthie not a baby—Ruthie a big girl." Yet whenever she could grab her baby cousin's bottle, she tried to suck it.

Ruth was drinking ginger ale and laughed, "It tickles my nose."

Ruth sucks only her left thumb and is definitely left-handed.

Is it possible children favor the hand of the thumb they find *first?* Ruth has always sucked her left thumb.

She loves to color, play "Which hand?" (is the toy in?), the game of alternating hands in a pile, the "job" of sorting and putting away forks, knives, and spoons, setting the table, etc.

Ruth is more sensitive to odors than to noises now.

2 years, 3 days.   July 22

WHEN Ruth visited the doctor for her two-year checkup, she screamed from the moment she stepped into his office and wouldn't let him touch her. (Height 34 inches, weight 27 lb.)

Ruth spilled a glass of milk on the table. As it ran down to the floor she cried out, "Looks like how it's raining milk." I said that I had to clean it up and that I was very tired. She replied, when she saw me on my hands and knees, "Just like poor Cinderella."

Polly Guserai is *not* an imaginary friend, as I thought. Ruth heard a commercial on the radio about polyglycerine, and shouted "Polly Guserai."

Ruth's uncle wanted to make her jealous, and put her doll against his shoulder and hugged it saying, "You're such a nice doll." Ruth watched intently, climbed on his lap, put her head on his shoulder, and said, "And *I'm* such a nice girl, *too.*"

References

Braine, M. D. S. The ontogeny of English phrase structure: The first phase. *Language,* 1963, 39:1–13.

Church, J. *Language and the Discovery of Reality.* New York: Random House, 1961.

Engen, T., Lipsitt, L. P., and Kaye, H. Olfactory responses and adaptation in the human neonate. *Journal of Comparative and Physiological Psychology,* 1963, 56:73–77.

Fantz, R. L. Pattern vision in newborn infants. *Science,* 1963, 140:296–297.

Harlow, H. F. The nature of love. *American Psychologist,* 1958, 13:673–685.

Hebb, D. O., and Riesen, A. H. The genesis of irrational fears. *Bulletin of the Canadian Psychological Association*, 1943, 3:49–50.

Hunton, Vera D. The recognition of inverted pictures by children. *Journal of Genetic Psychology*, 1955, 86:281–288.

Pratt, K. C. The neonate. In Carmichael, L. (ed.) *Manual of Child Psychology*. New York: Wiley, 1954, Chapter 4.

Shiff, W., Caviness, J., and Gibson, J. J. Persistent fear responses in Rhesus monkeys to the optical stimulus of "looming." *Science*, 1962, 136:982–983.

Uzgiris, I. C., and Hunt, J. McV. A scale of infant psychological development. Unpublished manuscript, 1964.

Weir, R. H. *Language in the Crib*. The Hague: Mouton, 1962.

Wertheimer, M. Psychomotor coordination of auditory and visual space at birth. *Science*, 1961, 134:1692.

SUMMARY AND COMMENTS

SPECIALISTS in the behavior of infants know that this is a lively field, as exemplified by Brackbill's invaluable compilation (1964), the recent symposium by Caldwell, Fantz, Greenberg, Stone, and Wolff (1965), the Merrill-Palmer conferences (1965), and the series under the editorship of Foss (e.g., 1963). With so much work being done by experts, one might well question the need for amateur efforts such as these three biographies. But while the professionals, the editor included, are quite properly concentrating on the systematic piece-by-piece analysis of psychological development, the present accounts remind us that there is still room in the life sciences for naturalistic, ecological, holistic observations which give us a picture of the baby-in-general, analogous to the portraits we have gained of dogs, cats, antelope, and, more recently, as in the work of DeVore (1960) and Schaller (1963), of baboons and mountain gorillas. Such observational studies provide a context in which to understand the results of analytic, laboratory-based studies, and furthermore serve to keep formal procedures oriented towards relevant analyses.

Here, then, are the lives of three babies developing in their natural habitat of home and family and society. In attempting to summarize these accounts and to derive what I see as some of the major implications, I shall not try to make detailed comparisons among the three babies. The index that begins on page 297 is designed to enable the reader to trace specific themes through the text.

These biographies seem, first, to have some implications for the study of learning, the way an organism's experiences are assimilated, and the effects of such assimilation on subsequent perceiving, feeling, thinking, and acting. Our three children exemplify every sort of learning process yet conceived of, and perhaps even some without any precedents in our formal conceptual schemes. These babies learn responses to particular situations, as in operant conditioning studies, they form conditioned associations, they learn perceptual discriminations. They learn about objects and their attributes, about their locations and extensions and excursions in space, how they operate and what their functions are. They learn causal sequences, and they come to comprehend a host of relationships binding things together in both concrete and formal systems. They learn language, both passively, by listening to people talk in a concrete context of space and things and actions and emotions, and actively, so that the verbal materials to which they have been exposed—including the unspoken "rules" of grammar and logic, and all the exceptions to the rules—become the raw materials out of which they can shape crude symbolic versions of their experience. For it must be remembered that language is learned not as an abstract system for representing and operating on the world, but in the process of so operating; it comes complete with subject matter, with content, so that in learning language the child simultaneously learns about the world and its properties, including innumerable moral and esthetic conventions. These three babies, like others, learn by active exploration and manipulation, by observation and drinking in, and by immediate and delayed imitation. Through empathic participation they take on cultural styles and values, they form cultural identifications so that they come to be like the people around them. Our three babies have picked up the styles of their families, but in idiosyncratic ways that suit and express their own individual temperaments.

Even more subtle are the ways that children learn to learn, in the case of our subjects to an extent that can only be described as high intelligence. For it is apparent that these three children, barring some calamity, are destined to keep right on being bright. What is less clear is the way the particular events of their lives have taught them a general framework of how things are, rich in corollaries and implications, so that they can solve problems, figure things out, and construct original formulations. In sum, the kinds of dealings these babies have had with people and things and symbols have made the world easy to perceive, explore, comprehend, and, in due time, manipulate in thought. Obviously, these accounts cannot tell us, except by implication, about those contrasting conditions of barrenness or turmoil in which great numbers of children grow up doomed to know the human condition in its least rewarding forms. This is not to predict that our three babies will grow up without stress or conflict or anguish or anxiety. It seems safe to say, however, that they have had early learning experiences that will make later learning come easily and that will both sensitize them to life and fortify them against emotional fracture.

We have thus been led to consideration of a second realm, that of emotion and motivation. Our three children show a high level of vitality and great intensity of feeling, which in my view are important components of their intellectual ability. They all display strikingly variegated emotions, from their manifestations of love and affection, through their reactions to music and other forms of esthetic appreciation, through slyness and coyness and vanity, to their capacities for rage or terror. They are not merely good-humored, but show a capacity for wit and humor, an early comic sense, a spirit of mockery and the absurd, a playful approach to the world, which promises well for freedom from the commonplace and a power to exercise imagination. We can see in all three babies something resembling the beginnings of achievement motivation, an urge to do things and to do them well—although it seems unlikely that any of these children would devote a life of hard work to purely economic achievement. Both our little girls show some oedipal tendencies, a readiness to cast the father in the role of mate and to banish the mother. All told, however, the visible libidinal component in the behavior of these three children seems slight, and the orthodox Freudian will find little support or solace in these accounts. Nor is there any reason to suspect that these three highly sophisticated mothers either missed or censored great quantities of erotic activity. If these babies came into the world as id-driven, lustful, tension-reduction-seeking creatures, the socialization process acted with remarkable and even miraculous speed to tame and civilize their surging impulses. These children's capacities for warmth and affection foretell powerful personal attachments, including sexual ones, in adult life, but at least during the period covered by these accounts little eroticism is evident.

An aspect of cognitive development that has been little studied at these early ages is awareness of self, whether in the matter of getting to know one's own body and its capacities for action and feeling or in that of having a sense of oneself as a person, of having an identity. These babies behave reflexively, toward themselves, from an early age. We can see such reflexive behavior in the babies' discovery of their hands and feet, and in the further discovery that they are *their* hands and feet, knitted into a total pattern of sensations that constitutes body experience. Reflexive behavior appears in the babies' coming to recognize themselves in the looking glass, in feeling possessive about belongings, in becoming autonomous and negativistic, in dressing up and preening, in assuming new identities in play, and in some rudimentary capacity to be amused at or by themselves. One can see early self-awareness in each baby's self-directions and self-instruction, in his observance of taboos, and in the way he acts when he has violated a taboo. Closely linked with one's identity is one's orientation to time, a sense of oneself as continuous, with a past and a present and, however dimly, a future. These babies are obviously at an elementary stage of temporal orientation, but it is clear that they remember and anticipate and have some knowledge of routines and stable sequences.

If we ascribe to the early environment a decisive role in the formation of character, as I do, one can look to these reports for some clues to successful child-rearing. All three sets of parents, in keeping with their various family styles, exemplify the modern look in parenthood, even though two sets are in middle age. Their dealings with their children are characterized by affection, respect, forthrightness, lack of anxiety, and lack of self-consciousness even with me, the perhaps-critical Expert, looking over their shoulder. They are able to take pleasure in children and children's coming to terms with the world, they are able to see and hear what is really happening without great upwellings of irrelevant moralism, they are able to talk to children even before the children can reply in kind, they can communicate the love and concern that they as parents feel, they have the strength to assert standards that are relevant and to impose reasonable demands. And they are able to provide richly varied experience at a rate that does not overwhelm the child or try to coerce him into forms of behavior inappropriate to his age. In all this, of course, these parents have had their lots made easier by the feedback they have received from their responsive and reciprocally stimulating children.

Rewarding as these accounts are, they do not tell the whole story of the first two years of life, and it is probably important to emphasize some things that we still do not know enough about as suggestions for further research. While these records clearly show that babies apprehend the world in ways radically different from what we as adults take for granted, as in early lack of object conservation, we still have the task of specifying systematically and conceptualizing coherently what these differences are. Only with such an investigation can we decide which aspects of the world are given in naïve perception and which come to take on perceptual significance as a product of experience. This, of course, is simply a statement in developmental terms of the problem of understanding individual and cultural differences in how the world is constituted, both factually and judgmentally.

It is part of my concern to try first of all to specify some of the early cognitive correlates of cultural differences, whether it be in such respects as style of movement, as pointed out by Mead and Macgregor (1951, pages 181–186), or in the timing of postural development (Geber, 1958), of posture and walking (Dennis and Najarian, 1957), and of visually directed grasping (White, 1963). We have additional evidence of the effects of early rearing experience from the literature of infra-human development (see, for instance, Denenberg, 1962). There is every reason to suppose that cultural differences in cognition, which are very conspicuous in adults, will also begin to appear quite early in ways that can be investigated formally and quantitatively.

Second comes the task of trying to find out which specific or general characteristics of child-world relations account for these cognitive differences. By the same token, such procedures should be of help in understanding the nature and early origins of those variations which we call psychopathology. One would also want to find out which cognitive operations and capacities hang together meaningfully in correlational clusters, and which cognitive operations are linked in an unvarying sequence, as passive language precedes active speaking.

A somewhat different line of research has to do with the contrasts between pre-linguistic and post-linguistic behavior, the way learning language, and learning a language with thus-and-such particular characteristics, affects cognition. Incidental to such research is the finding of categories for the analysis of linguistic acts. Here the antecedent-consequent relations may be far less direct and intelligible than with such things as the primacy of passive language over active. For instance, observations so far have led me to the hypothesis that representational drawing, as distinct from scribbling, is contingent on active language, that is, that no child draws recognizable pictures of things before he has begun speaking in words. This hypothesis has to be tested, of course, not only with normal children who begin speaking at slightly past age one and drawing at age two and a half, but with children in whom speech is greatly delayed, as in cases of deafness or expressive aphasia (Lenneberg, 1962). And it may have to be modified to take account of non-vocal speaking, as in sign language. Such research, obviously, aims at elucidating the Whorfian hypothesis which says that our perceiving and thinking are shaped by the linguistic forms peculiar to our culture. It is evident that we all subscribe to some version of the Whorfian hypothesis and assume that we can modify perception, thought, and action by symbolic manipulation, or we would give up on explaining things to children, on education by verbal means, on psychotherapy, or on telling the lost wayfarer how to reach his destination. On the other hand, we know that we have experiences that we cannot put into words, that there are verbal formulations which we cannot accept or credit for whatever reasons, and that sometimes we can accept the correctness or rationality of a verbal formulation and still not be able to make it a part of our lives. We know further, if only from the growth of dictionaries, that people are not completely the slaves of language as it exists, but are constantly changing and expanding their means of expression. Thus the relationships are unclear, and particularly as they enter into shaping the child's reality in accordance with his society's conception of how the world is and how it should be and how one must conduct oneself so as to be in tune with reality.

To close on some broader issues, it seems to me that these biographies teach us that reductionistic conceptions are hopelessly inadequate to describe the realities of human behavior even at its simplest, most primitive level. This is not to propose a doctrine of the soul, or even of a life force or mind, but to insist that babies who grow up in the proper humanizing conditions do more with their experience than register it and reproduce it. At best, they use their experience constructively, to decipher and think about and reconstitute the world, eventually to fabricate an identity, a set of values and of goals, and to strike a rational balance between enjoying present experience and working toward the future. This is not to say that human beings transcend their biological natures, but that human biology is a far more marvelous thing than we usually recognize. For what people transcend is our present conceptualizations of what biology is. We need a biology not only of growth and development and metamorphosis and homeostasis and self-repair and psychosomatics, but also of consciousness and thought and morality and learning and language and culture. Since none of these can be described in or reduced to the language of present-day biology, there seems to be no choice but to elevate and expand our biological conceptions so as to comprehend the indisputable facts of human behavior and development, including the clearcut emergents and discontinuities of psychological development. The alternative, it seems to me, is a dualism of biology and psychology, of mind and matter, of flesh and spirit, of natural and supernatural. There remains, of course, the possibility of escape into a solipsism where all is dream and science a delusion. And I think we have to begin by recognizing that there are two sorts of life processes, those devoted to the maintenance of equilibrium, internally and between organism and relevant environmental parameters, and those that vary and fluctuate and express the continually changing adaptations of the organism to its behavioral environment, including the environments it constructs symbolically or imaginally with little reference to material reality.

References

Brackbill, Yvonne. (ed.) *Research in Infant Behavior: A Cross-Indexed Bibliography.* Baltimore: Williams & Wilkins, 1964.

Caldwell, Bettye M., Fantz, R. L., Greenberg, N. H., Stone, L. J., and Wolff, P. H. New issues in infant development. *Annals of the New York Academy of Sciences,* 1965, 118:783–866.

Denenberg, V. H. The effects of early experience. In Hafez, E. S. E. (ed.) *The Behaviour of Domestic Animals*. London: Baillière, Tindall & Cox, 1962, pp. 109–138.

Dennis, W., and Najarian, P. Infant development under environmental handicap. *Psychological Monographs*, 1957, 71, no. 7.

DeVore, I. Socialization in free-living baboons. Paper read at meetings of American Psychological Association, 1960.

Foss, B. M. (ed.) *Determinants of Infant Behavior II*. London: Methuen; and New York: Wiley, 1963.

Geber, Marcelle. The psycho-motor development of African children in the first year, and the influence of maternal behavior. *Journal of Social Psychology*, 1958, 47:185–195.

Lenneberg, E. H. Understanding language without ability to speak: A case report. *Journal of Abnormal and Social Psychology*, 1962, 65: 419–425.

Mead, Margaret, and Macgregor, F. C. *Growth and Culture*. New York: Putnam, 1951.

Merrill-Palmer Institute. Papers from the 1964 Conference on Research and Teaching of Infant Development. *Merrill-Palmer Quarterly*, 1965, 11:91–179.

Schaller, G. B. *The Mountain Gorilla: Ecology and Behavior*. Chicago: University of Chicago, 1963.

White, B. L. The development of perception during the first six months of life. Paper read at meetings of the American Association for the Advancement of Science, 1963.

INDEX

[It is only a secondary function of this index to help the reader find what he is looking for. Its primary function is to tell the reader what he might look for, which strands of development can be traced through the book, which comparisons can be made among babies, and which cannot. In short, it is meant as a detailed, categorized, alphabetized table of contents. As anyone knows who has ever made an index, or a library catalogue or a curriculum, categorization is no simple matter. I make no claim to having found the right pigeon holes, the precise level of specificity and generality, or any system of logical consistency. I have tried, however, to find diverse headings with which to steer the reader to other possible categories. Since the categories overlap, an item of behavior may be multiply indexed or may appear under only one of a number of related categories. The reader is urged to have patience and, if a bit of behavior eludes him, to keep looking. Many forms of behavior (e.g., passive language) are interesting only in their early manifestations, and later occurrences have been indexed only when they seem to represent something new and different. Sometimes the age at which the baby performs some action does not correspond to the date of the entry. In such cases, if the occurrence can be accurately dated, the actual age is given in the index.]

A Note About the Editor

JOSEPH CHURCH is Professor of Psychology at Brooklyn College of The City University of New York. Before joining the Brooklyn College faculty, he taught at Vassar College in the Department of Child Study, at The New School for Social Research, and, most recently, at the University of Hawaii as a Visiting Professor. He is the author of *Language and the Discovery of Reality* (Random House, 1961), and co-author, with L. Joseph Stone, of the widely known *Childhood and Adolescence* (Random House, 1957), regarded as a leader in its field. Professor Church is a graduate of The New School for Social Research and was awarded his master's degree by Cornell University, and his doctorate by Clark University. He is currently doing research on early cognitive development and on group differences in value systems.

Church.

Three babies.